DEFINING CHILD ABUSE

Defining
Child Abuse

Jeanne M. Giovannoni
and Rosina M. Becerra

THE FREE PRESS
A Division of Macmillan Publishing Co., Inc.
NEW YORK

Collier Macmillan Publishers
LONDON

For our parents—
and for Joe, who brought
music to children

The Free Press
A Division of Macmillan Publishing Co., Inc.
866 Third Avenue, New York, N.Y. 10022

Collier Macmillan Canada, Inc.

First Free Press Paperback Edition 1982

Library of Congress Catalog Card Number: 79-7180

Printed in the United States of America

Paperback printing number

1   2   3   4   5   6   7   8   9   10

Hardcover printing number

5   6   7   8   9   10

Library of Congress Cataloging in Publication Data

Giovannoni, Jeanne M.
    Defining child abuse.

    Bibliography: p.
    Includes index.
    1. Child abuse--California. 2. Child abuse--United
States--Case studies. 3. Child welfare--United States--
Case studies. I. Becerra, Rosina, joint author.
II. Title.
HV742.C2G46 1979   362.7'1   79-7180
ISBN 0-02-911750-X
ISBN 0-02-911780-1 pbk.

Copyright Acknowledgments

Grateful thanks are extended to the following for permission to quote from their copyrighted publications.

From *Reporting Child Abuse and Neglect: Guidelines for Legislation*, by Alan Sussman and Stephen Cohen. Copyright © 1975 by Ballinger Publishing Company. Quotes from pp. 74 and 194.

From *Standards Relating to Abuse and Neglect*, The Juvenile Justice Standards Project. Copyright © 1977 by Ballinger Publishing Company. Quotes from pp. 3, 9, 10, 11, 37, and 184–185.

From *When Parents Fail: The Law's Response to Family Breakdown*, by Sanford N. Katz. Copyright © 1971 by Sanford N. Katz. Beacon Press. Quotes from pp. 3, 4, 5, 62–63, and 68.

From *Roots of Futility*, by N. A. Polansky, R. D. Borgman, and C. DeSaix. 1972. Jossey–Bass.

From "Foster Care: In Whose Best Interests?" by Robert Mnookin in *Harvard Educational Review*, Vol. 43, No. 4. Copyright © 1972 by President and Fellows of Harvard College. Quote from p. 616.

From "The Police" by Rudolph A. Pitcher in *Helping the Battered Child and His Family* (Kempe and Helfer, eds.). 1972. J. B. Lippincott Company. Quotes from pp. 242–243.

From "The Role of the Lawyer in Child Abuse Cases" by Jacob L. Isaacs, in *Helping the Battered Child and His Family* (Kempe and Helfer, eds.). 1972. J. B. Lippincott Company. Quote from p. 227.

From the Introduction to *Helping the Battered Child and His Family* (Henry C. Kempe and Ray E. Helfer, eds.). 1972. J. B. Lippincott Company. Quotes from pp. xi–xii.

From *Child Welfare Services*, by Alfred Kadushin. 1974. Macmillan Publishing Co., Inc. Quote from p. 235.

From *The Care of Destitute, Neglected and Delinquent Children*, by Homer Folks. 1907. Macmillan Publishing Co., Inc. Quote from p. 177.

From *Beyond the Best Interests of the Child*, by Joseph Goldstein, Anna Freud, and Albert J. Solnit. 1973. Macmillan Publishing Co., Inc. Quotes from pp. 4, 7, 8, 51, and 52.

From *Child Abuse and Neglect: Perspectives from Child Development*, by J. Giovannoni, J. Conklin, and P. Iiyama. 1978. R & E Research Associates, Inc. Quote from p. 88.

From *The Challenge of Social Equality*, by David Gil. 1976. Schenckman Publishing Co., Inc. Quote from p. 130.

From *Family Law in a Nutshell*, by Harry Krause. 1977. West Publishing Company. Quotes from pages 236–237.

From "Public Knowledge, Attitudes and Opinions About Child Abuse in the United States" by David G. Gil and John Noble in *Child Welfare*, Vol. 48, No. 7 (July 1969). From *Violence Against Children: Physical Child Abuse in the United States*, by David G. Gil. 1970. Harvard University Press. Quotes from pp. 395ff. *passim* and Chapter 3 *passim* respectively.

From "State Intervention on Behalf of Neglected Children" by Michael Wald in *Stanford Law Review* 27 (April 1975): 1000–1002, 1035.

From *Child Abuse Legislation of the 1970s*, by Vincent DeFrancis and Carroll L. Lucht. 1974. American Humane Association. Quotes from pp. 41–42.

From "Defining Emotional Neglect: A Community Workshop Looks at Neglected Children" by Leila Whiting in *Children Today* (Jan.–Feb. 1976). Quotes from pp. 3–4.

From *Standards for Child Protective Service*. 1973 (revision). Child Welfare League of America. Quotes from pp. 2, 5, 8, 12.

Contents

List of Tables

Foreword

JEANNE GIOVANNONI AND ROSINA BECERRA have amassed an extraordinary amount of data shattering a great many myths about
child abuse and neglect in American society. To begin with, in
their very thoroughly researched historical review of the problems
of child abuse and neglect, they demonstrate that these are not at
all new problems, spawned in the twentieth century. Indeed, they
go back to the beginnings of the country and before, and the issues
that surround their resolution are centuries old. Unfortunately, so
are some of the "solutions." As this book clearly demonstrates, increasing public awareness of the various forms of mistreatment of
children at the hands of their own parents and caretakers brings to
the forefront the growing crisis in the relationship between the
family and agents of the state.

Families are expected to be loving and to provide supportive,
secure environments for their children. Increasingly in America,
however, which boasts of being one of the most highly civilized
societies in the world, there are large numbers of children who are
not safe or secure within their families. When parents severely mis-
treat their own children they are not only damaging the children
and causing severe strains on the integrity of the family, but they
are also risking massive and not always enlightened confrontation
between the family and the agents of the state.

And when the state intervenes under a mandate to protect children from their own parents, it often does so in a manner that
makes the cure worse than the disease. Two factors among others
give this situation the aura of a gathering national crisis of major

proportions. First, the incidence of child abuse and neglect reports, by the best available information, is on the increase. Secondly, the society, through the state and federal governments, is devoting increasing attention, money, and state authority to mechanisms of intervention for dealing with the phenomena. Finally, as the authors document so cogently, the phenomena of "child abuse and neglect" are by no means homogeneous, nor are they confined to any social class stratum or ethnic group. Often, however, the government agents perceive the same behavior differently if it takes place in a different ethnic or social group from their own. What is more, the government often treats abuse and neglect differently as they arise among different ethnic and social groupings. At a time when the validity of cultural differences, and even neighborhood differences, is gaining greater recognition, the intervention of the state into different families, in the interests of protecting children, demands greater sensitivity to these differences and some radical changes in order to effectively carry out the protective function and to ameliorate the growing crisis between the family and the state.

The authors are careful not to overstate their findings. Indeed, the book may be viewed as a masterpiece of understatement, as befits serious social science scholarship. Yet it is very apparent that they have made an enormous contribution to our clearer understanding of major issues of national social policy.

The authors identify the nine major types of parental mistreatment of children that are most common today. These range from physical injury and sexual assault, among the severest forms of mistreatment, to failure to provide adequately for children's basic physical and emotional needs and their education. Matters that are perceived as less immediately damaging to the individual child are by far the more prevalent types and are the ones most conducive to clashes of values. These value conflicts go to the heart of the ambiguity that surrounds our basic beliefs about how our children should be reared.

Nor is there any homogeneity of opinions and values among professionals or lay people of various social class and ethnic backgrounds. Why, for example, as the authors document, should Black people see the failure to provide ordinary child care and protection as so much more serious than do others? Why do Hispanic families see moral infringement as so much more serious than other types of mistreatment? Why do well-educated white people react with particular abhorrence when their neighbors physically injure

their own children? As the authors point out it would be mislead-
ing to make ethnic generalities, as the agents of the state often do,
without a more enlightened understanding of the nature of cultural
pluralism in American society and the manner in which the society
conditions the quality of life for members of different ethnic and
social class groups.

Again with appropriate modesty and qualifications, the authors
prescribe approaches to public policy that might help the state and
the family get off their collision course and at the same time help
professionals and families take better care of their children. In
keeping with their own call for greater specificity in defining the
phenomena that are encompassed by the terms "child abuse" and
"neglect," they deal first with the policy issues that surround each
of the different types of mistreatment that they have delineated—
what parental actions should and should not be so defined and
under what conditions. Next they deal with the more general
policy issues, including those surrounding statutory changes,
research and evaluation, and resource allocation.

First, the authors demonstrate the need for more specificity in
the laws defining child mistreatment and prescribing state intervention. Too much discretion is now left to judges and to other
state authorities under the present vague and widely variant
statutes. The great latitude in discretionary action accounts for the
wide discrepancies in the treatment of abuse and neglect cases and
in the sanctions placed on parents judged to be abusive and
neglectful.

Secondly, the authors call for and provide much more precise
definitions to be used in research, in statistical reporting, and in
service accountability and evaluation. Only through such efforts
can we begin to provide the kinds of information needed for im-
proved education of the general population and for professionals
and policymakers as well, education about the nature and scope of
child mistreatment in this country, and on the nature and limitations of state intervention for its treatment and prevention.

With respect to resource allocation the authors call for greater
role specificity among the professionals dealing with child mistreatment. Given the complexity of interests involved, multiple professional orientations are needed for effective and equitable resolution
of these situations. Let the police be police, they say, and not have
to be lawyers, social workers, and physicians at the same time.
Ditto for the other professionals. More effective treatment of these

problems begins with interprofessional cooperation not interprofessional diffusion and confusion.

Finally, they hold, on the basis of their research, that it is indispensable that extraordinary steps be taken to bring more ethnically and culturally diverse persons into roles at all levels of dealing with the problems, from policymaking through research to direct treatment of child abuse and neglect. If children are to receive better care and if the growing crisis between the family and the state is to be attenuated, there must be representation of culturally diverse groups. The all too common practice of sending white, middle-class professionals into low-income, ethnic minority communities to rescue children from their parents without a sensitivity to cultural pluralism often produces more problems than solutions. Nor is it enough to give white professionals a more appropriate education. Affirmative action on a grand scale is required to deal with this problem. Consider the single fact that a large proportion of the Hispanic respondents in this research preferred to be interviewed in Spanish rather than English. The authors of this book were sensitive enough to ask about the preference as well as able to provide the service. When such families come into contact with the state, however, they are generally not offered this opportunity.

The readers of this book, by reading it and acting on its findings and conclusions, will be in a position to make a major contribution to the welfare of children, the integrity of the American family life, and resolution of the growing crises in relations between the family and the state.

> Andrew Billingsley, Ph.D.
> President, Morgan State University
> and Professor of Sociology

Preface

THE TERMS "CHILD ABUSE" and "child neglect" have come into common usage recently as growing national attention has focused on the problem of child mistreatment. Yet the labels are still ambiguous, and this ambiguity has hampered efforts to understand the problem better through research and to ameliorate it through social intervention. In seeking, through our research, to clarify child abuse and neglect, we have assumed that, like other forms of social deviance, they are socially defined phenomena. The research was thus focused on the opinions of the definers themselves—professionals and members of the general population. We solicited their views about a wide range of specific child abuse incidents that differed in kind and degree.

Through the facilities of the Survey Research Center of the Institute for Social Science Research at the University of California, Los Angeles, interviews were conducted with those professionals—lawyers, pediatricians, police officers, and social workers—who daily handle the problems of abuse and neglect for the County of Los Angeles and with a representative sample of the general population. In addition, a sample of actual cases of child abuse and neglect drawn from four counties in California were studied. We developed measures to assess the relative seriousness of the specific incidents of abuse and neglect that had brought the 949 families in the sample under the aegis of protective intervention, and then we analyzed the relationship between the seriousness of the incident and the way in which the family was handled. The participating counties were Contra Costa, Orange, Sacramento, and San Diego.

The book begins with an overview of the problems involved in defining child abuse. This is followed by a historical review of the changing conceptions of the problems over the past three hundred years. The survey of professionals is reported in chapter 3, and the survey of the general population in chapter 4. Examination of the actual cases is presented in chapter 5. The book concludes with a discussion of the policy implications derived from the research.

Acknowledgments

IT IS NOT POSSIBLE to thank individually all those who helped us with the research on which this book was ultimately based, and hence the book itself: the busy professionals who took time to give thoughtful answers to our questions, the members of the general population who let our interviewers into their homes and answered our questions; and most of all the suffering families who permitted us to gather information about them. We earnestly hope that the work they made possible will prove to be of service to them all.

No research endeavor—from the conception of the ideas that guide it, its design, execution, analysis, to its final interpretation—is ever the work of a single individual or even a few. At each step of the way many people helped us at one or more stages with a variety of their personal and professional talents and wisdom. The following people worked directly on many facets of the project: Mary Pori, Jerrald Freiwirth, Lyle Groeneveld, Shiri Pollack, and Margaret Purvine. Data collection and analysis were greatly enhanced through the efforts of the project staff—Jo Stumpf, Bonnie Behrens, and Mary Joyner—and by personnel of the UCLA Institute for Social Science Research: Vi Dorfman, Rita Engelhardt, Eve Fielder, Cheryl Groves, Antoinette Jenkins, Miles Rogers, and Donald Witzke.

As anyone knows who has attempted to do work in sensitive areas, access to crucial data is vital. These people were especially helpful to us not simply in providing such access but also in giving us useful insights: Lorraine Adler, Don Brown, Esther Cardoll, Nathan Cohen, Maurice Connery, Dorothy Dean, James Fisk,

David Freidman, Jackie Howell, Sylvia Kerr, Stephanie Klopfleisch, Laura Lee Saddick, William Stewart, Aaron Stovitz, Gerald Swan, and Walter Tasem.

Finally, we were immeasurably aided by the following people in a variety of overlapping roles—consultant, colleague, friend, and most important, challenger of our ideas: Cecelia Sudia, Andrew Billingsley, Howard Freeman, Wyatt Jones, Ethel Selvester, David Binder, Peter Rossi, and Sidney Sussman.

Numerous rewrites were made possible through the unstinting efforts of Iris Ross, Carey Miller, and Margaret Kisliuk.

From research report to digestible book is a harrowing road. For us it was made easier through the skillful efforts of Gladys Topkis of The Free Press.

The entire work was supported through a grant (#86–P–80086/9) from the Social and Rehabilitation Services, Office of Research and Demonstrations, U.S. Department of Health, Education, and Welfare. Sidney Netherey and Virginia White served as project officers.

The usual disclaimers that the final product is our sole responsibility apply, though we very much wish not to be disclaimed by any of the above who were so helpful to us.

J.M.G.
R.M.B.

CHAPTER 1

The Problem of
Defining Child Abuse

A THREE-YEAR-OLD in Tennessee was forced by her stepfather to walk for three days and three nights, until she died of exhaustion. A seven-year-old in California was locked in a room and tied to a chair by her parents for her whole life; when found she weighed only 35 pounds and was only 33 inches tall and unable to talk. An infant sustained permanent damage from maggots in her ears, maggots that swarmed over the feces-laden rags on which she lay. These situations, brought to public attention through the media, present no ambiguity. Would anyone question that these children have been abused and neglected?

But what of the following situations? Three children, aged two to ten, were found by Chicago police at 9:30 P.M. in an apartment to which the officers had been summoned by neighbors' complaints that the children had been left alone. The children, who were barefoot and in their underwear, said they had not been fed since morning, when their mother had left them locked in the apartment. The mother arrived at 10:30 P.M. from her job as a cocktail waitress. She angrily protested that she had done nothing wrong; the ten-year-old, she said, was perfectly capable of taking care of the younger children. The police refused to take action. The neighbors were incensed. In San Bernardino, a judge returned a seven-year-old to her deaf parents, admonishing the protective agency that had removed her from them and placed her in a foster home in the belief that the parents, because of their deafness, could not give

1

the child the emotional nurturance and intellectual stimulation needed for her development. Were the Chicago police right in not taking action or were the neighbors right? Was the San Bernardino judge right in returning the child, or was the protective agency right in removing her? These two cases illustrate some of the more problematic aspects of defining abuse and neglect and highlight the disagreements that can occur among professionals whose responsibility it is to arrive at these definitions, and between professionals and community members. The term "child abuse" for many people conjures up an image of a tiny baby with a mass of ugly bruises and swollen welts. But in reality, situations labeled as child abuse and neglect cover a very broad range of parental actions and failures, differing greatly in their nature and in the severity of harm inflicted on children through them. This book addresses the problem of defining child abuse and neglect.

Many assume that since child abuse and neglect are against the law, somewhere there are statutes that make clear distinctions between what is and what is not child abuse or neglect. But this is not the case. Nowhere are there clear-cut definitions of what is encompassed by the terms. The ambiguity of definition precipitates problems and disagreements among the professionals who work daily with abuse and neglect situations. These difficulties are less well known among the general public and even among peripherally related professionals, such as mental health workers and schoolteachers. But why should there be problems? Why are the legal definitions so imprecise? Why must there be so many different professionals involved in making the determination about a single case and why should there be disagreement among them? And, most important, what are the implications of the disagreement for children, for their parents, and for the society as a whole?

To begin with let us circumscribe the nature of the situations about which we are concerned: the abuse and neglect that children suffer at the hands of their own parents, within the confines of their families. To be sure, children suffer assaults at the hands of outsiders as well and are the victims of abuse and of neglect by social institutions other than the family. Resolution of these situations is not without its problematic aspects, but in neither instance does it entail the complexities involved in dealing with abuse and neglect that occur within the family, between parent and child. When it comes to defining parental actions as abusive or neglectful—or the failure to make such definition—the stakes are high.

And they are high for all involved—the children, the parents, and the society.

For children, their very lives may be at stake, their immediate safety, comfort, welfare, and future development jeopardized, as in the examples of actual cases just given.

But the consequences can be grave for parents as well. They can permanently lose their right to parent their children, as in cases in which the children are removed to the care of other parents through adoption. Or they may have their rights severely curtailed, perhaps indefinitely, as when the children are placed in a foster home or institution. At the very least their autonomy in rearing their children as they see fit can be eroded through supervision of the children in their own homes by a social agency. Such separation and such intrusion into the parent-child relationship and family life, of course, affect the children as well. These are the possible consequences for parents that must be weighed in defining abuse and neglect, and they must be weighed against the harm that might befall children, both in the present and in the future, if such definition is not made.

The potential consequences for individual parents and children inevitably are of import for the society in which they live and its instrumentality, the state. And here we come to the heart of the matter that makes violence by a parent to a child different from that between strangers, and makes neglect of children by their parents different from their neglect by other social institutions. At stake for the society are the welfare of the future generation and at the same time the viability and integrity of its most fundamental social institution, the family. Ultimately the society, the state, defines the minimum expectations of those entrusted with the rearing of the young, and the limitations of the authority of parents. Defining neglect is in essence defining what these minimal expectations are, and defining abuse is defining what those limitations of authority are. How those definitions are made ultimately determines the nature of the relationship between the state and the institution of the family, and that relationship, in turn, is the cornerstone of the social organization of the whole society, the expression of its most basic social values. In our society, given our interpretations of the value of freedom, the family is considered a highly autonomous unit. Hence any encroachment on that autonomy constitutes an erosion of this basic value, and an assault on the social institution of the family.

But the state not only bears the responsibility for protecting and ensuring the viability of the institution of the family. It also bears a responsibility to its individual members, particularly the powerless. Children are, in effect, captive within the autonomous family enclave. Ultimately, then, the state's exercise of its protective function toward children can come about only through interference with that autonomy.

Given the gravity of the consequences for children, their parents, and the society, should we not expect that the definitions upon which such crucial decisions must rest would be clear and precise? Should we not expect that the classifications of parental acts that subject families to forfeiture of their autonomy would have clearly designated parameters? And should we not expect that the social agents, the professionals who must make the designations, would both know and agree on what these parameters are? Ironically, it is the very gravity of the situation that mitigates against more precise and forthright definition and, in the absence of such definition, spurs disagreement among the professionals. When the stakes are high and the consequences grave, the definers understandably retreat into the haven of ambiguity, with its continuing options for retrenchment.

There is more to the problem, however, than a simple reluctance to come to grips with definition. For in order to set the parameters of child abuse and neglect, we must decide just what the minimum expectations are of parents in this society and what the limitations are on the exercise of parental authority. In essence, the definitions of child abuse and neglect get at the very fundamental issues of what is acceptable child rearing in our society. And here we are hampered by our lack of knowledge of the effects of varying child rearing practices and parental performance on children, but also, and perhaps more important, we are faced with disparate values about the very effects themselves. "Good" child rearing practices are those that produce "good" adults. Our uncertainty about the ways children are reared and the kinds of adults they become constitutes one kind of problem, one that may be answered through the gradual growth of knowledge about child development. But the value issues cannot be resolved through knowledge alone. Thus, to the complexities of the value conflicts inherent in resolving situations of child abuse and neglect are added the value issues of what we consider to be desirable or undesirable traits, in children and in adults. Such value issues are even more pronounced in a society such as ours, with its ethnic, religious, social, and economic diversity. Protection of these pluralistic interests and values is integral to the interests of justice and fairness, and failure to consider such value differences can also jeopardize the viability of family life among whole segments of the society.

If the issues that surround the definitions of child abuse and neglect are basically value issues, especially ones of conflicting values, can they be resolved in any rational way? We believe that they can, and that they must, and this conviction spurred the research that was the foundation of this book and that guided its purpose. Indeed, a major thesis of the book is that child abuse and neglect are matters of social definition and that the problems that inhere in the establishment of those definitions ultimately rest on value issues. It is rather commonplace to state that value questions are not ones that can be answered through empirical research, since value issues—what should and should not be—are not subject to tests of empirical validation. But the answers to the following questions can be sought through research: How commonly held are the values about different kinds of and degrees of child abuse and neglect? Who are the people who hold similar values? Around what issues are the more divergent values expressed and by whom? It is these answers that we present in this book.

Both the book and the research were motivated by a conviction that not only can the definitional issues in child abuse and neglect be addressed more effectively than they are currently or have been in the past, but also that they *must be*, before we can adequately deal with the problem. Now that child abuse and neglect have come into a focal position in our national social policy and in our social consciousness, we must act, and before we can act effectively in formulating our future social policies, the policies in our laws, and those that guide the allocation of social resources in overcoming the problems, we first of all must know what we are talking about. The general public should know, the social policymakers should know, the researchers should know, and families, parents, and children—who are the object of the definitions and the consequences—should know. But in the absence of precise definitions, none can know.

Let us now consider the current status of the definitional maze and its implications. First we look at the state legislation, which defines those circumstances of abuse and neglect that a state can intervene in to protect children. Definitional ambiguity at this level has serious implications for the efficacy of these laws in protecting children and in enabling those who enforce the laws to act in a just and fair manner. Next, we examine the professional standards and criteria by which those who deal with the actual cases interpret the laws and the mandates that empower them to intervene. Again we find these seriously deficient, with the result that professionals find themselves without clear-cut guidelines for action and, very important, for resolving disagreements. At the broader level of national social policy we again find vagueness in the very legislation mandating the largest allocation of federal resources for resolving the problems of child abuse and neglect that the nation has ever invested. Finally, we look at the definitions that have been used in research efforts to understand the scope of the problems, the effectiveness of interventive programs, and the underlying etiology of the problems. Here we find that vagueness of research definitions and lack of uniformity among the more precise ones stymie those attempting to use the research products in making policy decisions.

EVIDENCE OF DEFINITIONAL PROBLEMS AND THEIR IMPLICATIONS

State Statutory Definition

California's laws serve as an example of the range of specificity in statutory definitions of child abuse and neglect. California, like all other states, has three sets of laws relating to child abuse and neglect. One kind of law mandates physicians and certain other professionals, such as school superintendents and principals, dentists, and religious practitioners, to report to the local police any situation where they suspect that a child has "physical injuries or injury which appear to have been inflicted upon him by other than accidental means" (California Penal Code, sec. 11161.5). The concept of physical injury seems fairly straightforward. However, the other two sets of laws, those in the penal code that define criminal child abuse or neglect, and the others in the civil code that spell out grounds for making a child a dependent ward of the court, are not so straightforward. The criminal statute includes as a felonious crime, punishable by imprisonment for up to ten years, the following phrases: "willfully causes or permits any child to suffer or inflicts thereon unjustifiable physical pain or mental suffering . . . or . . . to be placed in such situations that its person or health is endangered" (California Penal Code, sec. 273A). The Welfare and

Institutions code provides that any child may be made a dependent ward of the court "who is not provided with a home or suitable place of abode . . . whose home is an unfit place for him by reasons of neglect, cruelty, depravity, or physical abuse of either of his parents" (chap. 1068, art. 6, secs. 300b and d). Terms such as "mental suffering," "endangering health," "suitable place of abode," and "unfit place" are not further elaborated anywhere in the statutes. In fact, the above descriptions *are* the legal definitions given for a "dependent child."

The vagueness of California's laws is no exception to the general rule. In Illinois, for example, a neglected minor is defined in part as "one who is neglected as to proper or necessary support . . . or other care necessary for his well-being." In that same state parental rights may be terminated and a child given up for adoption for "failure to maintain a reasonable degree of interest, concern or responsibility as to the child's welfare" (Illinois Revised Statutes, chap. 37, 702–4, 705–9).

In a 1974 analysis of reporting laws, Vincent De Francis and Carroll Lucht found only eighteen states that had attempted to enlarge upon what was specified in the law as a "reportable condition." In some laws, particularly those that limit reporting responsibility to physical injury, the language used to describe a "reportable condition" is so restricted that a statutory definition is not necessary. Iowa, for example, specifies as a reportable condition that "the child has had physical injury inflicted on him as a result of abuse and neglect." No statutory definition of abuse is given. On the other hand, the Texas reporting law specifies as reportable "a child's physical or mental health or welfare has been adversely affected by abuse or neglect," but it offers no definition of what might be encompassed by "health" or "welfare" or "adverse effects." De Francis and Lucht observed that among those reporting laws that do offer a definition, the degree of specificity varies greatly from jurisdiction to jurisdiction. "Colorado, for example, defines abuse in very specific medical terms, e.g. 'skin bruising, bleeding, malnutrition, burns . . .' " (1974, pp. 41–42). Many definitions, however, are nonspecific, especially in those states where conditions other than physical injury are reportable conditions. The Louisiana statute offers the following definition of "neglect," which is a reportable condition there: "the failure to provide . . . the proper or necessary support, education as required by law, or medical, or surgical or *any other care necessary for his well-being"* (emphasis added) (De Francis and Lucht 1974, p. 43).

While the reporting laws evidence the absence or ambiguity of definition, the civil and criminal codes describing management and disposition are even less precise. In part, this reflects the fact that reporting laws tend to be more restricted to physical injury and harm, while the criminal and civil codes cover a wide array of phenomena, especially those under the rubric of "neglect." In Katz and his colleagues' 1975 analysis of child neglect laws, the absence of statutory definitions of "neglect" or "neglected child" was noted:

> A large majority of jurisdictions (45) do not have a statutory definition for the term "neglect" and/or "neglected child." Only eight states define "neglect" . . . and less than half the jurisdictions (22) have a "neglected child" definition. . . . Twenty-three states use some other definition to refer to a "neglected child," such as "deprived child," "dependent or neglected," or "dependent child" [Katz et al. 1975, pp. 25–26].

These definitions themselves, as well as the grounds for determining child neglect that Katz tabulates, run the gamut from extreme specificity to generality. Such grounds might include "found begging or receiving alms," "failure to send child to school, " "child is habitually truant," "lack of education as required by law," or "lack of proper parental care, control or guardianship." In particular, the use of such terms as "proper," "adequate," "unfit," and "general well-being" in these statutes render them open to criticism not only of being vague but also of downright injustice, since those accused under such statutes are at the mercy of their accusers' interpretation of these terms. Similar criticism has also been levied at reporting laws that use the terms "serious" or "severe" in designating reportable physical injury, leaving much discretion to the reporters as to the "seriousness" or "severity" of a given injury (Daly 1969).

There is no controversy about the fact that all state definitions are vague, but there is controversy as to the desirability of that imprecision, controversy that itself is testimony to the definitional vagueness. On the one hand there are those in the legal profession who argue that vague definitions, including terms such as "unfit" and "unsuitable," permit judicial flexibility, which allows for individualization in specific cases. Harry D. Krause and Sanford Katz, both prominent in the family law arena, have made such suggestions. Krause states:

Due to the varied nature of the situations to be covered, the neglect and dependency laws are rarely specific. A legal finding of neglect typically is a composite of many factors and requires a highly individualized judgment on all the circumstances of each specific case. Statutes *need* to be flexible to provide the necessary broad discretion to the courts [Krause 1977, p. 236–37].

In addition to the potential benefits of individualization of specific cases, Katz has pointed to the advantage that broad state statutes can be interpreted with greater sensitivity to local community standards:

It seems clear that even the most detailed neglect statute . . . would probably be termed "broad" or even "vague" in areas other than family law. . . . The legislative purpose behind the broad language appears to be to allow judges wide discretion in deciding neglect cases. Presumably local judges have a knowledge of community resources as well as information about the area which they can call upon in the disposition of a case. At the same time juvenile and domestic relations judges are considered "closer" to the issues in any given case and to generally reflect local community attitudes [Katz 1971, pp. 62–63].

Neither of these legal authorities are unmindful of the dangers that inhere in broad statutes. Katz notes not only the potential for community representativeness but also the risk of the impositions of a given judge's idiosyncratic biases in case decisions. Krause also acknowledges such potential, but he believes that in reality such situations are unlikely:

As a practical matter, State intervention in the family typically takes place only in circumstances in which reasonable men and women would have little difficulty agreeing that the intervention is justified. This is an unintended, benign consequence of the heavy workloads of under-financed child protective agencies [p. 236–7].

Others in the legal profession have been less sanguine about the reliability of judicial objectivity and the reasonableness of judges' and social workers' expectations of parents coming before them. In a 1975 paper that later served as the conceptual framework for the model of child protective legislation produced by the American Bar Association, Michael Wald stated:

Most state statutes define neglect in broad, vague language, which would seem to allow virtually unlimited intervention. . . .

> The definitions of neglect offered by legal scholars are equally broad. . . . The absence of precise standards for state intervention is said to be a necessity even a virtue. . . . I contend that this position is incorrect. It is both possible and desirable to define neglect in more specific terms and with reference to the types of damage that justify intervention. . . . Vague laws increase the likelihood that decisions to intervene will be made in situations where the child will be harmed by intervention. Because the statutes do not reflect a considered analysis of what types of harm justify the risk of intervention, decision making is left to the ad hoc analysis of social workers and judges. . . . Their decisions often reflect personal values about children which are not supported by scientific evidence and which result in removing children from environments in which they are doing adequately. Only through carefully drawn statutes, drafted in terms of specific harms to the child, can we limit the possibility of intervention in situations where it will do more harm than good [Wald 1975, pp. 1000–1002].

Although all do not agree with Wald as to how the situation should be resolved, there is agreement that the present state of statutory vagueness has in it the strong potential for injustice and unfairness in dealing with parents and at the same time poses serious jeopardy to the states' efforts to protect children adequately.

Criteria and Guidelines for Professionals

Vague statutory definitions would not pose such a problem if there were clear-cut criteria and standards for interpreting them available to those who must make judgments about specific cases. There is substantial evidence that such criteria do not exist. In the previously quoted passage from Krause, in which he attested to the necessity for nonspecific statutes, he went on to cite a professional tool available to social workers in making their judgments about the initial determination of whether to intervene or not: "To help the social worker, the Children's Division of the American Humane Association has developed a lengthy list of 'things to look for' " (Krause 1977, p. 236). He had reference to the conditions thought to "prove" child abuse or neglect developed by Cynthia Bell and Wallace J. Mlyniec (1974, pp. 26–37). This checklist, entitled "Identifying Conditions of Child Neglect," deals with four types of conditions, and within each type is a listing of specifics. The four are "Physical," "Emotional," "Material," and "Demoralizing Cir-

cumstances." Although the checklist items certainly go far beyond
the statutes in their specificity, the items themselves tend to be
most explicit in the very same areas that the statutes are, the most
tangible ones—that is, the "Physical" and "Material." Some examples under "Physical" are: "physically abused," "lack of dental
care," and "malnourished and emaciated." Under the "Material"
heading are included "dirty, smelly, ragged (clothing) and generally in terrible disrepair," and "hazardous conditions existing for
children such as broken stairs, broken windows, broken porch, and
stair railings, etc." However, conditions listed as indicators of
"emotional" neglect and "demoralizing circumstances" actually
tend to be as vague as the statutes, requiring the same kinds of subjective judgments. For example, under "emotional" is listed,
"Denied normal experiences that produce feelings of being loved,
wanted, secure, and worthy." And listed among "demoralizing circumstances" are "immature parents," "values in home conflict
with society," and "failure to individualize children and their
needs."

Whether from the standpoint of statutory definitions or from
professional guidelines such as those above, the burden of interpretation ultimately falls on the various professionals, who must
make decisions about whether individual cases belong under the
broader rubrics of neglect and abuse. There is strong evidence that
these professionals feel this burden keenly and are extremely dissatisfied with the ambiguous criteria under which they must
operate. In 1974 a sociologist, Saad Nagi, and his colleagues at the
Mershon Center of the Ohio State University undertook a study of
the organizational effectiveness of county child protective systems
over the nation. The respondents in this study included social
workers from child protective services, public health nurses, school
systems, medical personnel, police, and juvenile court personnel.
With respect to the criteria available to them in making judgments,
Nagi reports that only small minorities of each professional group
considered available criteria sufficiently specific and clear:

> Much greater proportions of these responses, ranging from a high
> of 67.9% for respondents from school systems to a low of 43.5%
> for those from child protective agencies, found decision-criteria
> badly lacking in specificity and clarity. It is interesting to note
> that physicians, whose fields are based on the harder and more
> advanced technologies, expressed much greater skepticism about

the current status of decision criteria than did personnel from
child protective services [Nagi 1977, p. 21].

On the basis of this very comprehensive study, Nagi concluded:

> While cases closer to the two ends of any continuum are more
> readily identifiable, doubt increases as one moves from either end
> toward the middle. Although such vagueness is not uncommon to
> criteria defining social problems, the area of doubt in regard to
> child abuse and neglect seems to include a large proportion of
> cases. At the heart of the problem lies the question of when and
> what forms of maltreatment are to be considered disciplinary, ex-
> cessive, or abusive. Much has been written about this question,
> ranging from societal prescriptions denouncing violence to
> specific justifications for court rulings. Nevertheless, the
> numerous statements made about the subject thus far have
> neither significantly furthered the clarification of criteria nor
> narrowed the range of doubtful cases. . . . This lack of clear and
> objective criteria reflects fundamental limitations in the state of
> knowledge about child development; it constitutes the most dif-
> ficult obstacle to appropriate decision-making with child
> maltreatment [pp. 20–21].

It is little wonder that professionals, who must make serious decisions every day in the face of these obstacles, express dismay.

National Social Policy Legislation

Although the problems of child abuse and neglect go far back in
history, they did not become the object of legislation dictating national social policy until very recently. The most important legislation and the first of its kind to be national in scope was that passed
in 1974, which established the National Center on Child Abuse and
Neglect. The legislation was sponsored by Senator Walter F. Mon-
dale. Among the charges to the National Center, three specified in
the law are:

- compile, analyze, and publish a summary annually of recently
  conducted and currently conducted research on child abuse and
  neglect;
- conduct research into the causes of child abuse and neglect, and
  into the prevention, identification, and treatment thereof; and
- make a complete and full study of the national incidence of
  child abuse and neglect, including a determination of the extent
  to which incidents of child abuse and neglect are increasing in
  number or severity [P.L. 93–247, 93d Cong., S1191].

The bill authorized some $60 million to be expended toward these and other research and demonstration efforts. The bill itself is a clear example of a legislative body's request for the kind of information needed for future policy decisions. But what a difficult charge to the National Center. The only definition given of the problem of which they are to make "a complete and full study" is as follows:

> For purposes of this Act the term "child abuse and neglect" means the physical or mental injury, sexual abuse, negligent treatment, or maltreatment of a child under the age of eighteen by a person who is responsible for the child's welfare under circumstances which indicate that the child's health or *welfare* is harmed or threatened thereby [emphasis added].

How is one to go about finding the causes and making a full investigation of such broadly defined and diverse phenomena? What evidence is there that existing research efforts have been able to meet this very reasonable legislative request, in the face of the definitional problems involved?

Problems in Research Definitions

In 1977, after reviewing for the National Center on Child Abuse and Neglect all available results of research, Mary Porter Martin began her report with an observation of the definitional inadequacy in existing research and in scholarly writing about the subject:

> The issue of defining abuse and neglect is one of central importance and logically precedes any discussion of incidence, etiology, or treatment. The vagueness and ambiguities that surround the definition of this particular social problem touch every aspect of the field—reporting system, treatment program, research and policy planning [Martin 1978, p. 1].

Indictment of the inadequacy of research definitions is at once an assessment of the state of the art and of where we as a society are in our thinking and convictions about child abuse and neglect. The importance of adequate research definitions lies in the relationship between research and social policy. Social policy regarding social problems can begin to take on a rational stance only when informed by valid data as to the nature and scope of the problem. Thus the function of research is to supply such data. The nature of such data may entail a search for greater understanding of the phenomena in question, such as that directed toward the causes of the problem. Sound programs for prevention, treatment, or correction of the problems must be based on such data. Similarly, research evaluation of such programs is necessary to weed out the unsuccessful ones. Other kinds of research efforts can be directed toward the achievement of accurate estimates of the scope of the problem, the numbers of persons affected and the distribution of the problem in the population, and those most likely to be affected. Such data will be crucial to decisions that must be made at the policy level regarding the allocation of resources for amelioration of the problem. No one piece of research can supply all such data; the building of a body of knowledge can only come about through many research endeavors. The melding of the data into a useful and coherent whole can only be achieved if the findings from the diverse efforts are comparable. And crucial to such comparability is a clear delineation of just what was being studied, what was being counted, or what was being explained. Clearly the definitional ambiguities that surround the phenomena of child abuse and neglect preclude the necessary comparability vital to rational social policy formulation and enactment.

Some examples of the ways in which researchers have resolved the definitional problems they face serve to illustrate the difficulties in translating their findings into social policy and action. One method, and probably the one most commonly used, has been to simply use as an operational definition of the cases under study the label assigned to an act as by responsible agencies, including hospitals, child protection agencies, police, and courts. Estimates of the incidence of child abuse have been based on work using no further definition of "abuse" than that it was the label assigned to the act (De Francis 1963; Kempe et al. 1962; Kempe and Helfer 1972; Cohen and Sussman 1975; Nagi 1975). There is no way of knowing whether the cases being counted represent similar or diverse phenomena, and hence no way of knowing what the numbers actually mean, save for an indication of the volume of cases being processed under particular labels through various reporting and protective systems. A similar approach has been used in evaluating treatment demonstrations. In one, although ten different programs were compared by the researchers, no uniform definition was used, save admission to the program, of the mistreatment involved that brought the cases into the program in the first place. How, then, is it possible to compare treatment outcomes when this crucial datum on treatment inputs has been omitted? (Berkeley Planning Associates 1977).

A similar state of affairs maintains with respect to work intended to elicit correlates of abusive behavior, ones that might suggest causes. When researchers have relied on official designation as the only means of defining their samples, differences in results among them cannot satisfactorily be explained. Valid results may thus be rejected on the ground that they are not corroborated by similar work, when in fact the studies were not comparable in the first place because the populations being studied were different. Thus research intended to inform policymakers as to the nature of the problem may simply be exasperating to them because of the unexplained, conflictual findings.[1]

Not all researchers have relied on official designation for sample definition; some have formulated their own operational definitions for research purposes and selected their samples accordingly. With such an approach at least the consumers of their research have the option of accepting or rejecting explicit definitions and the work based on them. The problem, of course, is that it is very difficult to know if the findings of such research can validly be extended to populations that have been defined in other ways, including the officially designated ones, which may indeed be the populations of most interest from a policy standpoint.

It is easier to formulate more stringent definitions when the phenomenon under study is restricted, and especially so with respect to "physical abuse" as opposed to the more amorphous concept of "neglect." An example of such a definition is that used by David Gil in his 1968 national study of the incidence and epidemiology of child abuse. He used as a criterion for selecting cases from among all of those reported: "Physical abuse of children is the intentional, nonaccidental use of physical force, or intentional, nonaccidental acts of omission, on the part of a parent or other

---

[1] An example of conflicting findings stemming from differences in population definitions concerns two studies done in different settings, a hospital and a public department of social services. Findings from the hospital-based study were that high levels of maternal stress, measured by family mobility, broken homes, and a history of violence or neglect, differentiated children admitted to a hospital for "failure to thrive" or for "abuse" from children admitted because of an accident (Newbergher et al. 1975). The social services department study, which included no "failure to thrive" children and no abused children, only those identified by the department as "neglected," found that social and familial background factors did not differentiate neglectful mothers from adequate mothers (Giovannoni and Billingsley 1970).

caretaker interacting with a child in his care, aimed at hurting, in-juring, or destroying the child" (Gil 1970, p. 6). In selecting cases for his study, Gil had trained raters screen reports to see which were appropriate to be included under his conceptual definition. It is notable that he included not only physical injury as part of the definition but the crucial factor of intent as well. Such a definition calls for a rather subjective judgment, one that can be made by trained raters but would be difficult to use reliably in routine statistical reporting.

The more diffuse concept of "neglect" is much more difficult to operationalize, and very few attempts have been made to do so in research efforts. Yet all available evidence indicates that the more narrowly defined "physical injury" constitutes only a small fraction of the kinds of situations that make up the bulk of public child pro-tection efforts. These estimates vary, based as they are on data col-lected through reporting mechanisms that make a distinction be-tween neglect and abuse. The range in the ratios of neglect to abuse is from three to one (Nagi 1975; Polansky, Hally, and Polan-sky 1975) (based on data from Florida) all the way to ten to one (an estimate based on a sample of cases from twelve courts over the na-tion) (Cain 1977). Although these widely discrepant figures are themselves testimony to the kind of uncertainty that the defini-tional ambiguity produces, they do suggest some consistency of the finding that "neglect" situations are more common among ap-prehended cases. The more easily defined "abuse" is thus relatively rare. Yet it is "neglect," the more important concern from a prac-tical standpoint, that has been the least likely to receive attention in definitionally precise research. Two pioneering efforts deserve consideration here, both for the contributions made and for the dif-ficulties they highlight. The first is the effort of Leontine Young, who sought both to describe and to distinguish between cases of abuse and neglect. Her study, based on her doctoral dissertation at the Ohio State University and later published under the title *Wednesday's Children*, has by now attained the stature of a classic in the field (Young 1964). Young sought to delineate parental, child, and familial characteristics that distinguished abusive from neglectful families. This kind of systematic investigation was a landmark endeavor, acknowledging explicitly that the two phe-nomena might not be the same. She drew her cases from different sources, including both urban and rural public child welfare agen-cies and privately sponsored child protection agencies. The definitional process was complex, and relied mostly on judgmental ratings by supervisory personnel in the contributing agencies. In the first step the supervisors were asked to select for study cases according to the following criteria: (1) the cases had come to the attention of their agencies via a complaint of child mistreatment, (2) in the best judgment of the supervisors the case was representative of all the cases coming to them, and (3) the case records had the most complete information.

Once Young's sample of case records had been selected, she then established the criteria for not simply categorizing them as "abuse" and "neglect" but also distinguishing within each of these types the "moderate" from the "severe." Cases were identified as "severe abuse" when "either or both the parents beat the children violently and consistently, so that time after time the results of the beatings were visible." Subsumed under "moderate abuse" were cases where "parents beat their children only now and then, that is when they were drunk or under some stress, and the beatings tended to be less violent." For "severe neglect" the criterion was "inadequate feeding." The criteria for "moderate neglect" were lack of cleanliness and lack of adequate clothing for the children" or "failure to provide medical care" (Young 1964, pp. 9–10).

Young quite openly stated that these were arbitrary criteria. Whether one agrees with the distinctions she made or not, the effort to sharpen the research definition of just what she was studying was not only a commendable one at the time but remains a relatively rare effort.

A few years later, in 1967, another scholar in the field, Norman Polansky, undertook the more ambitious task of developing a measure of neglect that could capture a wide range of parental behaviors, from unacceptable to optimal care and degrees of child caring within these extremes. He developed this measure, the Childhood Level of Living Scale, not with a population of identified neglectful mothers but with a group of mothers known to a day care center in rural Appalachia. This scale contained 136 items that referred to physical care and emotional/cognitive care. Within physical care there were 14 subcategories, such as feeding patterns, disease prevention, and regularity of provision for rest for children. Among the 7 cognitive/emotional subtypes were "level of disciplinary techniques," "providing reliable role image," and "consistency in encouraging superego development." The following are some examples of items in the physical care part of the CLL:

"Child frequently arrives at Day Care center and complains of being hungry." "The child receives at least nine hours of sleep most nights." These items are among those in the cognitive/emotional: "Mother seems not to follow through on threatened punishment," and "Mother expresses pride in daughter's femininity or son's masculinity."

Each of the items was scored "yes" or "no" for the mothers under study, and the scale was scored in such a way that the total score equaled the number of problematic behaviors present. Lower scores thus represented higher levels of child caring adequacy, and higher ones inadequate levels. For purposes of his research Polansky rejected the term "neglect," stating that "for our studies, the term *neglect* was replaced by the more neutral, objective concept *adequacy* of child-caring. The CLL operationalizes that concept" (Polansky et al. 1972, pp. 46–51).

In 1976 Polansky and his colleagues revised the CLL for application to an urban population. In this later study the families involved included ones that had been officially designated as "neglectful" by protective agencies for comparison with a group that had not. Although the CLL scores of the mothers identified as neglectful differed significantly from the nonidentified mothers, by no means was there perfect agreement between the protective agencies' designation of neglect and the classification of the mothers according to their scores on the scale. In other words, there appears to be a discrepancy between the agency's definition of "neglect" and the researchers'. In spite of this, however, both of Polansky's studies are among the few where the operational definition of neglect used in the research is explicit, and thus of much greater utility to the research consumer than work where the definitions are shrouded in the ambiguities of officially designated cases. The rarity of such definitional precision in child abuse and neglect research underscores the validity of the earlier observation by Martin, that the most pressing need in the field is research directly focused on the definitional issues.

All these observations about the deficiencies in statutory definitions, in standards and criteria to guide their interpretation, in enunciating national social policy, and in the definitions to guide and implement research all point to the acuteness of the situation. The definitional problems exist, as do the actual situations, along a continuum. At one extreme are those matters that are neither ambiguous nor controversial, situations that clearly belong under the rubrics of "abuse" or "neglect." At the other extreme are those that clearly do not. But between the extremes are matters that generate conflict, and the lines of demarcation become blurred. What are the areas that are most clear cut and those that are most controversial? What is the degree of consensus, and of disagreement, among the professionals who must make these judgments? What are the opinions of different segments of the general population—rich and poor, Black and white, English-speaking and non-English-speaking? How do the opinions of the professionals compare with those of the lay population? How do the differences in opinions about abuse and neglect affect the ways in which professionals attempt to ameliorate the children's situations?

These are the questions addressed in this book. The information on which it is based was gleaned through systematic study of the opinions of lawyers, pediatricians, police, social workers, and members of the general population in metropolitan Los Angeles, and from a systematic review of 949 actual cases of abuse and neglect in four other California counties.

In the rest of this chapter the perspectives that guided the research are presented first, and then the methods used.

PERSPECTIVES ON DEFINITION

The task of defining child abuse and neglect shares the commonalities that accrue to the definitional process itself. That is, definitions are in effect classifications, and the essence of the definitional process is the setting of criteria or boundaries for specifying what does and what does not belong in the classification. The clarity of definition depends on the precision of the criteria for demarcating the concept being defined. This effort to demarcate different classes of events is evident in the very use of the terms "abuse" and "neglect." Both might be subsumed under the rubric of "mistreatment" or "unfit parenting," but the two terms, subclassifications of the broader concepts, are more commonly used. The most frequent distinction made between these two terms is between "acts of commission" and "acts of omission" (Kadushin 1974). While these phrases may accurately capture the semantic differences, they are not at all helpful in delineating those acts of omission and commission that do and do not belong under the respective concepts. The common usage of the two terms does imply that the matters of concern cover a broad range of events and behaviors. Thus, it is best at the outset to abandon the terms "abuse" and "neglect" and to rephrase the question: "What is child mistreatment?"

In attempting to resolve the issues involved in answering the question, different perspectives can be taken on the nature of the phenomena. The perspective adopted in this book is derived from the sociological concept of social deviance. One of the assumptions underlying this perspective is that the meaning of any social phenomenon derives from the social system in which it occurs and/or is defined. Particular behaviors cannot be understood or classified apart from the social context. In a sense, the behaviors themselves are considered to be neutral; they acquire or take on positive or negative connotations only as these are imputed to them within a given social system.

Closely tied to the concept of social deviance—in fact, integral to its definition—is that of social role. All social systems—all organized social groups—derive their order and are able to function through the capacity and willingness of their members to behave according to sets of expectations. These sets of behaviors, expected of persons occupying particular statuses in the social group, constitute social roles. Behavior that varies from those expectations can have negative connotations imputed to it; that is, it is judged to be not simply different but undesirably different, or "socially deviant." The designation of that which is undesirable, and the extent and kind of effort expended to control its occurrence, are predicated on the extent to which the deviant behavior is perceived to threaten the maintenance of the social system or the social order. Hence the imputation of negative values to given behaviors is dependent on the meaning of and presumed consequences of the behavior for a given social order. Insofar as the negative valuation of the behavior is derived from its meaning in a given social context, the designation of particular behaviors as deviant can be expected to vary from one social system to another, and within a given social system from one time to another. Thus, if one wishes to know whether a particular behavior is "deviant," one would seek the answer not in the behavior itself, nor in the person displaying the behavior, but rather in those who make the judgment about the behavior.

It is well at the outset to distinguish this perspective from another approach to the definitional issues, an approach that we term the diagnostic perspective, since it derives chiefly, though not exclusively, from medical science. Diagnoses, like other definitions, are also classification procedures. A diagnosis is in effect the fitting of a particular case into a general category. The nature of the diagnostic procedure, however, is highly contingent upon the reason for making the diagnosis in the first place: to intervene in a pathological process or condition. Hence the diagnostician is concerned with a complex interaction of factors that include not only the presenting condition—the symptom—but also the identification of the pathology producing it and the necessary interventions for eliminating or correcting the pathology. A diagnosis is not complete until the underlying pathology of the symptom is identified. The symptom is only a clue to be utilized in making the diagnosis. Hence the diagnostician looks within the individual for the pathology that is producing the symptom, with the ultimate goal of being able to correct the pathology.

While the diagnostic process does involve general categories or classifications, the focus of inquiry is always the individual. Even if some ultimate environmental cause might be sought, such as contaminated drinking water, such a search would not commence unless the individual displayed certain signs of pathological functioning. It is also possible in some cases that the diagnostician can identify pathological functioning even before it becomes evident to the sufferer through subjective experience of symptoms. Hence diagnoses of coronary heart disease, for example, can be made before a coronary attack has occurred.

The diagnostic approach to the definition of child mistreatment is well exemplified in the work of C. Henry Kempe and Ray E. Helfer, among the most prominent leaders in the field of child abuse. In discussing the definition of "battered child" (a term coined by Dr. Kempe) and of "child abuse," they state that they would define abuse on the basis of the characteristics of the abuser, the underlying source of the pathology, not primarily on the basis of the mistreating behavior or even on the evidence of its effect on the victim of the behavior. With reference to the term "battered child," they state:

> For some this term means only the child who has been the victim of the most severe form of physical punishment, i.e. that child who represents the far end of a child abuse spectrum. For others the term implies the total spectrum of abuse, beginning with the parents (*or future parents*), who have the potential to abuse their small children and ending with the severely beaten or killed

child. Our view of the battered child is one that encompasses the total spectrum of abuse . . . this spectrum has now extended beyond the early and mild cases of physical abuse to the point of *early recognition of those parents who have the potential to abuse* their small children. The confusion and lack of definition have limited communication between those working in the field and often are the primary sources of misunderstanding among those who wish to define the problem more clearly [emphasis added] [Kempe and Helfer 1972, pp. xi–xii].

The focal point in this definition, the source of the pathological functioning, is illustrative of the diagnostic, medical approach. As with coronary heart disease, it is assumed that the diagnosis of child abuse can be made prior to any behavior that might be classified as mistreatment or abuse. It can even be made before the individuals in question assume the social status of being parents. In this diagnostic perspective, the incident of mistreatment, the symptom, can become an irrelevant datum. The focal point of the social-deviance perspective, on the other hand, is first of all on the act of mistreatment itself.

For some time now, the application of the medical diagnostic models to the definitions of other phenomena involving human behavior has been questioned by those of a more sociological persuasion. Thus nonmedical approaches to the definitions of both mental illness and mental retardation have not only become part of the sociological and psychiatric literature but have found their way into laws regulating the lives of those medically diagnosed as "mentally ill" or "mentally retarded." In most states, medical diagnosis of schizophrenia is not sufficient ground to commit a person to a mental hospital. Rather, he must be "a danger to himself or others." A psychological diagnosis of mental retardation based solely on the basis of IQ tests is not sufficient ground for exclusion from the benefits of public education. Rather, the social regulatory mechanisms increasingly rely not just on the diagnoses but on the social functioning and behavior of those diagnosed as such and on the social responses to that behavior (California Welfare and Institutions Code, sec. 5250a; California Education Code, sec. 6902).

With respect to child mistreatment, are the diagnostic and the social-deviance perspectives necessarily incompatible? Is the focus on the social meaning of the behavior encompassed by mistreatment diametrically opposed to the diagnostic approach, which defines mistreatment in terms of the mistreaters' characteristics?

The answer, we believe, is "yes." And the reasons rest on some practical considerations, not solely on an abstract preference for one theoretical stance over another. While the clinician understandably is concerned ultimately with intervention and hence concentrates on the pathology to be corrected, the very exercise of that interventive method cannot be totally divorced from the social context in which it takes place. Within the social context, the legal right to intervene might be challenged and the social resources for providing the intervention withheld, depending on the social valuations placed on the mistreating behaviors in question. While the diagnostician is understandably most concerned with the pathology, the etiology of the mistreatment, the question must be raised, "Why is a source of pathology sought unless the behavior itself is considered socially pathological or deviant?" While it may be horrifying to contemplate, in societies that socially sanction infanticide, one does not seek answers to the question of "why" an individual kills a baby. Or at least one does not seek the answers in the individual.

In our search to clarify the definitional issues surrounding child mistreatment, we have sought answers, then, not among those who have been labeled as mistreating parents but, rather, among those crucial actors in the social system who play some part in the social act of defining mistreatment. It is a complex array of actors, including the general population and members of key professions, precisely because the issues involved go to the core of very basic social values.

DESCRIPTION OF THE RESEARCH METHOD

Research into the problems of definition was conducted in two phases. The first phase involved a survey of opinions of samples of professionals and of a lay population. The second phase consisted of a survey of actual cases of child abuse and neglect. From data collected in the second survey a method was developed for defining the kinds and degrees of mistreatment the children had undergone. These measures of mistreatment were then used in examining the relationship between the mistreatment and the kinds of decisions made by professionals handling the children's cases.

Opinion Surveys

No social definition of child mistreatment is possible unless there is agreement among the definers both as to what they see and how they evaluate it. The fundamental question addressed in the opinion survey concerned the extent of agreement among the various key definers of mistreatment—professionals and lay people.

Survey questions: The research instrument developed to assess these opinions was a set of vignettes depicting specific incidents of child mistreatment. The content of the vignettes was derived from existing laws, reviews of professional literature, case records, and the authors' own experiences—as practitioners and researchers—with actual cases. The vignettes were constructed so that they would represent all the different kinds of actions that might be considered as mistreatment. In all, thirteen categories of incidents were conceived. These categories involved cleanliness, clothing, drug/alcohol abuse, education, emotional treatment, fostering delinquency, housing, medical care, nutrition, parental sexual mores, physical abuse, supervision, and sexual abuse. Within each of these broad categories, an effort was made to construct the vignettes so that varying degrees of severity of mistreatment would be represented. For example, within physical abuse there was a vignette that depicted "burning the child on the buttocks with a cigarette," and one that described "spanking the child with the hand." An additional variation was systematically made in the vignettes. Each statement was constructed so that there was a version that only described what the action had been, and then a companion statement that described both the action and the consequences for the child. For example, there was a vignette that read: "The parent banged the child's head aganst the wall." With the added consequence, a separate vignette read: "The parent banged the child's head against the wall. The child suffered a concussion." In all, 78 pairs of vignettes were generated, for a total of 156, half with consequences and half without mention of consequence. From this basic set of 156 vignettes, 60 were randomly selected for presentation to each respondent in the opinion survey.[2]

The respondents were asked to rate each vignette according to how serious they thought each incident was from the standpoint of the welfare of the child.

Undoubtedly multiple criteria are used in designating individual cases of mistreatment, such as the parent's motivation, or

[2] A more detailed description of the vignettes and the ways that they were sampled and presented to the respondents is given in chapters 3 and 4.

mitigating circumstances like ignorance. However, if it can be assumed that societal interest in intervening in mistreatment is based primarily on a duty to protect children, then the primary criterion in defining mistreatment is the effect on the child. This is so even if the actions are of a nature that primarily offend the society and only secondarily are expected to eventually have adverse effects on the child. Thus, in establishing the criteria for ratings of the vignettes, the welfare of the child was made the point of orientation. Each vignette was rated with reference to the relative seriousness of its impact on the welfare of the child. The focus on the child's welfare captures the values attached to the different kinds of parental behaviors as well as the resulting effects on children. Hence questions of fact—whether one particular kind of behavior does or does not produce a specified effect on the children—can be avoided. Rather the social valuation of the behavior and of the effect itself can be addressed directly. While it may well be that knowledge of child development is limited in making long-range predictions about the effects of parenting on children, the social valuations of those effects remain a separate issue. With respect to social definitions of mistreatment, it is this evaluation that is crucial, not the factual probabilities of the outcome of a particular parental behavior. If the effects for children are not considered socially undesirable, the accuracy of prediction becomes irrelevant with respect to defining mistreatment. In essence, then, the criterion of seriousness—the welfare of the child—focused the research on the respondents' relative social valuations of different areas of child rearing and conditions in children.

Respondents: The lay population surveyed was a representative sample of people in the Los Angeles Metropolitan Area. All social strata and ethnic groups were included. A major purpose of the research was to ascertain the extent of agreement among various subgroups in the population. There were 1,065 respondents in the sample; 129 (12 percent) were Afro-American, 177 (17 percent) Spanish surnamed, 687 (65 percent) white, and 72 (7 percent) of other ethnic groups, Asian and Native American. In addition to being asked to rate the vignettes, the respondents were also asked a series of questions regarding their knowledge of child abuse and how they thought it should be handled. Respondents were given the options of reading the vignettes and of being interviewed in Spanish or English. Eighty-five of them chose Spanish.[3]

The professional respondents were 71 lawyers, 113 social workers, 79 pediatricians, and 50 police officers. All these professionals play key roles in the handling of child abuse and neglect in Los Angeles County. A detailed description of the various roles and functions that they performed is given at this point, not only to describe the sample but also in order to inform any reader who may be unfamiliar with the usual kinds of agencies and personnel that handle child mistreatment. Los Angeles County has a well-developed child protection system. In almost every county across the country, some semblance of the various elements in the Los Angeles system is also present. Child mistreatment is a legal problem, a social problem, and often a medical one. Indeed, the complexity of the mechanisms employed in its management is testimony to the complexity of issues involved in the relationships among the state, parents, and children. Each of the professions performs one or more functions in the process of protecting these various interests.

The *police* are charged with receiving reports of child abuse under the penal code of California. They investigate complaints, and for ones they consider valid, bring the case to the attention of the courts directly, or refer to the Department of Public Social Services for further action. In Los Angeles there is a child abuse unit of the police department that both does investigatory work and serves as consultant to other police officers. In addition to their roles in protecting children, the police have an additional one: apprehending criminals. Thus they must arrest persons suspected of having violated the law in the penal code. They make the judgment as to whether the mistreatment involved is subject to prosecution under those laws. In addition to the child abuse officers, in each precinct of the Los Angeles Police Department there are officers assigned exclusively to juvenile work, although not exclusively to cases of child abuse. Ten officers from the Special Child Abuse Unit and forty juvenile officers participated in the study.

Social workers in the Department of Public Social Services also have responsibility for investigating all complaints of mistreatment that come to their attention, either from the community at large or on referral from the police. When the social workers charged with

---

[3] A more detailed description of the lay respondents and the interview procedures is given in chapter 4.

investigation deem the complaint a valid one, they have two options. One is to refer the case for protective social services within the department, and to do so when they do not think court action is warranted. Social services are provided to families willing to accept them through this part of the department. If, however, a case is deemed worthy of court action, then the social workers are charged with preparing the petition to the court for a hearing and for presenting evidence that the situation comes under the laws that justify making a child a dependent ward of the court. If a child is so adjudicated by the courts, then the department is charged with providing a substitute home for the child, or providing supervison of the child in his own home, if the court deems that proper. The 113 social workers who participated in this study perform one or more of the functions just described.

Cases of mistreatment are heard in one centralized dependency court in Los Angeles. It is staffed by one supervising judge, four commissioners, and one senior referee. These court officers were not included in the survey because there were too few of them to draw any valid conclusions about their responses. All arraignments, detentions, adjudications, and dispositions of petitions filed under Section 300 of the California Welfare and Institutions Code (child mistreatment) are handled in this court. There are various *counsel* who represent clients in the court. The county counsel represent the Department of Public Social Services. Eight of these participated in this study. If it is deemed by the court that there is a conflict of interest between a child's interest and the Department of Public Social Services, then an attorney from a panel of private attorneys who serve the court is appointed to represent the child. The court may also appoint an attorney from this panel to represent the parents. Twenty-one such lawyers participated in this study. In addition, twenty-four lawyers from the Legal Aid Foundation who had served as counsel for parents or children in such cases also participated. Crimes against children, including various forms of mistreatment, are proscribed in the California Penal Code. Such crimes may be felonies or misdemeanors. In Los Angeles County felony charges are instituted and prosecuted by the staff of the district attorney's office, and misdemeanors by the city attorney's staff. Nine deputy district attorneys and eight deputy city attorneys served as respondents. Their work was not limited to cases of criminal mistreatment. In general the work of the lawyers in this study, save for the county counsel, was less specialized with respect to mistreatment cases than was that of the police and social workers.

Pediatricians, although their work is hardly limited to mistreatment cases, do play key roles in the handling of mistreatment. They are specifically mandated under the penal code to report suspected nonaccidental physical injury to the police. Furthermore, they are called upon to testify in both civil and criminal procedures. Their testimony concerns the nature of the injury—in other words, that it was nonaccidentally inflicted, not likely the result of disease or accident. In their daily practice they are also involved in mistreatment cases other than physical injury—for example, those involving malnutrition. The pediatricians participating in rating the vignettes were drawn from several sources in order to obtain representation of physicians practicing in different kinds of settings, and hence with exposure to a wide clientele. Twenty-seven practiced in teaching hospitals (University of California at Los Angeles and University of Southern California—Los Angeles County General Hospital). Thirty-three practiced in a prepaid group health plan, Kaiser-Permanente. Nineteen practiced privately and were drawn at random from the population of board-certified pediatricians in the Los Angeles area.

The professionals who participated in the research thus represented all those concerned with the various interests that are at stake in making decisions about individual cases of child abuse and neglect. In their daily work they must deal with situations identical to those described in the vignettes that they were asked to rate. Our research questions concerned the levels of agreement and disagreement among them in their perceptions of the incidents: Do they agree or disagree as to the seriousness of each of these incidents? Do they see the various incidents in the same way—that is, do they all perceive different types of incidents as having an underlying commonality? This is crucial, since if professionals and lay people alike do not see particular incidents as having a commonality, then there is little likelihood that they would judge such incidents as coming under the broader classifications. Hence, no conceptual definition of these broader classifications such as the kind that must be given in statutes and practice standards would be of any use. Do they differentiate among the various kinds of mistreatment, and, if so, do they agree on which ones are the more serious, and those less serious? Finally, to what extent do the professionals and the general population share similar perceptions and valuations of mistreatment? These were the questions addressed in this part of the research.

Survey of Actual Cases of Mistreatment

In this phase of the research 949 cases from the protective service system of four other California counties were surveyed. A lengthy schedule of information was completed by the workers handling these cases. This information included specifics of the mistreatment, characteristics of children and families, and the kinds of dispositions made and services offered. The cases themselves were drawn from all elements in the protective service systems, the voluntary protective services, and the courts, thus ensuring that the gamut of kinds of mistreatment and of seriousness would be spanned. For each case the specific incidents of mistreatment were recorded on a checklist. Examples from the checklist are: "Burn, scalding," "Child not fed over 24 hour period, more than once," "Child in need of dental care, in pain or experiencing difficulty in eating." From these data a method was developed for translating this information into a measure of the seriousness of mistreatment involved in each case. Then these questions were addressed: How is the seriousness of mistreatment, the degree and kind, related to what happens to the children and their families, including removal of the children, initiation of court action, and provision of different services? Are particular kinds of mistreatment related to particular kinds of familial situations? By what pathways do families come into protective networks, and who initially defined mistreatment in these cases? Answering these questions was an important goal of the research. An equally important purpose was to overcome some of the deficiencies of previous research based on ill-defined populations. All the cases were "officially designated" ones, but the nature of mistreatment in all was made explicit in the operational definitions used.

THE PLAN OF THE BOOK

Chapter 2 is devoted to examination of the historical context in which the issues that stimulated the research have developed. The history of child mistreatment is crucial to an understanding of the problems that now inhere in its definition and its management. Many of the issues around which today's controversies revolve, both the definition of mistreatment and the ways in which it should be handled and by whom, have deep roots in the development of American society and in the evolution of the relations among the state and parents and children.

In chapter 3 the opinions of the professionals studied are presented, and in chapter 4, those of the lay population. Each of these chapters is introduced by a review of the existing literature on the subject. That literature is scant on systematic research but abounds in speculations about attitudes toward abuse and neglect from various professionals and subgroups of the general public. The data, as we shall see, refute many of these speculations.

In chapter 5 the analysis of actual cases is presented, including how mistreatment was defined in each and the relationship between the definition of mistreatment and what happened to the children and their families.

Chapter 6 concludes the book with an examination of the social policy implications derived from the research findings. In this last chapter we offer our own opinions about solutions to the issues, and what the specific ingredients of more precise definitions might be, along with a framework for viewing the areas of controversy over what does and does not belong in definitions of abuse and neglect. A major thesis of the book is that the terms "child abuse" and "neglect" are matters of social definition. As such, they are terms that encompass phenomena subject to neither absolute nor immutable definition. These phenomena cannot be divorced from the broader social contexts in which the definitions are made. Crucial factors in the social context condition the definitions that are formulated: the perceptions of the definers themselves, including both their objective and their subjective views of reality, their social values, and the social consequences ensuing from the act of definition. The values of the definers and the social consequences of the definitions in turn reflect the social structure and the value systems of the broader society.

Thus we do not expect that all will agree with the answers to the questions "What is child abuse?" and "What is child neglect?" given in this book. We do believe, however, that its readers will come to a better understanding of their own definitions. They will not all agree with one another, but the areas of disagreement among them can be made explicit. And that is a beginning.

CHAPTER 2

Child Mistreatment:
A Historical Perspective

SINCE THE BEGINNINGS of the country, American approaches to child mistreatment have undergone many changes, both in the definitions of mistreatment as expressed in laws and in the kinds of social institutions designated to manage the problems. These changes have paralleled others in the society, particularly changing concepts about children themselves and about the role of the family.

As legal entities, the concepts of "abused child" or "neglected child" are creatures of the nineteenth century. They evolved out of and were part of an intricate mosaic of social movements that spawned new social institutions. These institutions themselves were both a stimulus and a response to the growing recognition of the specialness of children, who could not be adequately served within the context of the social and legal institutions established for adults.

The history of American approaches to child mistreatment is necessarily the history of shifting social values and shifting attempts to resolve the competition among values reflective of the interests of the state, the parents, and the children. As history reveals, resolutions of these value dilemmas have been unstable and conflictual. Understanding of the various positions in present-day controversies can be enhanced through an understanding of the historical antecedents of the controversies as well as of the participants.

We begin with the English colonial roots of our social and legal institutions, then trace nineteenth-century social reforms for children and their impact on the concept of mistreatment. Finally, twentieth-century developments leading to our present conceptions of the problem and its management are described.

THE ENGLISH SOCIOLEGAL HERITAGE

The English colonists brought with them a tradition of both laws and social institutions, which served as the fundamental basis for the development of American laws and institutions and for many subsequent social reforms. Most crucial to the development of American family law have been the traditions of English common law.

A key legal concept with respect to the handling of child mistreatment is that of custody. The ultimate cost to parents adjudicated by the courts as having mistreated their children is loss of custody. Custody refers to the rights of parents, or other legal guardians, to control their children without outside interference. Our present laws about parental custody are said to derive from English common law, but the ideas behind our laws are in fact of somewhat more ambiguous origins and have evolved by a rather circuitous route. One transition that is unclear is that from the concept of custody as limited to issues of property rights to the modern concept, which extends beyond property rights to the entirety of the personal relationship between parent and child. Katz has observed:

> The judicial doctrine referred to as the "parental right to custody" holds that any biological parent is entitled to the custody of his child unless the parent is affirmatively shown to be unfit. Many courts have claimed that the right is based on principles of morality and natural affection. However the common law history of the doctrine indicates that it may have been created for economic reasons, even though dictates of a moral code have also had a bearing. During the feudal period, custodial rights, which had commercial value were subject to transfer and sale; a child was primarily a financial asset to his father. . . . In time the emphasis shifted from the property theory of custody toward the personal status theory; that is, the natural parents, because of their relationship to the child, were presumed to be the custodians best fitted to serve the child's needs [Katz 1971, p. 4].

Because of the centrality of property in feudal society and thought, personal relationships were defined in terms of property.

Personhood was virtually synonymous with property ownership. Feudal law did not recognize the family as such. The only laws that existed were those relating to the relationship between father and son and between husband and wife with respect to property rights among them. The most crucial matters pertained to rights of inheritance and management of the revenues of the estates at issue. For example, the father was entitled to "wardship," the right to be a guardian of a minor heir. On the father's death, that right passed not to the child's mother but to the lord of the land of which the child's estate was a part. The guardian was obligated to provide for the maintenance and education of the minor ward, but such provision came out of the revenues of the estate (ten Broeck 1964, p. 287). The relationships to their parents of those without property and the siblings of heirs were not spelled out in law. However, insofar as children could be considered servants in the house of their father, the master, some analogue for defining the rights of the father could be found in the master-servant relationship.

The master-father thus had a right to the services of his servant-child. By this same analogy a father might make claims against a third party deemed to have injured the child. Damage to the child was assessed in terms of loss to the father of the services of the servant-child. A father, for example, could sue his daughter's seducer on the ground that her pregnancy resulted in a loss to the father of her services.

A very important distinction between child and servant, however, was that the child had none of the rights of the servant inherent in the master-servant contract, such as remuneration for services or maintenance while sick or disabled. In fact, it appears that the father did not truly have a legal obligation to support his children or to be liable for debts incurred by third parties in relation to his children. Ten Broeck elaborated on these distinctions:

> Not all of the rights between master and servant applied to the relationship between parent and child. The servant had rights in the relationship which could not be claimed by the child—rights to its continuance during the contracted term, to the payment of wages, and to maintenance during sickness and disability. Between father and child, there were no legally enforceable rights; the child was not entitled to the father's care, protection or support. He remained in his father's household at the complete sufferance of the father, who could turn him out at any moment without regard to the child's need or the father's ability. For

physical mistreatment the child had no right of action against his father, though here the criminal law might assist him [ten Broeck 1964, pp. 288–89].

It is out of this early thinking about parental custody, the stress on property, and the analogue with the master-servant relationship that the notion of children as the chattel of their parents emerged. It should be emphasized that such rights did not accrue to all parents but only to those vested with property rights. Serfs, for example, were virtually chattel of the masters themselves, and describing a serf's child as his chattel would hardly be an accurate description of that relationship.

The common law, unlike statutory law, was unwritten, and developed in the application of judicial principles to individual cases. As values and customs changed, the principles were subject to change. The unbridled authority of the father and the lack of specific obligations were gradually modified, but precise information on just when and how these changes in perceptions of the parent-child relationship came about is elusive at best, and whether in fact the ideas about aspects of the personal relationship are rooted in common law is open to speculation. With reference to the work of Sir William Blackstone, ten Broeck comments:

> Blackstone, reviewing the law governing the relationship of parent and child in the last half of the eighteenth century found little to report. The discussion . . . gives little solace to later opinions which emphasize parental rights to custody and to the child as property and assert that these are founded on the common law [p. 289].

Blackstone's comments on the parent-child relationship, published in his commentaries and based on lectures on the common law he gave at Oxford in 1758, are at least enlightening as to what the cumulative impressions were of what the parent-child relationship *should* be, based on "natural law," if not necessarily common law. Blackstone discussed the legal duties of parents to their legitimate children, and their power over them, and with respect to parental duties he cited maintenance, protection, and education.

> The duty of parents for the *maintenance* of their children is a principle of natural law; an obligation . . . laid down on them not only by nature herself . . . in bringing them into the world: for they would be in the highest manner injurious to their issue, if

they only gave their children life, that they might afterwards see
them perish [Blackstone 1793, as quoted in Abbott 1938*a*, pp.
9–13].

This was not an unlimited duty, and Blackstone went on to
point out the limitation: "For the policy of the laws, which are ever
watchful to promote industry, did not mean to compel a father to
maintain his idle and lazy children in ease and indolence." The
duty to maintain was tempered by the children's duty to work.

The duty to protect children, also cited as a natural duty, referred primarily to protection from injury by third parties or
avenging these. An example given by Blackstone was: "A man's son
was beaten by another boy, and the father went near a mile to find
him, and there revenged his son's quarrel by beating the other boy,
of which beating he afterwards unfortunately died; it was not held
to be murder, but manslaughter merely."

The last duty of parents to children is that of educating them, a
"duty pointed out by reason, and of far the greatest importance of
any." Blackstone criticized the municipal laws of most countries for
not making this duty explicit. While citing English laws as also being deficient in this regard, he took solace in the institution of apprenticeship through which the children of "the poor and laborious
part of the community . . . are taken out of the hands of their
parents and are placed out by the public in such a manner, as may
render their abilities, in their several studies, of the greatest advantage to the commonwealth." As we discuss below, the municipal
laws in colonial America were not so remiss with respect to the
duty to educate, and enforced this duty on segments of the community other than the "poor and laborious."

With respect to the power of the father over his children,
Blackstone cited ancient Roman law that virtually gave the father
power over their life and death. Such unbridled power was not the
case in England. "The power of a parent by our English laws is
much more moderate; but still sufficient to keep the child in order
and obedience. He may lawfully correct his child, being under age,
in a *reasonable manner;* for this is for the benefit of his education"
(emphasis added). What was "reasonable" was not elaborated.

Blackstone's *Commentaries* may or may not be an accurate
reflection of what English common-law prescriptions regarding
parent-child relationships had been up to that time. Nonetheless,
the sentiments expressed are reflective of the concept of parental
relationships the American colonists brought with them. The bio-

logical father had a right to custody of his child, but this right was tempered by duties and obligations to provide maintenance, protection, and education.[1] Hence the custody can be forfeited through failure to perform these duties. This basic notion is reflected in colonial legislation, and Blackstone's commentaries have been accepted as fundamental in the development of American law (Abbott 1938a, pp. 5–6; ten Broeck 1964, pp. 298–306).

Along with the traditions of the English common law, the English colonists also brought with them the tradition of the Elizabethan poor laws, and these laws had a profound effect on the family life of poor parents and children. These laws represented the codification in 1601 of numerous rules and practices relating to public provisions for the poor. They established the fundamental principle of the obligation of the community to provide relief for the destitute, and the obligation correspondingly of the members of the community to contribute to the relief-giving measures. The laws themselves carved out an intricate set of rules and regulations that were to govern the lives of those so relieved, not the least of these regulations pertaining to the relationship between parents and children. It can safely be said that the cost to parents of receiving poor relief was forfeiture of their children.

One means of alleviating the destitution of children, for instance, was through indenture and apprenticeship. Under the laws of 1601, the churchwarden in each parish, along with three or four "substantial householders," constituted the "overseers of the poor" in that parish. Among the duties prescribed for the overseer were the following:

> setting to work the children of all such whose parents shall not by the said church warden and overseers, or the greater part of them, *be thought able to keep and maintain their children* . . . it shall be lawful for the said church wardens and overseers . . . to bind any such children . . . to be apprentices, where they shall see *convenient*, till such manchild shall come to the age of fourteen and such womanchild to the age of one and twenty years, or the time of her marriage; the same to be as effectual to all purposes, as if such child were of full age, and by indenture of cove-

---

[1] The unquestioned exclusive rights of the father to custody maintained for all practical purposes in both England and the United States until the twentieth century. Only very gradually did states in this century pass legislation making the father and mother equal (Abbott 1938a, pp. 7–8).

nant bound him or her self [emphasis added] [43 Elizabeth, 1601-ch. 2, Great Britain, Statutes at Large, II 685–686, as quoted in Bremner 1970*a*, p. 65].

The heavy reliance in the statute on the judgment of the overseers, with no standards even as to whether the parents were able to maintain their children, hardly bespeaks any consideration of their rights, or even a recognition that such rights existed. Clearly, if one of the rights of parents was to the fruits of their children's labor, this was not a right to be accorded to the parents of public charges. The paramount interest at stake was that of the community, which hoped to reduce the public burden of caring for the destitute. The primacy of the community's interests with respect to public charges, which negated the parents' rights, if any existed, as well as the interests of children, dominated the administration of American public relief for more than three centuries.

Jacobus ten Broeck has carefully elaborated the ways in which the poor laws both in England and in America have to a great extent produced a stratified law with respect to family relations (ten Broeck 1964). The importance of the poor-law mentality in relation to child mistreatment cannot be overemphasized. Forfeiture of children because of economic dependency, with no other manifest reason, remained a fact of American life until well into this century. Indeed, as will presently be documented, that form of child mistreatment most commonly associated with poverty, physical neglect, was one of the last to be incorporated into laws dealing with mistreatment. And such recognition came only *after* devaluation of the practice of removing children from their parents for reasons of their poverty alone. Early definitions of child mistreatment evolved in a social context that not only permitted the practice of removing children from poor and economically dependent parents but sanctioned and encouraged it. As long as children could be removed for these reasons only, there was no need for further legal definition of the parental unfitness that could rightly provoke removal. Economic dependency equaled "unfitness."

The English colonists brought with them these traditions of common laws and the poor laws. They also brought with them their own social values and moral and religious principles, including those of family relationships. These values and principles shaped colonial life and found expression in the various statutes, ordinances, and edicts that structured the governance of colonial communities. The early statutes reveal colonial conceptions of the proper relationship between family and community and expectations of both parents and children. Many of them actually were the precursors of much later laws with respect to juveniles, including those that delineated parental mistreatment.

We have noted that in the hierarchy of values, the community's interests were primary. Parents were essentially community surrogates charged with rearing desirable citizens. Children were subordinate to their parents, and parents were subordinate to the community. Intrusion into family privacy and autonomy was commonplace and in fact was an accepted means of ensuring that children not only were being properly reared but also were contributing to community survival within the bounds of their capabilities.

The highly cherished qualities were industriousness and moral and social conformity. Parents' obligations were to provide their children with both a secular and a religious education and above all to prevent any inclination toward idleness. There were laws that empowered communities to take children from parents who permitted such idleness and to indenture them or apprentice them, even if the parents were not dependent on public poor relief. The institutions of indenture and apprenticeship were in fact utilized by some parents as a means of providing their children with educational and vocational advantages that they could not afford. Such separation was not considered harmful to either parents or children, and, if in the best interests of the community, was a virtue. Clearly, the values of working and earning a livelihood superseded those of the bonds of affection between parent and child.

A Virginia statute of 1646 exemplifies this preference of community need over parental wishes.

> Whereas sundry laws and statutes by Act of Parliament established have . . . ordained . . . that the justices of the peace should, at their discretion, bind out children to tradesmen or husbandmen to be brought up in some good and lawful calling. And whereas God Almighty . . . hath vouchsafed increase of children to this colony . . . who if instructed in good and lawful trades may much improve the honor and reputation of the county . . . but, forasmuch as for the most part the parents, either through fond indulgence or perverse obstinacy, are most averse and unwilling to part with their children: *Be it therefore enacted by authority of this Grand Assembly,* according to the aforesaid

laudable custom in the kingdom of England, that the commissioners of the several counties respectively do, at their discretion, make choice of two children in each county of the age of eight or seven years at the least, either male or female, which are to be sent up to James City between this and June next to be employed in the public flax houses under such master and mistress as shall be there appointed, in carding, knitting, and spinning, etc. [Quoted in Bremner 1970a, p. 65 from *VA Statutes at Large*, I, New York, 1823, pp. 336–37].

Parents' obligations to teach their children to read and write and to inform them fully of religious teachings were ensured in some townships through regular house-to-house inspection by designated citizens and various town officials. They were empowered to visit families and to examine the children in their catechism and reading and writing abilities. The parents could be fined or jailed if found to be failing in these responsibilities and their children could be apprenticed.

The office of tithingman was established in Massachusetts in the 1670s to supervise families. Each tithingman was assigned the inspection of ten or twelve families in his neighborhood.[2] Such tithingmen were to be chosen from "among the most prudent and discrete inhabitants" and had to "diligently inspect" the families under their supervision. The statute listed all types of people and behaviors that were not to be tolerated. Not the least of these were stubborn and disorderly children. The tithingmen, on the basis of their diligent inspection, were to give to the magistrate the name of anyone they deemed fell into the following categories:

all single persons that live from under family government, stubborn and disorderly children and servants, night walkers, tipplers, Sabbath breakers . . . or whatever else course or practice of any persons tending to debauchery, irreligion, profaneness, and atheism amongst us, whether by *omission of family govern-*

[2] The office of tithingman dates far back in English history to the time of Alfred the Great. Essentially tithingmen constituted a part of the local police system. England was divided into shires; within a shire an area where ten families lived constituted a tithing, and in each of these a man was chosen to see to it that all in the tithing obeyed the law. The tithingmen appointed in Massachusetts essentially had police power in that they could go into homes and inspect the inhabitants and if they found them wanting could turn them over to the magistrate, an act equivalent to arrest. This act is an early example of the use of local police in matters of family life (Bopp and Schultz 1972, p. 9; Pigeon 1949, p. 5).

ment, nurture and religious duties [or] *instruction of children and servants,* or idle, profligate, uncivil or rude practices of any sort [emphasis added] [Mass. Records, VI, 240–41 as quoted in S. Morgan, *The Puritan Family* (New York, 1966), pp. 148–49].

The consequences of being found to be such a person ranged from fines and binding out to imprisonment. Reliance on family government to maintain orderly and socially acceptable behavior throughout the community implied that the existence of such behavior reflected not only on the individuals in question but also on the failure of the family to carry out its charge. The interest of the community was primary, and family privacy was subordinated to that interest.

Because of the heavy stress on industriousness and moral and social conformity for all members of the community, obedience was viewed as the primary virtue of children. As the best insurance that conforming adults would be produced, obedience was not a matter to be left solely to parents. Parents of unruly, disrespectful children were themselves faulted and could be punished. Even more than that, public responsibility for children's obedience was mandated through statutes that empowered appropriate civic or religious bodies to chastise rebellious children, even to the point of putting them to death. The statutes themselves, while giving evidence of the strong value placed on the subjugation of a child's will to that of parents and elders, also give evidence of some respect for the limits of corporal punishment to be endured. Furthermore, as the following Massachusetts record indicates, excessive physical punishment was considered as a justification for a child to defy a cruel parent.

If any children above sixteen years old and of sufficient understanding shall curse or smite their natural father or mother, they shall be put to death, unless it can be sufficiently testified that the parents have been very unchristianly negligent in the education of such children or so provoked them by extreme and cruel correction that they have been forced thereunto to preserve themselves from death or maiming [Mass. Records III (1854) 101 as quoted in Bremner 1970*a*, p. 68].

While clearly indicating the harshness of the treatment of children, these statutes cannot be taken as evidence that wanton physical mistreatment of children was sanctioned. Such punishment as was to be meted out was first of all established within the law, with limitations put on the number of times children publicly whipped could be struck. Most important, such punishments were imposed by the courts. There was not a license for parents to kill their children, however rebellious. Chastisement through corporal punishment was considered a parental obligation, but there was a degree beyond which such chastisement became a vice.[3]

The value placed on industriousness and conformity and the subordination of family to community interests were very understandable in the colonial context, for survival itself depended on the productivity and social cohesiveness of the citizens. This was not survival in just an intergenerational sense but from one spring to the next. Furthermore, these were shared values, for colonial communities were peopled by members with similar backgrounds and faiths, who had come together out of a desire to be together. Simple social ostracism and shame no doubt kept as many parents and children in line as did the more formal mechanisms.

As the nation grew, however, and the population not only increased but became more diverse, and as cities grew, throwing together those who did not necessarily want to be together, both the potential for common sharing of values and the motivation and capacity to conform to them were diminished. More elaborate laws and social institutions were needed to ensure conformity.

The Nineteenth and Early Twentieth Centuries: The Emergence of Children as a Special Class

When the new nation was formed, with a federal government, and the Constitution written, one of the powers not delegated to that federal government by the states was power over matters of family public policy and law. The Constitution makes no explicit mention of families or children, or of relationships between husband and wife, parent and child, or of the family's relationship to the state. This was neither accident nor oversight, but testimony to the keen interest local communities had in the social unit of the family, an interest too jealously guarded to be entrusted to the

---

[3] Such laws, though not including so severe a penalty as death, were not limited to the colonies. New states, such as Illinois in 1819, began to pass similar ones providing for, among other punishments, public whipping. These laws were the precursors of those of today that refer to "status offenses"—i.e., specify acts that are illegal for children because of their age status, but not for adults (Abbott 1938*b*).

federal government, beyond the control of the local communities and the states. In fact, even state governments were slow to encroach on matters of the family, especially those relating to children. Diversity of values and interests could not be served by a single set of rules established at the federal level. The backbone of the slave system, for example, was the social legislation carefully designed to keep slaves from forming legal families and to ensure intergenerational slave status.

As Katz has observed, the U.S. Supreme Court has employed "substantive due process" to protect family relationships from undue governmental intrusion. However, definition and protection of the family as a social institution, especially the parent-child relationship, are not jealously guarded by the Constitution.

In comparing the constitutional protections of the family with those of other social and economic institutions, Katz had this to say:

> The law does not give the family protection as a social institution. Judicial cases may mention *family* privacy and *family* integrity, but in reality the family as a unit is less protected than corporations. . . . Extensive litigation, for example, has resulted in setting out explicit legal rights and duties for business corporations under the Fourteenth Amendment to the United States Constitution [due process and equal protection]. And in recent years, the United States Supreme Court has shown little reluctance to invoke the protection of the First Amendment's right of association to govern labor unions, religious groups, and political associations. A comparable clarification in regard to the family, however, is missing [Katz 1971, p. 3].

In considering how laws and social institutions related to child mistreatment have evolved, we have to look beyond the federal level of government at a myriad of local and state laws, ordinances, and court decisions. It is necessary even to look beyond government itself, at a diversity of social institutions. In the nineteenth century increasing reliance on private charitable and philanthropic work in effect empowered the private sector to intervene in the lives of families and children quite as extensively as any branch of government.

In one sense the concept of childhood itself emerged out of the nineteenth century. To be sure, children always had a special status. As our review of the colonial period demonstrates, the obedience demanded of children was peculiar to their status. However, save for schools and a few orphanages, social institutions special to children did not exist. There were, for example, no special laws relating to homicide or assault and battery of children: rather, children were assumed to be protected from such events by the same laws that protected adults. The same was true of sexual assault and incest, although definitions of rape did include a lower age limit for consenting females. Under the poor laws children enjoyed no special status. As public charges they were disposed of in the most efficient way, as were adults. Indenture and apprenticeship, though ideally suited to children, providing them with both board and keep as well as future employability, were not peculiar to them. Finally, children were subject to the same criminal laws and punishments as adults, though here there was a demarcation: the "age of reason," which is essentially a religious concept rather than a legal one or one based on knowledge of child development. In effect, deviant acts by or against children were handled pretty much as they were for adults.

This state of affairs changed during the nineteenth century. One class of children did not emerge, however, but rather several special classes of children, each with its own set of laws and social institutions. The title of the classic child welfare text, written by Homer Folks in 1902, captures well the delineations that were made: *The Care of Destitute, Neglected and Delinquent Children.*

Destitution, neglect, and delinquency constituted special social statuses for children. The social definitions that were the bases for assigning children to these three statuses were integral to the evolution of the statuses, with all the reverberations of such delineation for the children, their parents, and the society. Very crucial in the evolution of the social definitions of child mistreatment are the ways in which distinctions came to be made not between these three categories of children and all other children, but rather between "neglected" children and the other two classifications of deviant children: the destitute and the delinquent.

The distinction between the neglected child and the delinquent came much earlier than that between the neglected and the destitute. The reason is a rather simple one. The social response to the problems of all three "kinds" of children was the same: remove them from their parents. It was not until such a response became socially and economically unacceptable for destitute children that it became necessary to distinguish "neglected" destitute children from the masses of destitute ones. This did not happen until 1935, with the enactment of the Social Security Act, finally supplanting the poor laws as the primary means of alleviating destitution.

In discussing the emergence of the distinction between the neglected child and the delinquent, it must be pointed out that the vast majority of children deemed to be delinquent or neglected were the offspring of poor and often destitute parents. They were also for the most part children of immigrants, or immigrants themselves, whose language and customs were foreign to the Anglo-Saxon traditions of those empowered to make the distinctions among them.[4] They were, in fact, very often, save for the accident of who was defining their plight, the same children, and those who defined their delinquency or neglect were very often the same people, or at least people of the same ideologic persuasions about moral reform.

In tracing the history of both delinquent and neglected children, we find that formal delineation in law and refinements in definition have come about largely through the following sequence of events: The social institutions to deal with the children came first—the orphanages and reformatories—then came the laws prescribing the conditions under which the institutions were to be appropriately used. Then came challenges to the laws and their constitutionality. This is an important consideration. The laws governing both delinquency and mistreatment seem to have evolved not as a response to a general community concern but rather as a means of facilitating the management of particular children defined as problematic by a rather select group, well educated and often with the powerful economic backing of private philanthropists (Schlossman 1977).

The major social institutions specific to children developed in the first half of the nineteenth century. Both the orphanage and the reformatory were intended by their reformist originators to separate children from adults: in the case of the orphanage, destitute children from destitute adults; in the case of the reformatory, criminal children from criminal adults. In both cases, a primary motivation was to keep the adults from further affecting the children with their particular kind of viciousness, either their

[4] Although the majority of children in the Northern states were of European ancestry, children of African ancestry fared even worse than they under the existing institutional arrangements, by virtue of their exclusion from many institutions for children (Billingsley and Giovannoni 1972).

criminality or the pauperism that spawned their economic dependency.

The first reformatory was sponsored by a reform group, the Society for the Prevention of Pauperism, which had been founded in 1818 with ambitions of overcoming these twin evils. One of the endeavors that its members energetically pursued was the inspection of publicly run institutions, including both prisons and almshouses. Among the conditions that they deplored in both was the mixing of children and adults.

On the basis of the second annual report of the society, a new organization was formed in 1824, the Society for the Reformation of Juvenile Delinquents. In 1825 this society opened the New York House of Refuge, the first of what came to be known as reform schools (Abbott 1938*b*, pp. 345–49). Surrounding states quickly followed suit. Cities and courts were empowered to send young wrongdoers to such "schools" rather than to jail or prison. They were to be considered "juvenile delinquents," not adult criminals. The reformatories housed children whose only malfeasance was the destitution of their parents, as well as delinquents. It also housed children later to be called "neglected." Though they were not considered "criminals," and the institution itself not a prison, there was a heavy reliance on the police to do the case finding for the reformatories. In an 1832 report to the New York state legislature the Society for the Prevention of Pauperism described in part an institution for which they were seeking building funds as follows: "The design of the proposed institution is, to furnish, in the *first place*, an asylum, in which boys under a certain age, who become subject to the notice of our police, either as vagrants, or homeless, or charged with petty crimes, may be received" (as quoted in Abbott 1938*b*, p. 348).

Early on, the integral role of the police in juvenile work, including work that involved no crimes, was established, first in identifying delinquent children and soon after in finding neglected children. While the social reformers were intent on taking children's problems out of the legal arena, of necessity they relied on law enforcement to serve as gatekeeper to the social institutions they developed.

A few years after its founding, the charter of the New York House of Refuge was enlarged to include among its obligations "a child found to be destitute, if abandoned by its parents or suffered to lead a vicious or vagrant life."

In 1833 a law amending the New York City Charter (one of the first to refer to neglected children) made more explicit the conditions under which children might be brought under public commitment, but it was vague as to the kind of institutions to which such commitment might be made

> The mayor, recorder, or any two aldermen, or two special justices, might commit to the almshouse, *or other suitable place*, for labor or instruction any child found in a state of want or suffering, or abandonment, or *improperly exposed or neglected* by its parents or other person having the same in charge, or soliciting charity from door to door, or whose mother was a notoriously immoral woman [emphasis added] [Folks 1902, p. 169].

Among other suitable places was, of course, the reformatory, the House of Refuge. Since in the view of nineteenth-century reformers mixing children who had committed no crimes with those who had was as threatening to moral character as mixing children with adult criminals, they pushed for new laws that would make it possible to separate these children while still designating them public charges. Such separation is still a popular social cause in many local communities that do not separate delinquent and dependent children in juvenile detention facilities.

There were two reasons for the lack of specificity about the social institutions that were to respond to the array of children's needs, "wants," and "sufferings." One was that the children themselves did not display these problems separately. The great majority had one characteristic in common—they were the children of poor immigrants, and the common conditions of their lives were part and parcel of their problems. The other reason was a practical one. Commitment of children to reformatories or orphanages cost money. The destitute would become public charges in any case. If new institutions for special categories of children were to be developed, assumption of public responsibility for the nondestitute would incur a great cost that would otherwise not fall to the community or state. Thus, while communities pursued an interest in the protection of children, restraint of that interest also made financial sense. As the laws defining neglected children developed, no new social institutions were created to care for the children. They were separated from delinquent children, to be cared for like destitute children, which many of them also were. Hence the case of neglected children came within the purview of those who cared for the poor, the predecessors of modern social workers.

One organization did emerge that was devoted exclusively to mistreated children. This society is best viewed as a distinct kind of social agency with police powers and as a social movement, a part of the humane movement begun in England and other European countries in the 1820s. The actual social agencies that developed under the auspices of the Society for the Prevention of Cruelty to Children never became nationwide in scope. But as a social movement, the SPCC and its successor, the Children's Division of the American Humane Association, had a broad and profound influence and impact on the concepts of child mistreatment and its proper management. In 1874 formation of the society was sparked by appeals to the American Society for the Prevention of Cruelty to Animals (which had been established in 1866) to intervene in the case of a little girl daily beaten by her stepmother. The concerned parties had turned to the ASPCA on finding that the child could have no protection under the existing laws in New York City until the guilt of the stepmother had been established. The animal society handled that case, but subsequently the SPCC was formed. Within five years, ten more such societies were formed, and more gradually followed. In some instances the work was combined with work for animals, but this practice was controversial within the movement (McCrea 1910, p. 135–59). By 1900 there were 161 organizations either exclusively for children or combined with protection of animals. In 1877 the societies for children were incorporated into a national organization, the American Humane Association.

At the outset, the society served essentially a law enforcement function. In addition to seeking out mistreated children, it often placed agents in courts to investigate cases and to advise as to the proper handling of the children and the enforcement of any legal penalties that could be imposed on the perpetrators. The focus was on removal of children from their parents or guardians as the only means of protection and on punishment of the parents as a deterrent to others. "The Cruelty" became a common household term designating the societies, and as Folks has noted, the deterrent effects of their existence probably protected vast numbers of children "whose parents have restrained angry tempers and vicious impulses through fears of 'the Cruelty!' " (Folks 1902, p. 177).

As specialists the societies had a crucial influence in respect to both the definitions of child mistreatment and the evolution of thought as to how it should be handled. The organization took a keen interest in laws to protect children and were a dominant social force in spurring passage of these laws at the state level.

States Define "Neglected Child"

Municipal legislation empowering local authorities to take charge of mistreated children, such as the 1833 New York ordinance, was becoming commonplace by mid-century. However, state-level legislation was a product of the latter part of the century. An essential feature of these laws was the provision of grounds by which parental custody could be challenged and, if the parents were found wanting, forfeited. The children could be declared "dependent" and as such could become the responsibility of the states' charities. Many of the specifics of mistreatment defined in the laws had long been outlawed in the states' penal codes. However, the penal codes did not deal with what was to happen to a wronged child, only with the disposition of the wrongdoer.

Thus, these laws in effect created a new class of children, distinct from the destitute covered by the poor laws and the delinquents covered by the delinquency statutes. The earlier penal codes made it a crime for any person to commit the proscribed actions. The newer laws in civil code made commission of those acts by parents or guardians grounds for forfeiture of custody.

Although the laws of many other states had preceded it, the 1889 law of Michigan was considered a model. This law, the culmination of efforts to separate delinquent children from others dependent on the state, addressed itself specifically to the "ill-treated child." Several sections concerning matters that were already in statutes, essentially proscriptions against contributing to the delinquency of a minor or endangering the morals of children, pertained to all adults, not specifically to parents. These included prohibitions of the use of children in certain occupations—such as gymnast, acrobat, or rope walker—in public exhibitions, in begging, or in any occupation dangerous to life or injurious to health. The use of children for any indecent or immoral purpose was prohibited, and specific reference made it a misdemeanor to send or admit any child under sixteen to a saloon, house of prostitution, gambling hall, or variety theater. The sale or gift to minors of obscene books or papers or police reports, or of alcohol or tobacco, was unlawful, as it was to employ minors in the sale of such items. These were the same kinds of matters that defined a delinquent. What was new in the 1889 statute was that it dealt specifically with the following parental obligations in defining an ill-treated child.

> An ill-treated child is hereby declared to be: *First* one whose mother, father or guardian shall habitually violate or permit such child to violate the provisions of sections 1, 2, 5, and 6 of this act [those just described; parents were thus made responsible whether or not they themselves had violated the provisions]. *Second* one whose father, mother or guardian habitually causes or permits the health of such child to be injured, or his life to be endangered by exposure, want or other injury to his person, or causes or permits him to engage in any occupation that will be likely to endanger his health or life or deprave his morals. *Third* one whose father, mother or guardian is an habitual drunkard or a person of notorious or scandalous conduct or a reputed thief or prostitute, or one who habitually permits him to frequent public places for the purpose of begging or receiving alms or to frequent the company of or consort with reputed thieves or prostitutes, with or without such father, mother or guardian or by any other act or example or by vicious training, depraves the morals of such child [Reported in *Proceedings of the Conference of Charities and Corrections*, 1889, pp. 6–7].

The different sections of the law can be reduced to the following categories of parental failure: (1) endangering the morals of their children or permitting others to do so, (2) exhibiting morally reprehensible behavior themselves, and (3) endangering the life and health of children. Notably, the parts of the law dealing with moral aspects are considerably more explicit than those dealing with the life and health of the child. The outer parameters of "endangering" and "health" are not spelled out, but at least the ideas imply some criteria for judging parents' failures.

While the Michigan law was a model, it was not entirely typical of those passed at the time in that it included reference to actions to protect the physical well-being of children. In other states the matters concerning morals were enacted much earlier and physical matters came later.

In 1910 a summary of laws relating to the protection of children was published by the Henry Bergh Foundation for the Promotion

of Humane Education at Columbia University.[5] Eight categories
of dangers against which the laws protected children were
delineated.

The first, referred to as "general," had four subcategories: "To
willfully cause or permit, (a) life or health of any child to be endangered (b) or unnecessarily expose to weather (c) or cruelly torture or punish, (d) or neglect or deprive of necessary food, shelter
and clothing." Physical cruelty and torture were the most commonly proscribed, in slightly over half the states. The other matters
referring more to physical neglect were specific in the laws of less
than one third. States that did not have cruelty clauses specific to
children relied as they always had on the assault and battery laws
(McCrea 1910, pp. 390–431).

The second category of laws for children, labeled "Abandonment, Desertion and Non-support," obtained in forty states. Many
states relied on these laws to deal with matters pertaining to
deprivation of food, clothing, and shelter. Laws against "carnal
abuse" of children, the third category, existed in all but two states.
The remaining categories all dealt with matters of morals, similar
to those mentioned in the Michigan law. Reflecting the earlier concern with such matters, these laws existed in well over two-thirds
of the states.

An update of this report published in 1914 by C. C. Carstens,
head of the Massachusetts SPCC, took note of the relative lack of
concern with the physical care of children. He commended and
recommended a recently passed Massachusetts statute:

> The general provisions in the various states protecting children
> . . . have been but slightly modified during the last five years.
> The Massachusetts statutes have perhaps seen the most important
> addition. . . . By chapter 180 of the Acts of 1909 a child is also
> protected against the neglect to provide proper physical care
> because of neglect, crime, cruelty, insanity, drunkenness or other
> vice of its parents. Many states have not developed specialized
> statutes to protect children against their abuses, but depend upon
> those punishing assault and battery or non-support to serve this
> purpose [Carstens 1914, pp. 31–32].

[5] Henry Bergh is credited with starting the humane movement in this country.
After a journey to England to acquaint himself with the work of the Royal Society for the Prevention of Cruelty to Animals in London, he returned to interest
people in starting a similar society, and he was its first president.

Legal bases and legal challenges: Both the delinquency statutes and the later neglect laws empowered courts to take children from the custody of their parents. The legal basis for such empowerment was set down in 1838, in response to a challenge of the commitment of a child to the Philadelphia House of Refuge.

A teenage girl, Mary Ann Crouse, had been committed to that institution by a Justice of the Peace at the request of her mother. When the father, who had not been apprised of this action, discovered it, he hired a lawyer, obtained a writ of *habeas corpus*, and demanded his daughter's release on the grounds of the Sixth Amendment, that she had been incarcerated without a trial by jury. The managers of the House of Refuge countered that the Bill of Rights did not apply to minors. The court upheld the managers, not on the Bill of Rights argument alone but rather on the doctrine of *parens patriae:* "May not the natural parents, when unequal to the task of education or unworthy of it, be supplanted by the *parens patriae*, or common guardian of the community?" (*Ex parte* Crouse, 4 Wharton [Pa.] 9[1838]). The court further argued that the reformatory was a residential school, not a penitentiary, and hence not subject to any conditions of due process.

The origins of the doctrine of *parens patriae* date far back in history, but this appears to be the first invocation of the concept in American juvenile law (Schlossman 1977, p. 9). To be sure, the colonial tithingmen in their house-to-house family investigations were acting as "guardians of the community," but until the Crouse case, the legal enunciation of the doctrine had not been explicit. Notably the Crouse decision included the concept of unworthy parents, although nothing about their unworthiness was spelled out.

The doctrine of *parens patriae* remains to this day the fundamental legal principle underlying court intrusion into family life, whether for reasons of delinquency or mistreatment. In the nineteenth century, however, vast numbers of children were removed from their parents without ever coming into a court of law, or for that matter without even coming under the scrutiny of the poor-law administrators. A major movement in the second half of the century, founded by Charles Loring Brace, resulted in the wholesale transportation of children from Eastern cities to homes in the Midwest. The Children's Aid Society, which Brace founded, "rescued" homeless children and children of morally decadent or

cruel families by awarding them to farm families who came forth
to claim them. At least once Brace was publicly taken to task for
failing to observe parents' legal rights in the course of his rescue
work. The substance of that attack is noted here because it both exemplifies the casual way in which many children were removed
from their parents at that time and indicates a dawning awareness
that even poor parents might have some legal rights. At the 1872
Conference of Charities held in Saratoga, New York, a report on
Brace's Children's Aid Society was presented to the conference
(*Proceedings of the Conference of Charities* 1876, pp. 135–45).[6] In
the discussion that followed Thomas P. Norris, president of the
Board of Commissioners of Kings County, New York, inquired as
to the legal authority by which children were transferred out of
state. The reply was that children had to have a written statement
from their father or mother or legal guardian that they might be
taken West. Norris challenged this, stating that some children who
had been temporarily committed to institutions had been sent West
without the consent, and sometimes even the knowledge, of their
parents. He further noted that the parents of many children who
had been put in orphanages had been coerced into surrendering
them to the control of the private institutions. This was so because
it was by then against the law in many states to commit children to
almshouses, and the poverty-stricken parents were thus faced with
recourse to private orphanages, who would take children only on
their own terms. Norris states that he was not opposed to children
getting good homes but wished it could be done with some sensitivity to the parents' feelings.

Norris' plea was countered by the statement of George I.
Chance of Rhode Island, a representative of the State Board of
Charities there. He defended the placement system, saying that he
did not believe that mere paternity conferred rights to parents over
their children when they acknowledged no obligations to the child.
Rather, he believed that "when a parent is bringing up a child to
steal and drink, the rights of the parents are forfeited. They are an-
nihilated before the rights of the state" (*Proceedings* 1876, p. 147).
There was no mention that such "annihilation" might most properly take place in a court of law. Dr. Norris suggested to the conference that it endorse a statement that children should not be
taken out of the state without the consent of their natural or legal

[6] Brace had written the paper reporting on his and the society's work. The paper
was read by Moure Dupuy.

guardians. His was the only affirmative vote. Indeed the meeting ended with a commendation by its chairman, Theodore Roosevelt, then a member of the New York State Board of Charities. He called attention to the "important fact that Mr. Brace had offered to transfer every one of the delinquent boys in the New York institution on Randall's Island to western homes, boys, for whom he noted, the City of New York was paying thousands of dollars" (*Proceedings* 1876, p. 150). The simple economics of public child care appeared to supersede consideration of parents' rights.

Neglect statutes and custody issues: In spite of the fact that many poor parents were deprived of their children without any legal recourse, the neglect statutes did spell out some kind of due process for them and their children in the cases that got to the courts.

The Michigan statutes, like others passed in the last decade of the nineteenth century, provided for procedures whereby parents who had mistreated their children were to be handled. In Michigan, the Probate Court, which did not handle criminal matters but only matters pertaining to relations between persons, was made the tribunal for protecting ill-treated children.

When a complaint of ill treatment was brought to the attention of the judge of the Probate Court of the county where it occurred, the judge was to examine the complainant under oath. If satisfied that ill treatment under the act might have occurred, he was to issue a writ summoning the child, parents, and other witnesses. If the parents, referred to as "the accused" in the law, could not be found, proceedings would take place without them. If the child was without counsel, he or she was to be represented by the county prosecuting attorney. Parents were expected to provide their own counsel. On the request of the parents or counsel for the child or on the opinion of the judge, six jurors were to be empaneled according to the laws relating to courts held by justices of the peace. If the judge and/or jury were of the opinion that the allegations did bring the case within the jurisdiction of the law, the judge was to "make and enter an order that the accused has forfeited his right to the custody of the child during minority and the child be disposed of in the discretion of the judge or probate" (*Proceedings* 1889, p. 7).

In another portion of the act, referring to contested custody cases, the authority of the court was spelled out essentially on the basis of the doctrine of *parens patriae.*

For the most part these laws went uncontested. In 1870, however, one classic case did involve a challenge of the *parens patriae* doctrine and also took note of the vagueness of the 1867 Illinois statute under which a child had been removed and sent to a reformatory. Although the case in question actually involved the handling of a child as a delinquent, the opinion of the appellate courts might have had far-reaching effects on the advance of protective legislation and its reliance on *parens patriae*, if subsequently other courts had heeded that opinion.

Daniel O'Connell had been arrested on a charge of "misfortune" and sent to a Chicago Reform School. The statute, identical in wording to many others that defined a neglected child, authorized the arrest of any boy or girl aged six to sixteen who was a "vagrant, or is destitute of proper parental care, or is growing up in mendicancy, ignorance, or vice." Daniel's father demanded his release on the ground that his son had committed no crime. The appellate court upheld his demand, essentially arguing that the power of *parens patriae* was subject to the constraints of divine law and that the parent-child relationship was divinely ordained. The court asked, "Can the state, as *parens patriae*, exceed the power of the natural parent except in punishing crime?" (*The People* v. *Turner*, 55 Illinois, 280 [1870]).

Attacking the concept of the law as well as its vagueness, the court dealt with the matter of what standards were to dictate its interpretation: "What is the standard to be? What extent of enlightenment, what amount of industry, what degree of virtue, will save from the threatened imprisonment? . . . There is not a child in the land who could not be proved by two or more witnesses to be in this sad condition" (*The People* v. *Turner*).

The decision actually had little effect on the laws or on the courts, and none whatever in setting limitations on the doctrine of *parens patriae* (Schlossman 1977, p. 13). Indeed, that doctrine became the constitutional basis for the establishment of the major sociolegal institution that emerged to handle both delinquent and dependent neglected children, the juvenile court.

Establishment of Juvenile Court

The most important social institution to emerge out of the many decades of efforts to achieve reforms for children was the juvenile court. Spurred primarily, like the other reform efforts, by the wish to remove delinquent children from the adult criminal-justice system, the establishment of juvenile courts was equally important in the evolution of treatment of neglected and abused children. The legal management of mistreated children was transferred from the variety of courts where it previously had been handled to the juvenile court, where it remains to this day. The philosophy of the juvenile court has had a strong impact on the ways in which child mistreatment has been handled and the ways in which it has been defined legally.

Those who spearheaded the juvenile court movement were not lawyers but social workers. Their goal was to decriminalize juvenile procedures entirely. At the core of their philosophy was the idea that the court was there to cure and to treat juveniles, not to mete out punishment; to understand and to parent, not to make judgments about guilt or innocence. The role of the judge toward erring children was that of "wise and kind father." The children were not seen as criminals but as misguided and needing aid and encouragement, and should not be punished or treated as adult criminals in any way (Abbott 1938*b*, p. 331).

The ideal courtroom was a social-treatment agency as well as a court of law, and the ideal procedure was one that embodied informality and intimacy and facilitated the gathering of all kinds of information not strictly evidentiary. The purpose of the court proceedings was to provide judges with the best available information for making a disposition, regardless of whether it would be considered legal evidence. Parents and children alike, whether delinquent or neglected, were to be treated as clients of a benevolent judge with the best interest of the child at heart. As with matters of due process, issues of parental rights, if not overlooked, took on a new meaning.

Although the movement was spearheaded by social reformers—Lucy Flower, Julia Lathrop, Jane Addams—these women were not at all unmindful of the legal challenges that would meet a court constructed along lines of their ideal and saw their need to join forces with legal experts.[7] A committee was appointed at the 1898

---

[7] On a national scale the Chicago group shared the leadership of the juvenile court movement with Judge Ben Lindsey of Denver, Colorado. Lindsey also deplored treating children as criminals, and his concept of the juvenile court was essentially the same as that of the others who spearheaded the movement. Lindsey actually began his court earlier than the ones in Illinois. A Colorado school law had been passed in 1899, designed to strengthen the school's hand in dealing with truants and disciplinary problems. Lindsey took advantage of a section of this law under which it was possible to treat troublesome children as "juvenile

meeting of the Illinois State Conference of Charities to get a law drafted. This committee then arranged to work cooperatively with one from the Chicago Bar Association. Since the goal was to decriminalize juvenile court proceedings completely, the challenge was to get around constitutional guarantees of due process for accused criminals, guarantees that structured procedures in criminal courts. The strategy employed was the removal of juvenile cases from the jurisdiction of criminal courts to the Illinois courts of equity, which were subject to civil, not criminal, procedures. The framers of the first law reasoned that since American equity courts are analogous to the English high court of chancery, a legal basis could be justified for giving the judge the kind of powers they sought for their ideal court. In the English high court of chancery, principles of equity rather than rigid rules of law were applied. There courts exercised the Crown's prerogative of *parens patriae* in behalf of children. The court's parental authority included determination of just what the child's welfare was, to determine what was in the best interests of the child. We have seen how the doctrine of *parens patriae* had already served the cause of social reform as a justification for the reformatory. The ideals of those who sought a special kind of court for children could be realized through the complete removal of juvenile cases from the criminal courts, with their rigid procedures, to the equity court, where the judge could freely exercise the powers of *parens patriae* without regard to due process. The children were accused of no crime and hence were not in need of the usual protections afforded criminals.

The law was entitled "An Act to Regulate the Treatment and Control of Dependent, Neglected and Delinquent Children" (Laws of Illinois, 1899).

It applied to children under the age of sixteen. The definition of a "dependent child and neglected child" was similar to definitions in those earlier laws already described and included lack of proper parental care or guardianship, habitual begging, immoral association, and cruelty or depravity on the part of the parents. The act provided that the circuit and county courts were of original jurisdiction in cases coming under the act, and that in counties of 500,000 population or more, such courts should designate one of

disorderly persons" rather than as criminals. Lindsey got the district attorney to file juvenile complaints under this law, rather than under criminal law. In this way Lindsey established his juvenile court (Levine and Levine 1970, pp.191–192; Schlossman 1977, p. 58).

the judges to hear all such cases and should provide a special room for the hearings. The right of trial by jury on request was provided for. Procedurally, the act provided that anyone might petition the court, in writing, that a situation under the act existed, basing the claim on "information and belief." The judge was to issue a summons to the parents or guardian of the child in question and to the child. If a summons was not answered within twenty-four hours, the parent could be held in contempt of court and a warrant issued. On return of the summons, the hearing was to proceed. The child could be detained during the time prior to the hearing. The act authorized the appointment of "one or more discrete persons of good character" to serve as probation officers and to investigate cases for the judge.[8] Children found to be dependent or neglected under the act could be placed under the guardianship of an institution, private citizen, or social agency of the judge's choosing. Those awarded a child under the act had guardianship over the child but not over any estate of the child. Several similar laws were passed in other states in the next few years.

The constitutionality of the juvenile court was frequently claimed that the right to trial by jury had been denied, that due process had not been followed in bringing the children to the courts, and that the juvenile courts themselves were created in violation of the constitutions of the nation and the state. These challenges were refuted through invocation of the doctrine of *parens patriae* and the argument that since the juvenile court was not a new or a separate court, but rather a part of existing courts, there was no constitutional issue of the creation of a new court.

One challenge, involving a "neglected child" in Illinois, raised these issues concerning the constitutionality of the court and its

[8] The first probation officers attached to the Cook County Juvenile Court in Illinois were not employees of the court. Rather they were supported through private funds. The Juvenile Protective Association served the court with twenty-two workers, many of whom were settlement house workers at Hull House. Those, like Jane Addams, who had led the juvenile court and probation movement opposed, though unsuccessfully, the demise of the voluntary officer through the institution of probation services under civil service. They feared that civil service examinations would be insensitive to the necessary personal qualifications and also the negative effects of political corruption on publicly supported services. Probation services over the country developed in a variety of patterns and gradual professionalization of the occupation was uneven. Even today qualifications vary over the country. In some places those with professional social-work training may be given preference or share preference equally with persons from criminology programs; in others no one particular educational background is required or preferred (Levine and Levine 1970; Schlossman 1977).

proceedings and also alleged that the child declared by the juvenile court to be "neglected" was not and that his mother was not "unfit." The case involved a twelve-year-old boy whose mother was a follower of a religious leader, Otoman Zar-Adust Hanish. At various times Hanish had stayed in her home or she and the boy had traveled around the country with him, and on one occasion the boy had traveled around the country with Hanish and another man. When the situation came to its attention, the juvenile court had declared the boy to be a "neglected child" under the act in that he did not have "proper parental care," that his mother had wholly neglected and failed to care for him properly, and that she was an improper guardian, wholly unable to care for, protect, train, and educate the child. The appellate court ruled that the juvenile court was not a new court, as the judge of the court was a judge of the circuit court. Therefore it refused to hear any questions regarding violation of constitutional rights in the court's procedures, citing many cases that predated the juvenile court on the basis of the *parens patriae*, and struck down the legal challenges to the court itself. However, the decree of the lower court was reversed: the appellate court did not agree that the child in question was "neglected," or that the mother or Hanish or his religion was immoral, as had been charged. In their decision they noted the desirability of a broad interpretation of the statute, but warned the court against excessive imposition of values unnecessary for protection of the child:

> The purpose of the statute is to extend a protecting hand to unfortunate boys and girls, who, by reason of their own conduct, evil tendencies or improper environment, have proven that the best interest of the society, the welfare of the State and their own good demand that the guardianship of the State be substituted for that of the natural parents. . . . The statute should be given a broad and liberal construction, but it should not be held to extend to cases where there is merely a difference of opinion as to the best course to pursue in rearing a child. There should be evidence of neglect, abandonment, incapacity or cruelty on the part of the parent or that the child is being exposed to immorality and vice [*Lindsay* v. *Lindsay*, 257 Illinois 328 (1913)].

The juvenile court survived this and other challenges to the contitutionality of its existence and structure, and within a few years at least half the states had laws establishing special courts for juveniles. As evidenced in this decision, the statutes under which the courts operated, and still do, were vague, particularly with respect to the parent's behavior as opposed to the specification of semidelinquent behavior on the part of the children. This vagueness allowed for a high propensity of subjectivity in interpretation of the statutes. As in this case, disagreement by different observers as to what constituted deviance in child rearing, not just difference, was always possible. As was noted in chapter 1, observers of the juvenile court today still cite the high risk of imposition of the judge's own values, even idiosyncratic ones, in their decisions.

The combination of the imprecision of the statutes and the lack of procedural restraint on the judge's powers compounds such risk (Fox, 1971, p. 56). Nevertheless, appellate cases in neglect matters have been unusually rare. Katz speculates that the reason lies in the lack of sophistication and financial resources of the majority of parents affected. In the Lindsay case cited here, the mother obviously was sufficiently affluent to travel about the country in pursuit of her religious ideals. The kinds of cases that have been appealed most often have been appealed for reasons not necessarily linked to parent's socioeconomic status, such as an unwillingness to permit certain medical procedures and rearing children in unpopular religions (Katz 1971, pp. 69–82).

In recent decades, successful challenges to legal procedures, however, arising out of delinquency cases, have had an impact on the courts. These are discussed below.

At the opening of this century, the major legal antecedents of the current mechanisms for defining and managing child mistreatment were present. Laws defining what constituted a "neglected child" existed, as did the court that enforced these laws. The investigatory functions were carried out through a private agency, the Society for the Prevention of Cruelty to Children, or through the public sector, by the police and/or the probation services attached to the court. While these were primarily law enforcement agencies, a social-work orientation to the problem, rather than a legal one, was gaining ground within them, even within the police. The police had had an integral role in juvenile work throughout the nineteenth century, but there was no specialization of this particular function. However in the early 1900s juvenile police work took on a special character. This was spurred in part by the emphasis in the spreading juvenile courts on obtaining information not just about juvenile offenses but, more important, on the family background and circumstances of the youngsters. The police worked with the courts and thus were influenced by the developments. Specialization of juvenile work to meet the new responsibilities imposed by the juvenile courts came about first through the employment of women as police. The entry of women into police work had commenced in the late 1800s, when women were hired as matrons in the women's quarters of jails and to look after the physical needs of women and children in workhouses and police stations. In Portland, Oregon, in 1905 the first policewoman, Lola Baldwin, was assigned to do work with girls and women, especially to prevent prostitution.[9]

The policewomen's movement spread rapidly, and by 1915 in twenty states there were women police whose work was exclusively with the cases of women and children. The social service aspects of their work, particularly with reference to rehabilitating wayward young girls, quickly came to be recognized at the same time that social work was becoming professionalized through the establishment of schools of social work. Trained social workers were the preferred incumbents of these positions in many cities. Some schools of social work, including George Washington University and the New York School of Social Work, offered special courses and training for police work (Owings 1925).[10]

At the same time that the policewomen's movement was taking hold, the police departments in many large cities began to develop special approaches for both men and women police in working with juveniles—boys and girls. In 1914 in New York City a preventive program was launched that included an effort to avoid indiscriminate arrests of youths, to locate mental defectives among arrested youth, and to engage the police with youth in athletic events and other social group activities. Gradually the specializa-

[9] Shortly after Mrs. Baldwin's appointment a Department of Public Safety for the Protection of Young Girls and Women was organized, and she was made director of it. She did not wish the women officers to be known as "police," rather as "workers." In 1910 Alice Stebbins Wells, a graduate theological student and social worker in Los Angeles, was appointed and called "policewoman" and hence is credited with first actually having the title. Mrs. Baldwin's ambivalance about title perhaps reveals the ambiguity of the early policewoman's role—part police officer, part social worker (Owings 1925, p. 135–36).

[10] This merging of police and social-work education gradually waned as the professionalization of each developed separate pathways. At the university level, departments of criminology are the ones most likely to be giving advanced education to law enforcement personnel, including police, probation, and parole officers. There are still some joint programs—for example, at the University of Nevada's Department of Social Services and Corrections.

tion of juvenile police work began to take hold across the nation (Kahn 1951).

Protection of children from mistreatment was not a large part of the work compared with the efforts for delinquents. However, child protection was clearly within the purview of the police-women and the specialized juvenile officers that developed. Thus while the semiofficial investigatory agencies, the SPCCs, were shifting from a legalistic and punitive approach to mistreatment to a social-work one of prevention and rehabilitation, the police also were being influenced by social-work approaches. The movement for more direct involvement of social workers gained momentum in the early 1900s, eventually leading to the current predominance of social work in the identification, investigation, and treatment of neglect situations. More extensive involvement of social workers came about initially through efforts to distinguish the neglected child not from the delinquent but rather from the destitute child. Social work and its antecedents were the primary forces in the systems managing destitution.

Distinguishing the "Neglected" among the Destitute

Integral to the ideology of the many late-nineteenth-century social reformers was a belief in the preeminence of the family as the most benign center of child rearing. This value flew in the face of the four-hundred-year-old practice of the poor laws: separating children from their parents as a means of alleviating destitution. As the first juvenile court act symbolized the culmination of seventy-five years of juvenile reformists' efforts to distinguish child from adult criminals, so the 1909 White House Conference on Children symbolized the family proponents' efforts to break the poor-law tradition. The message of the conference, called by President Theodore Roosevelt, was that children should not be removed from their parents for reasons of poverty alone. Embodied in the decla-ration was a statement specifying which children and which parents should not be so separated.

> Children of parents of worthy character, suffering from tem-porary misfortune, and children of reasonable and efficient mothers, who are without the support of the normal breadwin-ner, should as a rule be kept with their parents, such aid being given as may be necessary to maintain suitable homes for the rearing of children. . . . The home should not be broken up for

reasons of poverty, but only for considerations of inefficiency or immorality [First Conference on the Care of Dependent Children 1909, pp. 9–10].

The obvious penalty for "inefficiency and immorality" was denial of the financial assistance that was necessary to maintain the family unit. The poor-law tradition of a separate set of rules regarding the parent-child relationship of the destitute was not to be broken in such cases. But who was to make the judgments about "inefficiency and immorality," and how were these to be made? The White House Conference declaration was not a law, but the conferees were highly influential people in the implementation of the message, for they represented the relief givers in both the public and private sectors. Insofar as denial of relief could result in removal of children, the laws governing provision of public relief, along with the rules and regulations of private charitable agencies, in effect constituted definitions of parental unfitness just as did the laws that defined the neglected child. Examination of these laws and agency operations is therefore integral to the examination of the evolution of definitions of mistreatment and of the agencies making the definitions.

Preservation of the family unit had to be implemented through provision of money. In the public sector, at the time, local poor relief was the only source available. The first major revisions of that system were embodied in the Mothers' Pension Laws, which marked a shift in the locus of relief giving from the local to the state level and the separation of a particular category of recipients from the general rules of the poor laws. They were a means-test form of public assistance and in effect were the precursors, at the state level, of the present-day federal/state program of Aid to Families of Dependent Children. The first laws were passed in Illinois in 1911, and within two years twenty states had such laws.

In addition to spelling out the degree of poverty that would make a widow eligible for benefits, these laws also spelled out the requirement that the mother be a fit person, morally and physically, to bring up her children and that it be in "the best interests of the children" to remain with her. The content and the specificity of the statute varied from state to state, but the integral tie to judgments of parental fitness as a condition of the receipt of aid was universal. In fact, in the twenty states with such laws, administration of the laws was placed with the juvenile courts. The very first law, in Illinois, was really an amendment to the Juvenile Court Act previously quoted, with the wording defining a "neglected" child intact. A paragraph was added to the effect that if the parents of the dependent child were poor but "otherwise proper guardians," the court could enter an order fixing the amount of money necessary to relieve them and could order the county board to pay it. In many states the investigators of relief eligibility were the probation officers. Many opposed imposition of these additional duties on the courts, including C. C. Carstens of the Massachusetts SPCC and Judge H. H. Baker of the Boston Juvenile Court. The fact was, however, that there was no other public local agency believed to be qualified to administer these programs. The majority of states with such laws were in the Midwest and Northwest. In many states the poor-law official administered the programs, and in some special county boards were established (Abbott 1938*b*, p. 229–36).

Although in some states the test of "fitness" of mothers was essentially the one embodied in the neglect statutes, in many others the test was much more explicit and imposed a standard of child rearing higher than that which would commonly be interpreted under the neglect statutes. Connecticut, for example, demanded that the widow be of "good character" and that she be a person "who will see that her children receive proper scholastic and religious training." It further stipulated that aid be denied or cut off at any time to families in which, among other things, "there is a record of intemperance, wastefulness or misconduct on the part of the widow," or "where the presence and behavior of lodgers are such to bring the widow into disrepute," or "where the home and the children are not kept clean and orderly, or where the children are unnecessarily kept from school or from work" (Connecticut Laws, 1919, chap. 323, sec. 9).

The provisions regarding parental fitness as a test of eligibility introduced a new element in poor relief. Eligibility, in terms of both finances and fitness, was a constant issue for those in the program, for continuing relief depended on the constant intrusion of home inspection and judgments about their child rearing practices.

It is notable here that the early child-neglect statutes placed heavy emphasis on and were most explicit with respect to matters that could be observed outside the home, especially by law enforcement, including such things as begging, immoral associations outside the home, and even observable physical injury of children. To be sure, probation officers investigated homes, but only after some event or situation had brought them to the court's attention. Ongoing, routine inspection of homes added a new dimension not only to the location of cases of mistreatment, which might otherwise be hidden in the privacy of the home, but also to the scope of what might be considered as mistreatment, including, as in the Connecticut law, "cleanliness" and "wastefulness."

The passage of the Mother's Pension Laws by no means eliminated private-agency relief giving. The strength of private charity at the time is evident in the fact that public relief had been abolished in many Eastern cities. The private agencies bitterly opposed the public laws as socialistic and as tending to increase pauperism and dependency.

Although their work was not child-focused, as was that of the protective agencies and the children's institutions, the private relief organizations bore a very direct relationship to both the definition and the handling of child mistreatment. In distinguishing "neglected children" from the mass of destitute children, they were in an important position both practically and ideologically, quite as important as those in the public sector. The private agencies had been making such distinctions for a long time. The "friendly visitors' " judgments about parental fitness and the denial of aid could be just as effective as the SPCC in stimulating the removal of children, albeit without the legal and criminal sanctions.

Some idea of the criteria of "unfitness" used by the charity organizations can be gleaned from a systematic survey of their work in nine cities done by Mary Richmond in 1909. The participating societies completed questionnaires on the cases of 985 widows that they had handled over the years. Data included in the study pertained to the reasons some of the children had been separated from their mothers.

During the time of the survey about 15 percent of the children in the study had been separated from their mothers. The majority had been committed to institutions and the rest sent to friends or relatives. Richmond categorized the reasons for the separations. Two categories reflected on the treatment of the children: "character of the mother" and "doubtful home influences." The others pertained to the mother's incapacity due to illness. Detailed examples of what was meant by "character" are not given, but a general description is stated:

> In the "character of the mother" most of the commitments were after the mother had been judged by the courts to be improper guardians for their children. In the other cases the woman was

frequently just as immoral or otherwise unfit to keep her children, but the commitments were accomplished with the woman's consent. In all such situations the decisions that the societies are obliged to make are comparatively easy. . . . The "doubtful home influence" cases are especially hard to classify. They represent those borderline situations which vex the souls of social workers in their efforts to give the right treatment [Richmond and Hall 1913, p. 34].

Richmond subdivided the "home-influence" cases into four groups, summarizing the situations in each group. The first dealt with suspected immorality of the mothers, which could not be proved. The second group was more varied, pertaining to aspects of the mother's character other than morals. Some of these aspects might well be considered as contributing to "emotional neglect" today—for example, "The widow was extravagant and bad tempered," and "The widow was lazy and inefficient." The third group included cases where the children's behavior was considered beyond the control of the mother—for instance, "The widow feared that her boys would grow up bad like an older brother," and "One boy was getting into bad habits." The last group were older children who would not work to support the young children (Richmond and Hall 1913, p. 35).

It is clear from Richmond's discussion of the handling of these cases that controversy existed between the societies and other agencies as to proper disposition. In some instances the SPCCs had refused to take cases. In others the charity societies objected to the removal of children by county officials at the request of the parents because such action interfered with the treatment being offered by the friendly visitors. In still others the societies disagreed with SPCC and other agencies that the homes in question were in fact unfit.

The ideological change in how the poor were to be dealt with spurred the distinction between "neglected" children and others. The result was the addition of a new category of definers of child mistreatment, social workers attached to both public and private sectors. Visits to the homes of the poor for relief-giving investigation, including judgments of parental fitness, had the potential for expanding the concept of mistreatment to include matters not usually publicly observable. It also had the potential for broadening the concept of mistreatment to matters of subjective judgment about the propriety of certain family living and child rearing practices. As the interpretation of morality spurred conflict in the legal system (as evidenced in the Lindsay case), the Richmond data indicate that similar conflicts existed among social agencies' observations of family functioning. Disentanglement of the definitions of mistreatment from situationally imposed "life styles" of the poor remains an issue to this day.

PROFESSIONALS IN THE TWENTIETH CENTURY

The Rudiments of Present Protective Systems

In the early part of this century the roots of all of the elements in the present-day community systems to protect children had been established. In the social welfare subsystem, the definition of mistreatment was made by social workers and relief investigators. The results could vary from removal of the children with the consent of the parents, without the involvement of any other agency or the courts, to referral to a protective society for investigation and possible court action, to direct petition to the court. The relief-giving agencies therefore played a direct role in disposing of cases of parental unfitness, as well as a case-finding role for the legal and law enforcement agencies.

In the legal subsystem, there were the statutes defining the conditions under which a child might be declared "neglected." The juvenile court was the agency empowered to make that decision and the decisions as to disposition. The decision-making power was in the hands of the judge, assisted by the police, probation services, and/or the SPCC. The SPCC, along with the police, performed both a case-finding function and an investigative one in many communities. Given the philosophy of the various juvenile courts, the judges and their probation officers also undertook a treatment and rehabilitative role. The balance between the legal and investigative functions of the courts and the treatment and rehabilitative roles was largely dependent on the orientation of individual judges and the qualifications of the probation officers, which varied enormously from one juvenile court to another.

Together, the social welfare agencies and the legal system constituted a curious commingling of the exercise of legal authority and the rendering of social service, with much overlap and blurring of roles. That tensions should arise in any system with such unclear role definitions is inevitable. And in fact they were observable early on.

In 1919, ten years after the first White House Conference on Children, a similar conference was called by the newly created U.S. Children's Bureau, itself an outgrowth of the first White House Conference. The later conference consisted of a series of meetings held over a two-month period, the proceedings of which were published in a volume entitled *Standards of Child Welfare* (1919). Neglected children received attention in meetings devoted to "Children in Need of Special Care." The major paper with reference to such children was given by Judge Victor P. Arnold of the Cook County (Illinois) Juvenile Court: "What Constitutes Sufficient Grounds for the Removal of a Child from His Home?" In making the delicate decisions that came before him, Judge Arnold placed a very heavy stress on the rehabilitation potential of the parents of the child in question (U.S. Children's Bureau, No. 60, pp. 345–50). His paper enunciated his expectations of probation officers, stating that if they were not dedicated and specially trained, there was no way that judicial intentions, embodied in decrees, could be carried out. Clearly the role of the court in his eyes was one that transcended legal functions to merge with the social service and the therapeutic. The judge, in making predictions about the rehabilitation potential of parents, in effect was to assume the role of behavioral scientist, and the probation officer to assume the role of social worker, in providing the rehabilitative treatment.

From the discussion that followed the judge's paper, it was clear that the merging roles of social workers and law enforcers elicited criticism of the efficacy of the performance of both. Social work and social agencies were criticized for not doing enough for families before bringing them to court, in effect leaving the court to do their work. Judges came under criticism for not being properly trained to carry out their diagnostic role in assessing the potential of both parents and child. The representative of the Brooklyn SPCC stated that judges needed to be educated in child psychology. Social workers came under criticism for their lack of knowledge about the law and legal procedures. The representative of the SPCC stated that "schools of philanthropy should train social workers more in the principles of evidence." And the chief probation officer of the New York City Children's Court also chided social workers who brought cases to court with no knowledge of what constituted evidence or of the functions and powers of the courts. He admonished the social workers, "The court is a court of law, call it by whatever name you like, and it must be governed by the rules of evidence. It is not a psychopathic laboratory." Thus one set of criticisms leveled against the court was that it was not a well-functioning psychopathic laboratory; the other centered on the intrusion into the legal arena of people better equipped to carry out the psychological component.

All these issues discussed sixty years ago at that conference persist to this day. Some are in fact more intense, and proponents perhaps more polarized. Insofar as some of today's underlying tensions stem from the intermingling of the legal and the social service dimensions, dissention can be expected to have been exacerbated by the developments in the field. There is the potential for polarization that inheres in the conflicting interests of the parties in the situation. There is also the potential for conflict that arises out of the spread of orientations of a broader array of actors due to: (1) the entry of social workers into primary roles in all phases of the protective process, including investigation, presentation of evidence, and service provision in both the legal and extralegal subsystems; (2) the assumption of a leadership role by pediatricians, especially those with a psychodynamic orientation; and (3) changes in the legal system, especially with respect to due process, and increased involvement of lawyers as counsel.

Child Mistreatment and Social Work

The dominant influence of professional social work in the area of child mistreatment has come about in two ways. The first was at an ideologic level, exemplified in the transformation of the SPCC from a quasi-law-enforcement agency to a social service one. The other way was through recent federal social service policies, in which federal funding for protective services had been allocated to public social service departments.

A change in the orientation of the SPCC from law enforcement to social work evolved gradually. Eventually this agency took the lead in defining child protective work as a social-work endeavor. The Massachusetts Society pioneered in this movement. The shift in emphasis embodied a broadening of the types of situation into which protective work was appropriate and hence a broadening of the concept of mistreatment. C. C. Carstens captured this shift in orientation in this statement:

> Children still need to be protected from the brutality of parents
> . . . rescued from degrading surroundings . . . but the Society
> believes it has a duty toward the children whose circumstances

are, each week that the family is left to itself, becoming worse, *but which are not yet so bad that court action is advisable or possible.* . . . *It must avail itself of every reasonable opportunity to reconstruct such families as are moving on to inevitable shipwreck* [emphasis added] [McCrea 1910, pp. 143–53].

Decades passed before this newer orientation was to become widespread. Its enunciation, however, was crucial in the evolution of conceptions of child mistreatment. The early "preventive work" Carsten and other pioneers of the SPCC talked about was translated into "child protective services," an endeavor that came to be defined as a specialization within the profession of social work and not only as an activity that went beyond the scope of cases under court jurisdiction, but also as one that was preferable to invocation of court authority. While bringing cases to court was a part of the work, it was regarded as a virtual admission of failure of the work attempted through the relationship between the professional social worker and the voluntary client. The concept of child protective services in the following definition by the American Humane Association *evidences the redefinition of protective work as a part of professional social work:*

> A specialized casework service to neglected, abused, exploited, or rejected children. The focus of the service is preventive and nonpunitive and is geared toward rehabilitation through identification and treatment of the motivating factors which underlie the problems (AHA 1955, p. 2).

The legal components of the social-work role are at best viewed as peripheral. Although this orientation and definition of child protective work originated within the Humane Association, it is fully representative of the approach to child protective services by the social-work profession in general.

The assumption by social workers of key roles in all aspects of protective services is attributable in part to the growth of public child-welfare services. Although such services began increasing in number in the 1920s, the great impetus was the passage of the Social Security Act in 1935. That act, and its subsequent amendments, have shaped all child-welfare services, including those for dependent children. The courts and probation continued to be the first line of defense until the early 1970s, when more federal monies became available for social services to neglected children, especially in Title XX, which expanded services to those other than public assistance recipients (Social Security Act, Title XX, sec. 2002). Hence, it was to the great advantage of states and communities to shift all functions related to neglected children to the welfare, or social service, sector, where federal social service monies were available. Although the shift is still not complete, we can state that the most typical pattern now places social workers employed in departments of public social services in the foremost position to carry out the functions of child-mistreatment management. These include protective services outside the purview of the court, investigative functions, and the responsibility for carrying out the disposition of the courts. The social workers have brought with them their special orientation to and definitions of the problems and modes of managing them. The nature of the ideal social-work intervention is one of therapy and rehabilitation, not one of social control. Social workers' authority rests on professional competence rather than legal authority. Justification for use of the authority is thus not customarily sought on legal grounds but rather on the grounds of the benefits to the clientele. Since the intervention itself is viewed as a means of helping, broadening of the scope of definition is a means of expanding the arena wherein the help the help can be given. Of particular importance is the emotional sphere, since casework and psychotherapeutic measures are particularly suited to intervention in emotional problems (Mulford 1958).

Pediatrics and the Discovery
of the "Battered Child"

Paralleling these developments in the social welfare arena have been major developments in the medical sphere. In a narrow sense the discovery of the "battered child syndrome" amounted to little more than a technological advance in pediatric radiology, which made it possible to detect willfully inflicted injuries in children, previously not detectable. But the impact of that discovery has far transcended a mere technological advance. The actual term "battered child syndrome," as we have noted, was first used by C. Henry Kempe at a 1961 symposium of the American Pediatric Society devoted to the new pediatric information (Radbill 1974, p. 19). Kempe and his associates at the University of Colorado Medical Center spurred a wave of national interest, which has had an impact on legislation, on the allocation of federal research and demonstration monies, and on conceptions of child mistreatment that far exceed the rather narrowly defined phenomenon that the radiological discovery encompassed.

Although medicine had always been at least peripherally involved in the problems of child mistreatment, as a profession it had not exercised a role of leadership, and no particular role had been assigned to physicians in the organizational apparatus designated to manage the problem. This changed with the "discovery" of the "battered child." Within just a few years after 1961, all the states had passed laws requiring physicians to report suspected cases of willfully inflicted injuries on children. These new laws, unlike those long on the books dealing with "neglected" children, dealt with reporting, not with management after reporting. In addition, physicians have increasingly been called upon to offer expert testimony in adjudicating cases of child abuse, in both criminal and juvenile court proceedings. The rather late entry of the medical profession into the arena has perhaps hampered an unrivaled ascendancy into a leadership position. In spite of their pronounced influence, so observable in the passage of the reporting laws, at least some pediatricians feel that their impact on day-to-day management of the problems has not reached its desired peak. The tenuousness of pediatric leadership in the area of child mistreatment was noted by Ray Helfer:

> Physical, nutritional, and emotional abuse is one of the most common maladies of the young child. . . . The medical profession has exhibited almost a complete lack of interest in this problem until recent years. . . . Pediatrics still lags behind certain social and legal agencies in providing leadership, service, understanding and even research in the field of child abuse. We in pediatrics have found ourselves in the position of saying, "We must hurry and catch up for we are their leader." It is the responsibility of the medical profession to assume leadership in this field [Helfer 1974, p. 25].

Helfer's perspective on medical leadership constitutes a redefinition of the entire problem of child mistreatment as primarily medical rather than legal or social. Thus the locus of management becomes the hospital. The courts and social services are reduced to a backup role and are to be called upon only when deemed necessary by the physician. At the core of the recommended medical approach is provision of a therapeutic relationship with the parents—a view compatible with, and in fact reinforcing of, the perspective of social work. Compatibility of both with the legal approach is another matter.

Developments in the Legal System

The developments in the legal system paralleling those just described in the social welfare and medical spheres are almost paradoxical. As both social work and medicine have come into prominence in the field of child mistreatment, the approaches of each have become increasingly therapeutic in nature, with a strong preference for nonlegal intervention.

Law enforcement: Of all the professionals currently playing key roles in the management of child mistreatment, the ones that have been involved the longest, in historical terms, are the police. As juvenile work has become a specialization within police work, the handling of child mistreatment has become a specialty within juvenile work in many communities. There is, of course, great variation from one community to another in the kinds of police resources available, and it is not possible therefore to make universally applicable statements about the role of the police or their particular preparation and skills in dealing with the problem. Law enforcement officers, whether specialized or not, have a dual responsibility. Since some acts of child mistreatment are crimes, the police have a duty to arrest in such cases, and at the same time a duty to protect children and to take them into custody, if necessary, to ensure that protection. In most communities, even though social workers may do the bulk of investigatory work, usually the police are the only ones empowered to enter homes on warrant and the only ones available twenty-four hours a day and seven days a week.

In spite of the fact that police clearly have, and have always had, clear functions in relation to child mistreatment, the propriety of their role is controversial. The rehabilitative approach to the problem of mistreatment as opposed to the punitive one of criminal prosecution has tended to becloud the perception of the dual police role—apprehending criminals and protecting children. Major Rudolph A. Pitcher of the U.S. Army Military Police Corps made the following observations about the present status of law enforcement in child mistreatment:

> The proper mission of law enforcement agencies relative to the child abuse phenomenon continues to remain unresolved. . . .

General disagreement over the most suitable role for the police among the social work, medical, law enforcement and legal professions has not been substantially modified. . . . The definition of an acceptable police role in dealing with cases of child abuse has been particularly hampered by the tendency of some members of the social work and medical professions to stereotype all law enforcement officers as "authority" figures whose mere contact with abusive families is undesirable due to a possible detrimental effect on subsequent family therapy [Pitcher, 1972, pp. 242–43].

Jack G. Collins, of the Los Angeles Police Department, made a similar observation, particularly with reference to misunderstandings between social work and law enforcement, and the failure of social workers to understand that just as they have changed their orientation since the early days of the SPCCs, so also have law enforcement personnel:

It seems apparent that the social work profession as a whole has failed to realize that the law enforcement agency's attitude toward the handling of child abuse cases has also undergone a transformation. It is still the belief of the police that pertinent laws must be enforced, but law enforcement has long since recognized the importance and need for referring the various aspects of these most complex cases to those persons and agencies primarily concerned with rehabilitation and the changing of the environment in which the illegal acts occurred. The law enforcement agencies maintain, however, that these referrals and rehabilitation programs must be handled within a legal framework [Collins 1974, p. 182].[11]

Such negative attitudes toward police can place them in an extremely difficult situation, the most difficult of any of the professions. They must interface in a unique way with the legal, social service, and medical systems, and playing cooperative roles simultaneously with all three must indeed be trying.

Court system: Tension among the various professionals has not been eased by changes that have occurred in the legal system:

[11] Some empirical evidence for these general observations is found in a survey conducted by Stephan J. Cohen. Questions concerned which agencies should receive initial reports of child abuse and which should investigate them. Seventy-eight percent of local social services workers preferred their own professional agency as the recipient of initial reports and 79 percent favored it for the investigation work. The majority of police respondents in the survey chose police departments to both receive and investigate reports (Sussmon and Cohen 1975, p. 142).

toward a reemphasis of a legalistic, over a therapeutic, perspective. The laws themselves have changed very little, save for the addition of the reporting laws. However, the juvenile court has been undergoing change. Furthermore, lawyers, as opposed to judges, have taken a much keener interest in the entire problem. As with most reforms in the legal management of neglected children, the changes were manifested first in the treatment of delinquent children. But the repercussions of these changes are now visible among neglected children as well.

According to a survey done in 1963, the presence of counsel in juvenile court proceedings had been a rarity in delinquency cases and almost nonexistent in neglect cases. In almost half of the courts studied, lawyers appeared in neglect cases less than 5 percent of the time (Isaacs 1972, p. 227). But this situation is changing.

The issue of legal representation and due process in delinquency cases culminated in the U.S. Supreme Court decision in the Gault case: the court declared juveniles to have the same constitutional rights to due process as adults do (in re Gault, 387 U.S. 1, 1967).[12] However, mounting criticism of the court's autonomy and omnipotence had already been felt in the revision of juvenile court legislation in New York and California in the early 1960s. New York pioneered with the system of "law guardians" established in 1962, a system that provides legal representation for minors in neglect as well as delinquency proceedings.

In the Gault decision, the legal representation of minors in delinquency cases was enunciated as a constitutional right. The decision did not extend such rights to minors involved in neglect pro-

---

[12] Fifteen-year-old Gerald Gault of Globe, Arizona, had been taken into custody by the police and placed in the children's detention home, accused of making a lewd telephone call. The petition for Gerald's juvenile court hearing was never served on his parents. Neither Gerald nor his parents were told that he had a right to counsel. Gerald was detained further, and at a third hearing, the judge committed him to the Arizona State Industrial School for the period of his minority. With the help of the American Civil Liberties Union the Gaults filed a petition of *habeas corpus* so that Gerald's case could be brought before a court for investigation of possible illegal imprisonment. That petition was dismissed in the Maricopa County Court and an appeal to the Arizona Supreme Court followed, which also was rejected. The case came then to the U.S. Supreme Court, and on May 15, 1967, an eight-to-one opinion favorable to Gerald was handed down. Gerald had been denied four constitutional rights—notice of the charge, right to counsel, right to confrontation and cross-examination of witnesses, and privilege against self-incrimination. The key point of the decision is that a juvenile in a delinquency proceeding is entitled to the same constitutional rights and safeguards as an adult in a criminal proceeding.

ceedings. However, the addition of legal services for delinquency cases in many places has expanded to coverage of neglect cases as well. Legal representation of children and of their parents is by no means uniform or universal. The juvenile court at present is perhaps best described as in flux. But the fluctuations are clearly in the direction of more legalism, not less. In some places the right to counsel means little more than the appointment of overworked public defenders, inexperienced with this kind of case. In others it means the appointment of private attorneys by the court at public expense, representation of the public agency bringing the complaint of neglect by counsel regularly employed for that purpose, and, when the child's interests are deemed incompatible with those of the parents and/or the agency, a court-appointed attorney for the child.

Fox has speculated that lawyers' interest in an array of legal rights, including those of parents and of children, were advanced by the whole atmosphere of the 1960s, including the civil rights movement in addition to the Gault decision. Legal services for the poor have been extended through federal programs and through the legal aid societies, and some law schools have taken a special interest in providing such services in juvenile court proceedings (Fox 1971).

It certainly would be inaccurate to claim that juvenile court proceedings have become totally adversarial or that judges no longer wield considerable discretion in their decisions, for the laws continue to be vague and open to a wide range of interpretation. However, it is quite fair to state that the legal professional has been awakened to unprecedented interest in the handling of child mistreatment. This interest, transcending individual cases, is evident in the active involvement of lawyers not only in issues regarding legal representation but in issues of the content of the laws as well, and in the entire matter of what should legally be considered as mistreatment.

These newer legal perceptions will be dealt with more thoroughly in the next chapter. They are still controversial within the legal profession itself. Disagreement exists among lawyers and between judges and lawyers. And these perceptions are not without criticism from the other professions involved.

CHAPTER 3

Professionals View
Child Mistreatment

OVER THE PAST hundred years American society has developed a complex sociolegal mechanism to handle the problems of child mistreatment. Four key professionals have become integrally involved: law, pediatrics, social work, and police. They have entered the arena at different times and with different orientations, and they perform different and sometimes conflicting roles in managing mistreatment. From the early part of this century on, there is scattered evidence that these professionals have not always been fully in accord either as to what should be considered mistreatment or as to the proper ways to deal with it.

These differences of opinion among professionals have been expressed in two ways. The first is through published writings of leaders in the different disciplines concerned with conceptual definitions of mistreatment, designating criteria as appropriate or inappropriate for categorizing specific cases. Such writings essentially reflect policy stances within the particular disciplines. The other way differing viewpoints are expressed is in the actual work setting, where professionals must interact around specific cases, requiring them to agree at least partially on criteria for categorizing these cases. Agreement and disagreement are evident among the professions at the levels of both policy and practice. Yet there has been little systematic investigation of the *degree* of agreement or disagreement, what the focal points are, and just which professions agree and which disagree on what aspects of mistreatment. In this chapter we present research that has addressed just these issues.

AGREEMENT AND DISAGREEMENT

The Policy Level

In an earlier chapter we traced the development of two approaches dealing with mistreatment, the legal perspective and the social service perspective. In part the conflict between these views is rooted in the potential conflict between the rights of parents and the rights and needs of children.

At the present time the most explicit controversies center on the types and degree of severity of mistreatment that constitute sufficient justification for removing children from their parents. While the rights of parents are an important consideration in this controversy, the welfare of children is of greater importance. Specifically at issue is the relative harm that might befall children by leaving them with their parents versus the harm caused by separating them from their parents and placing them in temporary foster families. This issue of relative harms has led some, especially in the legal profession, to recommend much more stringent criteria for mistreatment that justifies coercive court intrusion into family matters. In their estimation, the issue is not only the matter of relative harms, but also the *immediacy* of the harm and the *certainty* that it will occur if children are left with their parents. Of special significance are questions regarding the types of parental behavior that *might* have a future impact on children, particularly in the emotional realm, since there has been no research-based knowledge to determine the probabilities of the future occurrence of undesirable outcomes for children as a result of parental emotional treatment.

Although the book with the most profound impact on thinking about separating children from their parents focused primarily on the issue of child custody in divorce cases, its findings and recommendations have been carried over into questions of child placement in abuse and neglect situations. At the outset of *Beyond the Best Interests of the Child* (1973), Joseph Goldstein, Anna Freud, and Albert Solnit state their own value premises with respect to issues of child placement: a preference for the child's interests over those of all other parties, and a preference for minimum state intrusion into family life.

First, we take the view that the law must make the child's needs paramount. . . . Second, we have a preference for privacy. To safeguard the right of parents to raise their children as they see fit, free of government intrusion, except in cases of neglect and abandonment, is to safeguard each child's need for continuity. This preference for minimum state intervention and for leaving well enough alone is reinforced by our recognition that law is incapable of effectively managing so delicate and complex a relationship as that between parent and child [pp. 7–8].

Although they do not deal directly with the "neglect" referred to above, the authors do offer a standard by which determinations of such neglect might be made. They suggest supplanting the standard of "the best interests of the child" as a judicial decision-making guideline with one they refer to as "the least detrimental available alternative for safeguarding the child's growth and development."[1] Basically they reject the "best interests" standard as being hypocritical, a term by which adults have done what they wish under the guise of the children's interests: "Many decisions are 'in-name-only' for the best interests of the specific child who is being placed. They are fashioned primarily to meet the needs of competing adult claimants or to protect the general policies of a child care or other administrative agency" (pp. 53–54). The concept "least detrimental" they see as more forthright, at once acknowledging that the child in question is already a victim and that the available alternatives for alleviating his/her circumstances are themselves not totally benign, only less detrimental.

One criticism the authors levy at courts and child-placing agencies is the subordination of children's emotional interests to their physical state. With reference to curtailing parental custody in child neglect situations, they state: "The traditional goal of such intervention is to serve 'the best interests of the child.' In giving meaning to this goal, decision-makers in law have recognized the necessity of protecting a child's physical well-being as a guide to placement. But they have been slow to understand and to acknowledge the necessity of safeguarding a child's psychological well-being" (p. 4). They introduce a crucial concept with respect to children's emotional well-being, attachment to a "psychological

---

[1] In essence, the "best interests" standard is one that has prevailed in our courts since the supremacy of the biological parents, especially the father, to custody rights has been eroded. Rather than automatically deciding custody issues on a basis of biological ties, the "best interests" standard dictates that judicial decisions be guided by whatever is in the best interests of the child.

parent." Drawing on psychoanalytic theory, they proclaim that the most crucial contributor to healthy development of the whole child is the continuity of a relationship with such a person. Separation from the psychological parent inevitably takes its toll. Depending on the age of the child and length and severity of the breach in the relationship, the outcomes for the child can range from death to personality defects in adulthood. They define a psychological parent as "one who on a continuing, day-to-day basis, through interaction, companionship, interplay, and mutuality, fulfills the child's psychological needs for a parent, as well as the child's physical needs" (p. 98).

If the "psychological parent" is so important in making a determination of "least detrimental alternatives," a cardinal consideration in removing a child must be that a child would be in greater jeopardy by remaining with such a parent than the psychological jeopardy incurred through separation from that parent. Given their stance on the equality, perhaps even primacy, of psychological over physical concerns in child placement decisions, one might think that the authors would consider emotional neglect a valid reason for removing a child. However, this is not the case. Because of the primacy of the psychological parent-child relationship, the competing harm with that of separation must not only be greater, it must be certain. The authors reject the certainty of developmental assaults other than those of separation.

> Our capacity to predict is limited. No one—and psychoanalysis creates no exception—can forecast just what experiences, what events, what changes a child, or for that matter his adult custodian, will actually encounter. Nor can anyone predict in detail how the unfolding development of a child and his family will be reflected in the long run in the child's personality and character formation [p. 51].

Thus the authors assert that the certainty of trauma due to discontinuity in the parent-child relationship is known; estimates of other kinds of psychologically harmful situations are less factually based. They caution not only against intrusion through removal of children but against any kind of ameliorative intrusion into the relationship.

> The law will not act in the child's interests but merely add to the uncertainties if it tries to do the impossible—guess the future and impose on the custodian special conditions for the child's care.

This merely leads to harmful and threatening discontinuity by leaving the decision for placement open and subject to special challenges [p. 52].

Those who seek support in *Beyond the Best Interests of the Child* for extending "emotional neglect" as a matter worthy of court intrusion can find little solace for their cause. Since the authors of the book are highly authoritative figures in their respective disciplines—law, psychoanalysis, and pediatrics—these pronouncements have been accorded widespread acceptance. Yet the weight of the authors' arguments rests more on the absence of research evidence than on the presentation of positive research findings. The thrust of their argument is evident in the policy stances taken by members of the legal profession. Robert Mnookin, a lawyer influential in drafting revisions of child protective legislation in California, summarized their views well in arguing that children should not be placed in foster care only because of emotional mistreatment.

> No concensus exists about a theory of human behavior, and no theory is widely considered capable of generating reliable predictions about the psychological and behavioral consequences of alternative dispositions. This does not imply a criticism of the behavioral sciences. Indeed, Anna Freud . . . has warned that theory alone does not provide a reliable guide for prediction: "there remain factors which make clinical foresight, i.e. prediction, difficult and hazardous" not the least of which is that "the environmental happenings in a child's life will always remain unpredictable since they are not governed by any known laws" [Mnookin 1973, p. 616].

The impact on the legal profession of the logic presented in *Beyond the Best Interests of the Child* has not at all been limited to issues about emotional mistreatment; rather it has been extended to establishing criteria for intervention into all kinds of mistreatment. The underlying philosophy is clear in the standards set down by the Juvenile Justice Standards Project with respect to court intrusions into situations of child abuse and neglect. This project examined the entire juvenile justice system, particularly with reference to the rights and responsibilities of juveniles. The project was initiated in 1971 by the Institute of Judicial Administration, and in 1973 the American Bar Association joined as cosponsor. One of the committees established as part of the project was devoted to drafting standards for the conduct of child neglect proceedings. The drafting committee included social and behavioral scientists as well as lawyers and judges. In 1977 a report of that committee was published, *Standards Relating to Abuse and Neglect* (hereafter we refer to the standards as the JJSP/S and the overall project as the JJSP).

The underlying philosophy of the standards recommended is stated clearly in the report. Stringent and specific criteria are proposed as grounds for court intervention, criteria that would dramatically curtail judicial discretion. It is stated that "a basic tenet of the volume is that great deference should be given to 'family autonomy.' This tenet is adopted because it is most likely to lead to decisions that help children" (p. 3). This tenet is compatible with an explicit goal "to allow intervention only where there is reason to believe that coercive intervention will in fact benefit the child, given the knowledge available about children's needs and the means of helping children . . . to insure that when an intervention occurs, every effort is made to keep children with their parents." At the core of the intent of the proposed standards is restriction of the kinds of situations that can come within the scope of court jurisdiction through limitations on the definitions of child abuse and neglect. Crucial to the definitions is the idea of relative harms, an idea compatible with the concept of "least detrimental."

This is evident in the general principles that undergird the standards with regard to the purpose of intervention and the statutory guidelines (given on p. 9):

1.2   Purpose of intervention.
      Coercive state intervention should be premised upon specific harms that a child has suffered or is likely to suffer.

1.3   Statutory guidelines.
      The statutory grounds for coercive intervention on behalf of endangered children:
      A. should be defined as specifically as possible;
      B. should authorize intervention only where the child is suffering, or there is a substantial likelihood that the child will imminently suffer, serious harm;
      C. should permit coercive intervention only for categories of harm where intervention will, in most cases, *do more good than harm* [emphasis added].

In keeping with the focus on specific harms to children, the

JJSP/S recommends elimination of the terms "neglect" and "abuse" in statutory definitions of the grounds for intervention. Instead a new term is suggested: "endangered child," a term that captures the notion of specific and immediate harms. The proposed definition of an endangered child is one suffering from six kinds of harms given in the standards for establishing statutory grounds for intervention. Sharp restrictions are placed on parameters of what may be interpreted as constituting these harms.

Physical harm is defined as one "inflicted non-accidentally . . . which causes or creates a substantial risk of causing disfigurement, impairment of bodily functioning, or other serious physical injury." These same criteria are used to define the second harm, situations that result from *parental negligence,* not necessarily willfully inflicted. In essence this standard would limit interpretations of neglect to situations where the neglect resulted in or was likely to result in physical injury. *Emotional* damage constitutes a third harm, but it is limited as follows: "A child is suffering serious emotional damage, evidenced by severe anxiety, depression, or withdrawal, or untoward aggressive behavior toward self or others, *and the child's parents are not willing to provide treatment for him/her*" (emphasis added). Parental cooperativeness is thus an additional dimension added to the stringency of the criteria of manifest emotional damage, rather than merely a potentially harmful emotional family milieu.

Sexual abuse is a stated harm, whether inflicted by a parent or other household member. (Appended to this standard is an alternative one that would limit intervention in sexual abuse to cases where the child is "seriously harmed physically or emotionally thereby.") Failure to provide *medical* treatment is specified as a criterion for intervention, but the standard is limited to cases where the resultant physical harm would equal that degree of harm established for physical harm. As with emotional damage, intervention is contingent upon parental unwillingness to provide the treatment. The final harm refers to *contributing to the delinquency* of the child, but the contribution must be a direct one, not simply exposing a child to a delinquency-prone environment. The standard is: "A child is committing delinquent acts as a result of parental encouragement, guidance or approval" (pp. 10–11).

These six standards refer to guidelines for coercive intervention. The JJSP/S suggests much more limited criteria for laws mandating the reporting of child abuse to authorities. They would limit such laws to physical injury as defined in the standard for physical harm.

The standards and the philosophy expressed in them represent the stance taken by a significant constituency in the legal profession. There is by no means, however, universal ascription to them. In a dissenting opinion, appended to the JJSP/S report itself, Judge Justine Wise Polier, a very prominent New York City jurist, who also served on the commission that oversaw the entire JJSP, had this to say (pp. 184–185):

> The standards would eliminate neglect, abuse, abandonment or destitution as grounds for juvenile court jurisdiction. They would be replaced by a single category—"endangerment." Endangerment is defined as primarily limited to serious physical harm. Serious emotional harm is excluded unless there is also clear and convincing evidence of the child showing symptoms of severe anxiety, depression, withdrawal, or untoward aggressive behavior, *and* of the parents being unwilling to provide treatment. This position is also taken in regard to cases involving family incest.
>
> The proposed standards assume that children subject to physical harm are at greatest risk, and that, therefore, the limited resources available should be reserved for them. This assumption is not supported by data. More important, it fails to consider the experience of those who have worked with neglected children. Crippling harms including delinquent behavior have been found to result when children suffer neglect by reason of the mental or emotional disabilities of parents who cannot cope with parenthood.
>
> In conclusion, this volume challenges many of the wrongs perpetrated against children who are neglected by their families and the community. Unfortunately it was prepared during a decade when disillusionment, frustration, and increasing avoidance of concern for human problems dominated the ethos. The response is too largely one of lowering goals required to protect children.

The particular issue of including emotional grounds as a basis for judicial intervention had been observed several years before the JJSP/S report by Sanford Katz. His opinions of resolution of the matter, though cautious, do not coincide with the JJSP/S stance, but his views are representative of many others in the legal profession who at least would open the doors to judicial discretion in dealing with emotional mistreatment.

It is highly desirable that legislative recognition be given to "emotional neglect" as an independent legal standard. Specific statutory reference to mental health would provide the needed "peg" upon which to hang a finding of emotional deprivation. Because we have not yet acquired sufficient knowledge about normal and abnormal child development, it is not suggested that an elaborate or detailed definition of "emotional neglect" be frozen into a statute [Katz 1971: 68].

But Katz is mindful of the hazards involved in vague statutes:

Of course, merely listing "emotional neglect" as a standard for intervention will not cure neglect statutes. Nor will it necessarily revolutionize the handling of child neglect cases. It was in Minnesota, with its statutory provision recognizing emotional disability, that a mother was subjected to termination proceedings for writing bad checks. And in Maryland, with a similar provision in its neglect statute, a child was removed from its mother merely because it was in a home with other illegitimate children. The recognition of mental health as a relevant factor, however, will open up an avenue of judicial inquiry that takes cognizance of the complexity of individuals and the unreliability of depending exclusively on "conduct-based" or "event-based" classifications [p. 68].

The controversy over restrictive versus liberal definitions of what is to be construed as mistreatment is by no means confined to the legal profession, nor are discrepancies limited to issues of emotional mistreatment, though that is probably of paramount concern. Those in pediatrics and social work espouse definitions that go far beyond the limited scope suggested by the JJSP and its proponents.

In chapter 1 we quoted the definition of child abuse given by two prominent pediatricians, C. Henry Kempe and Ray E. Helfer. There we noted not only the breadth of circumstances included but the fact that the focal point was on parental, rather than child, characteristics. Some social-work definitions also embody this orientation.

Like Kempe and Helfer, social-work definers have approached the matter in very comprehensive terms, and their definitions beg the question of the demarcation between less than optimal environments and those that are outright neglectful or abusive. David Gil, who did pioneering work on the epidemiology of child abuse (1971), has since set himself apart from other writers in his very

sweeping definition of child abuse. This is the definition he presented to the Sub-Committee on Children and Youth of the U.S.
Senate, at hearings on the Child Abuse Prevention Act (S. 1191):

> Every child, despite his individual differences and uniqueness, is
> to be considered of equal intrinsic worth and hence should be en-
> titled to equal social, economic, civil and political rights, so that
> he may fully realize his inherent potential and share equally in
> life, liberty and happiness. Obviously, these value premises are
> rooted in the humanistic philosophy of our Declaration of In-
> dependence.
>
> In accordance with the value premises, then, any act of com-
> mission or omission by individuals, institutions, or society as a
> whole, and any conditions resulting from such acts or inaction,
> which deprive children of equal rights and liberties, and/or in-
> terfere with their optimal development, constitute, by definition,
> abusive or neglectful acts or conditions [Gil 1976, p. 130].

This very sweeping definition is at once a statement about child
abuse, in its very broadest sense, and a pronouncement of a socio-
political philosophy. Many might consider Gil's stance as "far out."
Certainly in all its ramifications it is not a practical one to act upon
in the foreseeable future. Yet as Martin has so aptly observed, "a
whole range of practical questions is generated or eliminated by the
philosophical statement underlying any definition" (Martin 1978,
p. 1). Indeed, one can speculate on the philosophical underpin-
nings of the much more limited and explicit definitions offered by
the JJSP/S, yet the basic expressed tenet of the value of family
autonomy and minimal state intrusion only skims the surface of an
obviously much deeper and more pervasive orientation as to how a
society should be ordered. Apart from these kinds of considerations, Gil's definition shares with others, considered as more practical, the ambiguities that surround the ideas of optimal development. We have noted that one premise of the very conservative
approach to a definition of emotional mistreatment by the JJSP/S
rests on the lack of empirically based data on what does and does
not enhance psychological development. The following approaches
to definitions of abuse and neglect, while not so far-reaching as
Gil's in their indictment of perpetrators and identification of victims, still hinge very crucially on the question of agreement not
only about what constitutes contributions toward optimal development but also about just what optimal development is.

Norman Polansky, whose work on developing an operational

definition of neglect was quoted in chapter 1, in 1975 offered this definition of the amorphous concept of child neglect:

> Child neglect may be defined as a condition in which a caretaker responsible for the child either deliberately or by extraordinary inattentiveness permits the child to experience avoidable present suffering and/or fails to provide one or more of the ingredients generally deemed essential for developing a person's physical, intellectual and emotional capacities [Polansky et al. 1975, p. 5].

The stance on optimal development and the assumption that the concept has a shared meaning for all observers is not limited to definitions offered by individual scholars such as Gil and Polansky. The Child Welfare League of America, an organization that accredits agencies, both public and private, serving children, in 1973 published standards for child protective service. In that standard-setting document, essentials of healthy development are spelled out as well as a description of a child in need of protective services. The essentials of healthy development are said to be:

- It is presumed that the well-being of a child is jeopardized when he is deprived of the love, care, protection, guidance and control considered essential for his healthy growth and development; and when he is denied the opportunities and experience he requires for development of his innate capacities.
- In order to develop to his fullest potentiality, a child needs to have a feeling of being loved and worthy, and a sense of trust, of belonging and of security.
- He needs opportunities for learning, recreation and leisure time pursuits under safe and adequately supervised auspices. He needs precepts and examples from adults who are important to him, in order to develop a pattern of conduct and moral values [CWLA 1973, p. 5].

In describing children for whom protective services are appropriate, the CWLA standards are more explicit about the essentials of development that might be missing and hence constitute abuse and neglect (p. 12).

> The child on whose behalf protective service should be given is one whose parents or others responsible for the care of the child *do not* provide, either through their own resources or through the use of available community resources, the love, care, guidance and protection a *child requires for healthy growth and development:* and whose condition or situation gives observable evidence

of the injurious effects of failure to meet at least the child's minimum needs.

It is presumed that physical, emotional and intellectual growth and welfare are being jeopardized when, for example, the child is:

—malnourished, without proper shelter or sleeping arrangements
—without supervision, unattended
—ill and lacking essential medical care
—physically abused
—sexually abused or exploited
—denied normal experiences that produce feelings of being loved, wanted, secure and worthy (*emotional neglect*)
—emotionally disturbed due to continuous friction in the home, marital discord, mentally ill parents
—exploited, overworked, *exposed to unwelcome and demoralizing circumstances* [emphasis added]

As with Gil's and Polansky's definitions, this statement from the CWLA rests in part on an implicit assumption that requirements for "healthy growth and development" are known and that beliefs about children's needs are shared. One category of the jeopardies listed bears note—that referring to "unwholesome and demoralizing circumstances." Matters pertaining to the moral behavior of parents, especially their sexual mores, are a less prominent issue of controversy among professionals than are those pertaining to emotional nurturance. Despite the lack of explicitness, there is evidence of controversy. Historically, as we noted in chapter 2, mistreatment statutes were concerned with issues of morality long before matters of physical care, and in some states even before physical brutality. The CWLA is not alone in its inclusion of morality as a matter of concern. The Children's Division of the American Humane Association (1972) goes along with this view, and in a leading child-welfare text Alfred Kadushin lists as a failure in the parental role that endangers the children "exposure to unwholesome or demoralizing circumstances" (Kadushin 1974, p. 235). In describing what is meant by this term he quotes Thelma Garrett Wilson's 1960 American Humane Association publication:

> The child may be living in an illegal environment, such as a house of prostitution or a gambling establishment, or . . . in an environment that is likely to contribute to his "moral degradation and/or delinquency." An example is that of a mother and teenage girl living above a bar where the only entrance to the apartment is between a bar and a pool hall [Wilson 1960, p. 5].

Notably the JJSP/S did not include among harms to children justifying court intrusion any reference whatsoever to parents' moral behavior. It did include as a harm actually engaging a child in a criminal act, but explicitly omitted immoral or criminal parental behavior that did not involve the child. Clearly there is a difference of opinion, then, on issues of morality.

There is some evidence of a rising discomfort with sweeping definitions, especially of emotional neglect, among a variety of professionals, including social workers. In 1975 an interdisciplinary seminar was held in Montgomery County, Maryland, with the express purpose of developing a practical definition of "emotional neglect" (Whiting 1975). Among the 120 participants there were psychiatrists, public health nurses, attorneys, and social workers. In her report on this seminar Leila Whiting, a social worker and child protection coordinator for that county, took note of the great difficulty participants had in distinguishing between children's behaviors described under "emotional neglect" and "emotional disturbance." In attempting their definitions, the seminar participants rejected an approach that focused on the family milieu rather than on the behavioral manifestations in children of the disturbances precipitated by that milieu. An example of the former approach is that taken by Vincent De Francis of the American Humane Association: "A child may become emotionally neglected when there is a failure on the part of the parents to provide him with the emotional support necessary for the development of a sound personality . . . when the climate in the home lacks the warmth and security essential for building in the child a sense of being loved and wanted" (De Francis 1963, p. 17).

In contrast to this focus on the possible precipitants of emotional harm, the initial definitions of the workshops in the seminar, while including references to such precipitants, also added qualifying phrases that described effects on the child such as "handicapping stress" resulting in "inappropriate behavior." When they then attempted to list specific "inappropriate behaviors," they inevitably found themselves listing symptoms of emotional disturbance. Whiting (1975) notes: "The list of behaviors was the same as may be found in any book of child psychopathology—hostile aggression, enuresis, encopresis, fire-setting, sadistic behavior, poor peer relationships, persistent under-achieving, truancy, immaturity, etc." (p. 5). Faced with the similarity of definition between the neglected and the disturbed child, their attention shifted to the parents' willingness to obtain help for the child as the criterion of neglect. The definition that they endorsed consequently was very similar to the standard developed by the JJSP/S, having in it the same two essential ingredients: (1) overt manifestation of disturbance in the child and (2) parental refusal to obtain treatment.

> The complex issues involved in defining *emotional disturbance* and *emotional neglect* may be resolved in terms of parental response to the identification of the problems. The child is emotionally disturbed; parental response determines whether or not the situation becomes one of emotional neglect. Perhaps more definitively stated, emotional neglect of a child equals the parents' refusal to recognize and take action to ameliorate a child's identified emotional disturbance [p. 5].

Such a definition is considerably more restrictive than ones endorsed by the CWLA or the AHA. There are others in the social-work profession who have raised questions regarding the state of knowledge about child development—physical, emotional, and moral. After an extensive review of child development literature and an interview survey of twenty child development experts addressing the question "what is known to be harmful to children," the authors concluded:

> There are definite factors known to be harmful to all children, but they must be qualified. Physical factors in the extreme are the clearest, at least in comparison with more subtle, less obvious manifestations and particularly with reference to children's psychosocial development. It becomes more difficult to answer any question that calls for fine lines of discrimination. Hence, even where the data are more clear-cut such as in the area of nutrition, the threshold between relatively less harmful and not harmful is blurred. Further complicating these fine demarcations is the fact that the variables are not linear: too much or too little can be harmful.
>
> The lack of clarity and certainty does not lie merely in the absence of a factual basis on which to answer the question of harm. It also lies in the nature of the question. What is "harmful" to children can only be answered with respect to some questions on the basis of social values. Scientists, including the social and behavioral scientist, can answer with facts about given sets of conditions and about the likelihood that they will lead to particular outcomes. The "harmfulness" of these outcomes, or conversely their desirability, becomes a question of values, not of facts [Giovannoni, Conklin, and Iiyama 1978, p. 88].

In evaluating the difference in definitional approaches taken by lawyers and those of social work and pediatrics, an important distinction must be made between the definitional purposes of the various definers. Understandably lawyers and judges are concerned with court standards and statutory definition. Members of the other professions do not limit their sphere of concern to the courts. Their concern rather is in describing the parameters of those situations where their particular kinds of help are appropriate—help for the children and for their parents. Hence they seek to widen, rather than limit, the definitions. Their definitions differ not only in scope but in focus. Concerned as they are with conditions that might prove harmful to children at some time in their lives, they focus not only on the condition of the child but also on the behavior of the parent and on the family milieu. They seek not only to protect children but to better the conditions under which they live, even if the conditions are not immediately harmful.

The Child Welfare League of America, in establishing standards for Child Protective Services, took note of this distinction between the legal and the social service sphere of concern: "The definition of a neglected or abused child, for whom social work help should always be available, is more encompassing than that of the neglected or abused child who comes within the jurisdiction of the court" (CWLA 1973, p. 2).

Vincent De Francis, who served for decades as head of the Children's Division of the AHA, also pointed to this difference in purpose with specific reference to issues of emotional neglect:

> The question of the legal definition of neglect becomes important only for those cases where court action is deemed necessary for the best interests of a child. This is a step taken in not more than ten per cent of a protective agency's caseload. Therefore, in the great preponderance of cases an agency will treat a problem of emotional neglect without using the court—without concern over a technicality which does not affect its right to extend preventive services [De Francis 1961, p. 13].

Although the different approaches based on different purposes are understandable, the controversies are not easily dismissed by distinguishing the social service from the legal domain. Two areas of controversy exist over how clearly the two arenas can justifiably be separated. One area of controversy centers on the right of social service agencies to intrude into the privacy of families without court sanction. The other concerns the use of the legal mechanism

of reporting laws as a case-finding mechanism for protective
agencies.

With respect to families' rights to privacy and autonomy, social
service agencies have been accused of using the threat of court action as a means of eliciting "voluntary" cooperation of parents with
their plans. Even if cooperation is not elicited through threats,
overt or covert, social service intervention is still seen by some as an
intrusion, an intrusion that merits the same kinds of justification
that coercive court intrusion does. In criticism of the statement by
De Francis cited above, two lawyers, Stephan J. Cohen and Alan
Sussman (1975), stated: "What De Francis overlooks, however, is
that nonjudicial intervention by a child protection agency may still
violate the rights of others, including their rights to property,
privacy and the right to be let alone" (p. 74).

The controversy about the use of reporting laws in part reflects
a more basic confusion of the purposes of reporting laws. The laws
themselves, first passed in the various states in response to the issue
of the battered child, have gradually increased in the scope of the
mistreatment that must be reported. In part this broadening of the
laws has been intended as a means of extending the investigatory
powers of protective agencies. One purpose of the laws is to bring
to the attention of protective agencies situations where children
may be in need of protection. A second purpose is to collect
statistics on the incidence of mistreatment. And a third, and highly
controversial one, is the establishment of central registries of
perpetrations of mistreatment for purposes of detection and identification of repeating offenders. This last purpose is clearly one
that concerns invasion of privacy, as does any kind of central
registry or data bank where information is kept about individuals,
with or without their knowledge, information that can be used to
their detriment (Sussman and Cohen 1975, pp. 168–69).

The first purpose of the reporting laws, to set into motion the
protective mechanisms that exist for children, is not challenged in
the same way that the central registry function is. However, there
are several issues inherent in the explicit objectives of the laws with
respect to mobilizing protective actions. These issues are exemplified in the wide range of differences in the various states' laws
with respect to who is mandated to report, what is to be reported,
and who is to investigate the reports. Mandated reporters range
from physicians only to anyone who suspects mistreatment is occurring. Reportable conditions range from narrowly defined

physical injuries only to anything that interferes with a child's welfare. In some states only law enforcement can accept reports, in others only departments of social services, and in some either can.

This wide range reflects the distance between the therapeutic and the legalistic approaches. Broad reporting statutes facilitate the investigation of a wide variety of situations, even situations that would not be likely to come within the purview of subsequent court jurisdiction for further intervention. Narrower reporting statutes exclude situations that are subject to coercive court intervention under other kinds of laws. As noted earlier, the JJSP/S would restrict reporting laws to situations of physical harm, while including certain emotional and moral circumstances in standards for court intervention. At the heart of the controversy is the fact that regardless of the purpose of the investigation, those mandated to accept reports are empowered to investigate the reported situations, and the investigation itself can be construed as an invasion of family privacy.

The arguments for separate definitions of mistreatment in the legal and social service arenas thus break down on the issue of family privacy, whether the focus of the argument concerns social service activity beyond the jurisdiction of the court or the use of reporting laws for purposes of social-work case finding. On both counts all the issues surrounding definitions for purposes of coercive court intervention emerge and cannot be dismissed on the basis of any distinct demarcation between the legal and the social-work domains. Should such power be given to social service agencies to enhance case-finding capacity to extend social-work help to children whose situations, in the words of the Child Welfare League, are "more encompassing than that of the neglected or abused child who comes within the jurisdiction of the court in a given state"? Among those who wish to see expanded definitions of mistreatment in reporting laws, the answer is "yes." Among those who would restrict such definitions in the interest of protecting family privacy, the answer is "no."

There is evidence that the majority of the people working in the field—not just social workers—do answer the question affirmatively. This evidence comes from the opinion survey, referred to in chapter 2, conducted as part of a study to develop a model child abuse reporting law. (The study was also part of the JJSP's total effort in establishing standards for the juvenile justice system.) The study surveyed the attitudes and opinions of a national sample of

1,439 people engaged in child abuse and neglect reporting and service systems (Sussman and Cohen 1974, pp. 137–38). Among the questions asked were ones relating to the scope of definition of reporting laws. Questions were asked separately about abuse and neglect. With respect to abuse, 90 percent thought that the scope of definition should not be restricted to physical injury, with 85 percent favoring inclusion of emotional abuse, defined as "the infliction of mental injury." With respect to "neglect," 92 percent thought it should be included along with "abuse." Eighty percent thought that emotional neglect ought to be a reportable circumstance. Sussman and Cohen do not give a breakdown of responses by discipline of the respondents, but with these very high proportions of responses, no one discipline could have accounted for the degree of unanimity. (Notably, however, legal representation in their sample was limited to the judiciary and prosecutory branches, rather than lawyers engaged in defending parents.) The majority (68 percent) of the respondents favored a social service agency as the one mandated to receive and investigate reports (pp. 137–38, 140). This indicates a willingness to entrust investigation of reports to social service agencies for a wide range of circumstances.

All these public statements of both individuals and organizations suggest that professionals are not totally in agreement, at least at the general conceptual level, as to either the kinds of actions encompassed by "mistreatment" or the degrees of severity within any given type of mistreatment that would constitute grounds for sociolegal intrusion. We turn now to a review of how these disagreements at the policy level may be reflected in practice around specific cases.

The Practice Level

Little systematic work has been done to measure the degree of interprofessional agreement in defining specific cases of mistreatment, although there is considerable speculation, based largely on clinical observation, that dissension exists and considerably more speculation as to the underlying reasons. These observations have focused on two types of situations: disagreement among individual professionals in identifying cases of physical injury as the result of willful child abuse, and disagreement over definition.

The most recent major legislative activity in the field has been directed at overcoming the failure of some professionals to report possible instances of willful child abuse. The enactment of mandatory reporting laws was predicated in part on the supposition that individual cases of physical injury, while treated medically, were not being properly diagnosed as "child abuse"—a diagnosis that brings the proper sociolegal protective mechanisms into play as well as medical treatment. The failure of medical personnel to make such diagnoses has long been observed by pioneers in the field from both social work and medicine (Boardman, 1962; Elmer, 1960; Kempe et al., 1962; and Helfer, 1975). This has been recognized not only by clinical observers but also by researchers who find discrepancies between the rates of cases reported by physicians and the statistical expectations of what such rates should be (Nagi 1975; Groeneveld and Giovannoni 1977). All of these observations assume implicitly that the failure to define specific cases of physical injury as "child abuse" results from a failure to recognize that the observed injury was inflicted on the child by a parent or other caretaker, not from the belief that the injury was not serious enough to constitute mistreatment.

In their efforts to explain why professionals do not recognize and subsequently label individual instances of child abuse, numerous observers have pointed to the potential psychological discomfort inherent in such designation. Potentially severe ambivalence may be generated from the professionals' dual identification, with both the abused child and the abusing parent. The psychic strain produced by this ambivalence is relieved by suppressing recognition of the situation as one of abuse in a form of psychological denial. Hospital staff, including both social workers and physicians, have been cited as succumbing to such intrapsychic resolution (Boardman 1962; Elmer 1960; Holmes et al. 1975).

Another potential reason for denial centers on the professionals' fears of their own destructive impulses. Repugnance at the thought of parents deliberately injuring their own child is one way of distancing the observed abuse from the professional's own impulses. Elmer especially has noted how this repugnance serves to deter recognition. She observed that hospital personnel frequently react to child abuse either by becoming intensely angered and seeking to punish the alleged abuser, or by ignoring the problem and refusing to consider any evidence of maltreatment. She went on to hypothesize a general societal taboo in the area of abuse. Middle-class professionals, she claims, feel uncomfortable about abusive behavior, preferring to think of themselves as "civilized" and therefore immune to such impulses. The repugnance itself can then generate attempts to blot out the incident altogether by openly disregarding evidence of abuse (Elmer 1966).

Silver and his colleagues (1967), interpreting data from a survey of 179 physicians in Washington, D.C., found that 20 percent of those surveyed rarely, if ever, considered the possibility of abuse when examining child-injury cases. They concluded that some physicians might experience difficulty in accepting the reality of willfully abusive behavior. In an article describing the problems arising from such incidents of medical nonrecognition, Sanders (1972) described practical matters that might contribute to nonrecognition, such as ignorance of and disdain for legal involvement, as well as psychological difficulties. He also noted the physician's unconscious feelings that result in deep-seated ambivalence toward acting on child abuse cases. Kempe and his associates (1962) frequently have noted the psychological dimensions in the failure of physicians to make the necessary diagnostic tests or to diagnose accurately the "battered child syndrome." They point out that doctors are often reluctant to question suspected abusive caretakers, even in the face of obvious circumstantial evidence of abuse, and often attempt to block the problem from their consciousness. Attempting to explain this phenonemon, the authors raise the possibility that these incidents create such great anger in physicians that they tend to repress the occurrence altogether.

Similar comments have been made about social workers. Holmes et al. (1975) made such observations on the basis of experience with individual treatment procedures at a family agency and with group therapy through Parents Anonymous, a self-help organization for abusive parents. Resistance to treating abusive parents emanated from more general problems that caseworkers experienced in dealing with incidents of abuse. Avoidance patterns were noticed among caseworkers whenever the sanguinary specifics of abuse were discussed, and details were often not solicited. It is not uncommon for caseworkers to identify strongly with an abused child and to become enraged with the alleged abusive parent. Yet it is also not unusual for a caseworker to deny continued abusive parental behavior in cases where the worker has established a warm, ongoing relationship with the parent.

Other professions also have been said to exhibit this ambivalence toward child abuse. The psychodynamic problems for lawyers were raised by Isaacs (1972) in his review of ethical, social, and legal problems relating to child abuse. He stated that lawyers share the same feelings of revulsion toward abusive acts and parents as do other professionals who come into direct contact with the problem. Pitcher (1972), in his discussion of the police and child abuse, did not deal so directly with these psychological factors per se, but he did observe that the police have tended to be punitive toward alleged abusers. He believed that such punitive, retributive attitudes are lessening now.

These observations, based largely on clinical impressions, refer to professionals' failure or reluctance to obtain the necessary information in order to designate a case as child abuse and are essentially limited to matters of physical injury. Other kinds of evidence exist, however, that professionals disagree among themselves even when faced with the same information. This evidence covers a broader spectrum of mistreatment than physical injury per se.

Polansky (1975) conceptualized the different approaches of the legal and social-work professions in demarcating situations of neglect. According to him, the legal perspective is concerned with neglect as a definable and separate entity, while the social-work perspective approaches child care along a continuum ranging from excellent care at one extreme through adequate care, to care that gives rise to great concern, and finally to neglectful and abusive care. Additionally, he and his coworkers expressed the view that social workers in general are more likely to be sensitized by their training to emotional matters than are other professionals.

Meier made a similar observation in 1964 in her review of the state of knowledge about child neglect, in which she discussed the definitions used by social workers and by the courts. In her view, social workers make no qualitative break between what is considered "acceptable" and "unacceptable" child rearing. Rather, they view parental behavior as existing along a relatively unbroken continuum of values. Meier noted the potential for conflict between the courts and social workers resulting from this perspective. She also noted the potential for conflict within the individual social worker as a result of the dual obligation to uphold societal values and at the same time to protect and enhance the welfare of the individual child.

If these observations are accurate, the potential for conflict between courts and social workers is clear. Perspectives on child rearing may exist along a continuum, but interventive action does not. Children are either removed from their parents' care or they are not; court intervention is invoked or it is not. Hence the nature of protective work makes demarcations along any continuum imperative at some point.

The potential for conflict between the police and social workers has been noted by Pitcher (1972). He believes that social workers are overoptimistic in assessing the potential for change in abusive families and naive in assessing the potential danger to children. In his view, police are much more realistic in their assessments of the change potential and the consequent risks imposed on children who remain with their parents.

These observations of interdisciplinary definitional controversy are impressionistically based. Nagi (1977) has provided the most extensive empirical data on the existence of such differences. In his survey of personnel in a nationally representative sample of child protective systems, he found that practitioners from the various disciplines were highly dissatisfied with the imprecise definitions under which they must operate. He reported that 56 percent of social workers and 64 percent of police agreed with the statement "It is difficult to say what is and what is not child maltreatment." Even higher proportions of hospital personnel and of judges were in agreement (Nagi 1977, p. 15).

Additional data presented by Nagi, while not specific to definitional controversies, reflect the generally conflicted relationships among the disciplines. These data concern the reports of difficulties experienced by various agency personnel in dealing with other agencies in their system.

> Perhaps because of their central role, child protective services experienced more difficulties than any other agency in the survey. Child protective services and hospital medical personnel showed a high level of mutual dissatisfaction, as did the police and child protective services . . . while the courts were ranked fairly high as sources of problems by most respondents' agencies. Finally, it should be noted also that child protective services were frequently and in a fairly consistent manner viewed as sources of problems [Nagi 1977, pp. 123–24].

Another source of empirical data indicates lack of agreement among disciplines regarding the definition of individual cases of child abuse and neglect by citing the proportion of reported cases that are subsequently sustained by investigating agencies mandated to receive these reports. It is generally conceded that the percentage of unsustained reports is relatively high. In an analysis of cases from five states reported to the National Clearinghouse for Child Neglect and Abuse, it was found that only 48 percent of the total cases reported in 1974 were later sustained (Groeneveld and Giovannoni 1977). The largest group of unsustained cases were those reported by private individuals, but lack of substantiation was by no means limited to them. The overall rate of substantiation among cases reported by physicians and hospitals, for instance, was 64 percent.

There was greater ambiguity in the definition of cases of neglect than in those of abuse, reflected in the breakdown of cases reported by medical sources: 70 percent of abuse reports but only 54 percent of neglect reports were sustained. Further evidence in these same data suggests that the likelihood of substantiation is much greater when definers are of the same discipline, indicating that agreement is greater within than among disciplines. The overall substantiation rate for cases reported by law enforcement, most of which were investigated by Departments of Social Services, was 70 percent. However, when a law enforcement agency both reported and investigated the report, the substantiation rate rose to 88 percent (Groeneveld and Giovannoni 1977).

Two very germane pieces of work are those by Boehm and by Billingsley and his colleagues, although they are related more to agreement on the disposition of different kinds. Boehm studied a variety of professional workers and community leaders in different settings, while Billingsley studied social workers in different kinds of social service organizations.

Boehm (1962) focused on the concept of "neglect" used by the community and by the social agencies. Utilizing a mailed questionnaire, she obtained 1,400 responses from community leadership groups, including professions concerned with child care, such as medicine, law, education, nursing, social work, and the clergy; community policymakers, such as legislators, and agency board members. The questionnaire contained six case vignettes drawn from case records and from casework literature, representing three general types of mistreatment situations: physical abuse or neglect, situations where there was evidence of disturbed behavior in the child or in the parent-child relationship, and situations where parental behavior was contrary to community norms and values but not necessarily threatening to the child's welfare. For each case the respondents were requested to choose one of the following responses: (1) no outside help is needed; (2) family is encouraged to seek the help of a community agency; and (3) there should be intervention by a community agency regardless of the family's wishes.

Boehm analyzed her data with respect to differences among occupational groups. She dichotomized the three options of response into two categories, "non-intervention" (no outside help) and "intervention" (coercive or voluntary). Social workers, clergy, nurses, and teachers were significantly more likely to perceive a need for outside help than were business managers and lawyers. Boehm's interpretation of these differences relates to the employment conditions of the various groups. The former work in bureaucratized settings, while the work of the latter is organized along entrepreneurial lines. Those with an entrepreneurial orientation are expected to adhere more to values of individual freedom, legal rights, and minimal intervention by the state in family matters. Social workers, while they may also subscribe to these values, may come into dissonance with other occupations, not over the issue of coercive intervention but over the issue of any kind of intervention versus no intervention whatever.

In his study of social workers' roles in two different kinds of agencies, a private protective-services agency and a voluntary family-service agency, Billingsley (1964) concluded that differences in the kinds of actions and treatment specifications varied markedly by agency type. Again using the case-vignette technique, including cases of physical abuse and neglect, he found that the workers in the family-service agency perceived both cause and treatment of the problems entirely in psychological terms. Protective-service workers, on the other hand, perceived both cause and treatment in more socially oriented terms. These data support the idea that differences in work milieu and agency function may be reflected in differences in perceptions, even among members of the same profession. Hence, it is reasonable to expect that such differences will also exist among different professions, working in different kinds of settings and carrying out different functions.

In a related work Billingsley et al. (1969) found that differences among social workers in perceptions of the proper disposition of hypothetical abuse and neglect situations were related to the kind of organizational unit in which they worked. Legalistic dispositions were more often recommended by those rendering social services to a general clientele, while therapeutic interventions were more typical of those in specialized protective child welfare services.

Two recent pieces of work are quite germane to our topic, although in both the focus on definition overlapped with one on opinions about causation of malnutrition (Gelles 1977; Lena and Warkov 1978).

Gelles used a mailed questionnaire to survey professionals in the state of Rhode Island. His respondents included 148 physicians in various kinds of practice, an additional 9 physicians working in emergency rooms, 49 social workers in the state's family and children's service, 106 police officers, 96 social workers from private social agencies, 109 school principals, and 68 elementary school guidance counselors. The respondents were asked if they considered thirteen different circumstances to be "child abuse." Some of the harms to the children were essentially the same—physical injury and malnutrition—but the contents changed along a dimension of willfulness on the part of the perpetrator.

"Willful malnutrition" received the highest proportions of affirmative answers—"Yes, consider as child abuse." Over 95 percent of each group of professionals responded affirmatively. When mitigating circumstances were added to the statement, this level of endorsement dropped dramatically. For "malnutrition due to ignorance," the range of "yes" answers was from 38 percent of the police down to 12 percent of the state social workers. Even fewer positive endorsements were received when the statement read "malnutrition due to finances," 23 percent of police going down to 6 percent of school principals. "Overfeeding" was considered to be child abuse somewhat more often than the above two instances of underfeeding: about a third of all the social workers thought it was abuse, while only a fifth of the physicians thought so.

Slightly less than half of each group of respondents considered "lack of emotional and intellectual stimulation" to be abuse. School principals (26 percent) and physicians (34 percent) were least likely to think so. A more dramatic kind of emotional mistreatment, "locked in a dark closet," was considered abuse by at least 85 percent of each profession, except physicians (73 percent). "Poor health services" was rated as abuse most often by police (33 percent) and least often by state social workers (10 percent).

The questions relating to physical injury showed wide variation when mitigating circumstances were added to the question. Over 95 percent of each respondent group, except the police, thought "willfully inflicted trauma" to be abuse. About three-fourths of each group considered as abuse "injured when struck too hard," except emergency room physicians, 44 percent. Two very similar statements received rather discrepant ratings: "Injured due to carelessness" ranged from 73 percent positive responses from counselors down to 45 percent of state social workers. When the wording "Child injured due to inadequate precautions taken by parents" was introduced, affirmative answers dropped, with a range of 56 percent of emergency room physicians to 30 percent of the other physicians. Injury least likely to be seen as "abuse" was that "due to poor housing." Thirty percent of the counselors thought this was abuse, ranging down to only 11 percent of the emergency room physicians.

Gelles underscores the wide discrepancy in these professional responses. It should be noted, however, that the discrepant responses were attained in items that mixed the condition with mitigating circumstances. There was near unanimity on willful malnutrition, willingly inflicted trauma, and sexual abuse. Over 95 percent of the professional groups (slightly fewer of physicians, 92 percent) saw sexual abuse as child abuse. Another factor that should be noted is the question posed, "Is this child abuse?" Had there also been a question "Is this child neglect?," the answers might have demonstrated more unanimity of response. Nonetheless, Gelles' data do suggest that there is variation among professionals in what they consider to be child abuse, and that this variation is related to the circumstances of the abuse.

Lena and Warkov were much more focused on opinions about causation. They utilized self-administered questionnaires to obtain the opinions of 100 probate judges, 120 teachers, 173 nurses, 113 social workers, and 52 police officers in Connecticut. They were posed two questions: "When you hear the term 'child abuse,' which of the following conditions comes to mind?" Six conditions were given as options, identical to six used by Gelles: Malnutrition due to willfulness or poverty or ignorance; trauma due to willfulness or carelessness, and lack of emotional/intellectual stimulation. The second question asked about causes, and respondents were asked to select from among nine possible causes: drinking, mental illness, anger, immaturity, nervousness, provocation, egocentricity, hating children, and sadism. When the authors used factor structures in the responses of the different professional groups, they found substantial commonalities. With respect to what constitutes child abuse, all the professionals saw two different kinds of phenomena as constituting abuse: "neglect" and "physical abuse." Causes also were dualized: "psychological rejection" and "uncontrollable behavior." Unlike Gelles, these authors concluded that there is homogeneity in the perceptions of child abuse held by different professionals (p. 20).

Although the empirical evidence is scant, when augmented by clinical impressions it suggests that disagreement in designating individual cases of mistreatment is common enough to be problematic. Explanations of the disagreement range from the purely psychodynamic, unrelated to professional status, to those that attribute it to diverse functions and socialization in different work settings. But there is little indication of what the *degree* of consensus or disagreement might be. Which professions agree most about what, and which least? What kinds of mistreatment generate greater or lesser disagreement? These are the questions we now try to answer.

THE STUDY OF PROFESSIONALS

We have seen that on both the policy and the practice levels, professionals responsible for the case management of child mistreatment exhibit areas of agreement and areas of disagreement and that there are two major areas of disagreement: (1) the kinds of actions to be included (for example, acts that might harm a child physically versus those that might cause emotional harm) and (2), within a given category of actions, the degree of actual or potential harm to the child. Even as regards physical abuse, which given its tangibleness might be expected to be more widely recognized as mistreatment, there is disagreement about severity. There are extreme cases of injury, such as broken bones, but what about abuses that cause bruises, reddening of the skin, or even no observable impact at all? Hence these two dimensions—the classification of acts and the relative degrees of harm within and among categories of acts—were the central areas of concern.

In chapter 1 we presented an overview of the research techniques used. Here we give a more detailed description of the vignettes and the ways in which they were presented to the respondents.

In several studies, opinions about specific incidents have been obtained through the vignette technique, which consists of the presentation of verbal descriptions of actions to research participants with the request that they rate each vignette by specified criteria. This technique has been used not only in research on child abuse and neglect but also in research on adult criminality and juvenile delinquency.

In the previously mentioned works by Boehm (1964) and Bill-ingsley (1965), both investigators used similar vignettes, depicting a fourfold category of mistreatment: emotional abuse and neglect and physical abuse and neglect. The vignettes included informa-tion beyond the specific actions, such as the race and marital status of the parents. Both researchers asked their respondents what ac-tion they would endorse in each of the situations, such as removal of the child, legal action, and so forth.

Rossi et al. (1974) surveyed a sample of the general population of the city of Baltimore to elicit opinions about the relative serious-ness of crimes committed by adults. He and his colleagues used statements describing criminal acts that corresponded to those categorized in the Uniform Crime Reports. Respondents were asked to rate each crime described on a scale of one to nine, with nine being the most serious and one the least.

The work of Sellin and Wolfgang (1964) most closely approx-imates the task undertaken here. They developed a method for scoring the relative seriousness of acts of juvenile delinquency. Vignettes were constructed that described acts of various categories such as murder or robbery, and that also varied the seriousness of the acts within categories along such dimensions as the amount stolen, the method of inflicting harm, and the degree of harm done. The acts ran the gamut from murder to public nuisances. Their method thus captured the two dimensions along which opin-ions of seriousness about mistreatment also vary—among different kinds of acts and within categories of acts. The construction of vignettes for this research was modeled after the method used by Sellin and Wolfgang.

Construction of the Vignettes

Construction of the vignettes involved three tasks: (1) selection of the kinds of incidents to be described; (2) selection of relevant dimensions along which the vignettes were to be varied in order to capture relative seriousness within categories; and (3) composition of the actual vignettes. There was one constraint at the outset: the vignettes had to be held to a number that the respondents could reasonably be asked to rate without getting tired or bored.

The categories were drawn from those in existing laws and

from those devised by experts in the field. The existing neglect statutes have been summarized by Meir (1964) and by Katz (1975). In addition the Child Welfare League of America and the Children's Division of the American Humane Association have delineated areas of child rearing practices that each organization recommends be considered as grounds for taking protective action (CWLA 1973; AHA 1972). From this composite of categorizations thirteen classes of incidents were developed. The categories themselves were considered as hypothetical in that there was no reason to assume that respondents would in fact share common views about each of the classes of events or that all would be perceived as mutually exclusive. An important goal of the research was to obtain empirical validation of the nature of the shared perceptions of the different kinds of mistreatment.

In identifying dimensions along which the severity of incidents could be varied within categories, there existed some literature on what experts thought these to be. For example, the Child Welfare League distinguished between leaving a child alone in the daytime and at night, inside and outside the house. For others these variations could only be designed on an *a priori* basis, such as varying degrees of underfeeding children. One uniform variation was introduced across categories. This consisted of pairing a stem statement simply describing the parents' behavior with the same vignette incorporating a consequence of the behavior for the child. For example: "The parent banged the child's head against the wall" (stem statement); "the parent banged the child's head against the wall. The child suffered a concussion" (stem plus consequence). This was done for all categories except for those dealing with parental behavior not directly related to child care, such as "the parents permit a relative who is a prostitute to bring customers to their house." Vignettes in these cases included the addition to the stem of a statement of the child's knowledge—for example, "the child knows this"—as an addition of consequences in the child's behavior ran the risk of contamination with other categories, such as the emotional one. The purpose of varying consequences was to establish the relative seriousness of acts as distinct from the seriousness of the effects of the acts on children.

A pool of 185 vignettes was developed. These were pretested with 60 graduate social work students and 38 undergraduate sociology students. On the basis of this pretest, 29 vignettes were eliminated because they received uniformly very low or extremely high ratings. In the low-rated vignettes were such things as ill-fitting clothing. The high-rated vignettes were ones combining physical assault and sexual molestation, and vignettes of physical injury where the consequence was death. The final pool contained 156 vignettes, 78 stems, and 78 stems plus consequences.[2]

The content of the incidents themselves was drawn from actual case records, examples in literature, and the authors' own experiences. The 13 categories, and the variables along which they varied, were as follows.

Cleanliness: Five vignettes dealing with the cleanliness of the child's body, hair, teeth, and bedding. The consequences included child has sores, impetigo, hair matted with old food, and a green film around teeth.

Clothing: Three vignettes dealing with the adequacy of clothing. The consequences referred to the child's discomfort with cold.

Drugs/alcohol: Eleven vignettes describing use of drugs by the parents or other adults in the household. The drugs varied—alcohol, cocaine, and marijuana. The consequences described the child's use of the drug in question.

Educational neglect: Three vignettes dealing with the child's absence from school either with the parents' knowledge or consent or willfully kept out by them, and one with failure to do homework. The consequence for all was "the child is failing in school."

Emotional neglect: Ten vignettes intended to portray emotional mistreatment. Five of these simply stated that the child was disturbed, and the willingness of the parents to obtain treatment

[2] The final set of 156 vignettes was tested for reliability. The testing of the reliability of the vignettes was carried out in a variety of ways with a total of 95 respondents. Because of the way the vignettes were developed (vignettes without and with consequences), two equivalent sets of 78 were available. Each set contained representation from each of the thirteen categories (cleanliness, emotional neglect, physical abuse, etc.) and vignettes with or without consequences, but never the stem vignette and its counterpart (stem and consequence) together. Thus, two similar sets, A and B, were generated. The test-retest and equivalent testing methods were used to determine reliability. Eleven respondents took set A twice and 14 respondents took set B twice—at least a week elapsed between retesting. Thirty-seven respondents took set A first and later took set B, and 33 respondents took set B first and later took set A. The degree of reliability was measured by Cronbach's alpha. The reliability coefficient varied from a low of .70 to a high of .98. See Jum Nunnally, *Psychometric Theory* (McGraw-Hill Book Co.: New York, 1967); and Lee J. Cronbach, "Coefficient Alpha and the Internal Structure of Tests," *Psychometrika* 16 (September 1951): 297–333.

for the child and/or themselves was varied. The others depicted verbally abusive behavior, favoring one child over another, locking a child in a room, and dressing the child in clothes appropriate to the opposite sex. The consequences for these were either the child fights with other children or does not play with them.

Fostering delinquency: Three vignettes concerned acts of stealing by the parents or another in the household, an uncle. The consequence added was involvement of the child in the act.

Housing: Eight vignettes describing unsafe, overcrowded, dirty housing, inadequate cooking facilities, and unsavory neighborhood. The consequences varied with the specific housing deficiency—for example, the consequence for skid row neighborhood was "child accosted by derelicts in doorway"; for house with broken windows, "child cut his hand."

Medical neglect: Seven vignettes depicting parental failure to obtain medical care for a sick child or routine medical care, including dental and ophthalmic. The consequences attached to each concerned an actual illness or dysfunction in the child. (Statements dealing with parents' refusal to permit care on religious or moral grounds were not included, as these kinds of actions represent conflicts with the law that transcend the usual parental role-performance failure.)

Nutritional: Five vignettes intended to capture parental failure in feeding children—varying degrees of not feeding at all or under- or overfeeding. Consequences referred to weight loss or gain, or to iron deficiency in the child.

Parental sexual mores: Seven vignettes depicted sexual activity on the part of the parent, including prostitution, promiscuity, and homosexuality. Child's knowledge of the activity was varied rather than a direct consequence for the child.

Physical abuse: Seven vignettes dealt with physical assault. The method of assault—with an instrument, closed fist, or open-handed—was varied. The consequences for the child ranged from concussion to red marks on the skin. Two other vignettes described burning the child—with a cigarette or with hot water—with the consequence being second-degree burns.

Supervision: Eight stem vignettes dealt with leaving a child alone or with an unreliable caretaker. The vignettes varied the time (length and day or night) the child was left. Consequences described the child wandering off or setting a small fire.

Sexual abuse: Five vignettes referred to sexual activity between parent and child ranging from intercourse to fondling, or verbal suggestion. Three of these vignettes did not have specific consequences but rather the frequency of the act (once, repeatedly) was varied. The consequence added to the other two was the child suffers recurring nightmares.

The Rating Task

There was no validated basis for establishing what the degrees of seriousness might be. An arbitrary nine-point scale was selected with the upper point, nine, being the most serious and the lowest point, one, the least serious. While the judgments of the raters were constrained by this arbitrary range, there was no intention of making any forced choices. The rating of each vignette was to be made independently of every other one. In effect raters were asked to give an absolute rating of each vignette in one of the categories from one to nine. The measure of their relative weightings emerged from the analysis.

In order to limit the effect that one vignette might have on the rating of another, the presentations were randomized. A computer program was designed to produce packets of 60 vignettes, printed on cards. Each packet of 60 vignettes included selections from the 13 classes and a random selection of vignettes without and with a consequence. Once a vignette was selected, its counterpart, with or without consequence, was not selected, so that the two related vignettes never appeared together in the same packet, to avoid the possibility that whichever of the two was first might influence the rating of the second. A final randomization of the ordering of the vignettes further ensured that no two packets of vignettes were alike. In order to ensure that raters would start from the same reference point, the first 4 vignettes were the same for everyone. They were designed to cover the span from maximum to minimum seriousness. For example, one described a parent who broke the child's jaw while forcing the child into an act of mutual masturbation. A less serious one concerned a child dressed only in hand-me-downs that were always ill-fitting. Thus, each rater rated 64 vignettes, of which the first 4 were not used in the analysis.

In order to facilitate independence of ratings, a vignette board was developed. The board was a cardboard rectangle to which were attached nine legal-size envelopes. The board fitted easily on the respondents' laps, propped up by a desk top or by hand. On each envelope was written a number from 1 through 9. The rater read the vignette and slipped the card into the envelope with the rating number chosen. At the conclusion of the ratings, the envelopes were sealed and returned for data processing.

The interviews with the respondents were conducted by trained survey-research personnel. After giving the respondents the vignette board and the packet of cards, the interviewers asked them to read the instruction card that preceded the vignettes:

> Many incidents have been classified as child abuse or neglect. Some are considered very serious acts, while others are not considered serious. Each card in your packet contains a short passage describing a potential incident of child abuse and/or neglect. Please rate the incident on a scale of increasing seriousness from 1 to 9, assigning high numbers to incidents which you believe are very serious and low numbers to incidents which you believe are not so serious. Next, place the card into the envelope marked with the digit (1–9) corresponding to your rating.

> Thank you for your cooperation.

The reading of the instructions was followed by the interviewer's instructions to the respondents:

> Rate each of the cards on a 9-point scale according to the seriousness for the welfare of the child; use 9 for the most serious acts and 1 for the least serious acts. There are no repeats; similar cards will differ by at least one word, such as day–night or always–sometimes. Base your decision on your professional experience with children and assume that the statements refer to a seven-year-old child. Are there any questions?

If the respondents expressed difficulty with a particular card, interviewers were instructed to provide two general answers:

1. "There is not enough information on the card to make a decision about the appropriate professional action, but your opinions are still important."
2. "You may have seen a variety of cases similar to this one, but please make your rating on the basis of the average case."

The Respondents

As detailed in chapter 1, the respondents represented four groups of professionals, all of whom play key roles in the protective services system in Los Angeles County—lawyers, social workers, police, and pediatricians. In table 3–1, selected characteristics of the professional groups are presented. These include their age, sex, and whether or not the respondent had had experience in rearing a child. (This information was gathered on a card placed at the end of each respondent's packet of vignettes.) Age was gathered for descriptive purposes. Sex and child-rearing experience were inquired about because these personal characteristics might influence perceptions of mistreatment in a way that would transcend professional orientation. Information about the respondents' education, income, and ethnic status was not gathered. The major social class indicator, education, clearly would have been totally confounded with professional groupings, hence there would have been no way of separating the effects of profession on ratings from that of socioeconomic status. Similarly, it was known that ethnic representation was very uneven across professions, some being almost exclusively white, while others, though somewhat more representative of other ethnic groups, were still predominantly white. As can be seen in table 3–1, the selected characteristics were not evenly distributed across professional groups. Social workers tended to be somewhat older and predominantly female; the others predominantly male. Police were much more likely than the others to have had experience with child rearing and lawyers least likely.

We now present the results of the data analyses. The presentation is organized with reference to these major research questions:

1. What were the effects on seriousness ratings of the addition of a consequence? Were these effects similar or different across professions? Did the effects vary with the nature of the mistreatment described?
2. What was the extent of agreement among professions as to the absolute and relative seriousness of specific incidents of mistreatment?
3. Do professionals agree on the underlying commonalities of specific incidents? Do they perceive common categories of mistreatment?
4. Do professionals agree as to the absolute and relative seriousness of different categories of mistreatment?

PROFESSIONAL RESPONSES TO
SPECIFIC INCIDENTS OF MISTREATMENT

Perceptions of seriousness of consequences: Do professionals agree about the seriousness of specific acts of mistreatment? To ap-

TABLE 3-1. Characteristics of the Respondent Groups

Profession (N)	Mean Age	Female	Child-Rearing Experience
Lawyers (71)	34.7	17%	49%
Social Workers (113)	40.3	82	69
Police (50)	33.4	20	80
Pediatricians (79)	37.4	28	52
Total (313)	37.2	44%	59%

proach this question the issue of the effect of a known consequence of the action was examined first in order to determine whether additional information radically changed perceptions of seriousness. To achieve this goal, a statistical comparison was made between the ratings of the basic vignettes and the ratings of the same vignettes with the consequences added, for the respondents as a whole, and between each professional grouping.[3] The questions posed in the analyses were these: Are some acts considered serious in themselves, regardless of the consequence for the child? Do members of different professions perceive the relationship between the seriousness of an act and the seriousness of the consequences in the same way?

Table 3-2 shows that the effect of the addition of consequence was a significant increase in the seriousness of the overall ratings in 43 of the 78 pairs of vignette statements and a significant decrease of the overall ratings in only 9 pairs. Therefore the addition of a consequence made a statistical difference for the total sample in 52 out of the 78 pairs of statements. The consequences (noted by "*" in the table) that tended to decrease the seriousness ratings were often those in which the child knew of the parents' action or the child was engaged in unacceptable behavior.[4]

For the most part this pattern did not deviate among the professional groups. In general the addition of consequences tended to increase the seriousness of the ratings of the vignettes more often for the lawyers and social workers than for the police and pediatricians.[5] For the police there does not seem to be a clear pattern for explaining this occurrence. Many of these actions were those in-

---

[3] Statistical test used, two-way analysis of variance (ANOVA). (See B. J. Winer, *Statistical Principles in Experimental Design*, 2d ed. [McGraw-Hill: New York, 1971], for discussion of ANOVA designs.)

[4] See vignettes 8, 13, 18, 19, 21, 23, 25, 63, 64.

[5] Number of times ratings increased: lawyers, 67, social workers, 65, pediatricians, 62, and police, 62.

TABLE 3-2.   The Vignettes and Ratings by Four Groups of Professionals[1]

VIGNETTES[2]	OVERALL RATING[3]	GROUP RATINGS			
		Lawyers	Pediatricians	Social Workers	Police
Sexual Abuse (6.95)[4]					
1. On one occasion, the parent and the child engaged in sexual intercourse.	8.15	7.96	7.81	8.21	8.61
OR					
The parent and the child repeatedly engaged in sexual intercourse.	8.33	8.08	8.13	8.38	8.89
2. On one occasion, the parent and the child engaged in mutual masturbation.	6.98	5.85	6.66	7.21	8.00
OR					
The parent and the child repeatedly engaged in mutual masturbation.	7.60	7.47	6.91	7.95	8.41
3. The parent repeatedly suggested to the child that they have sexual relations. (The child suffers recurring nightmares.)	6.85	5.80	6.86	7.29	7.46
	7.22	6.38	6.88	7.69	8.12
4. The parent repeatedly showed the child pornographic pictures. (The child suffers recurring nightmares.)	5.50	4.38	5.44	5.36	7.17
	6.60	5.59	6.26	7.18	7.09
5. On one occasion, the parent fondled the child's genital area.	5.10	4.64	3.94	5.19	7.29
OR					
The parent has repeatedly fondled the child's genital area.	6.97	6.65	6.00	7.24	8.44
Physical Abuse (6.24)					
6. The parent burned the child on the buttocks and the chest with a cigarette. (The child has second-degree burns.)	8.34	7.71	8.57	8.45	8.76
	8.53	8.38	8.36	8.69	8.63

Item						NO AGREEMENT
7. The parent immersed the child in a tub of hot water. (The child suffered second-degree burns.)	7.56 / 8.27	6.08 / 7.96	8.00 / 8.12	7.67 / 8.33	8.65 / 8.79	
8. The parent hit the child in the face, striking him with the fist. (The child suffered a black eye and a cut lip.)	7.25 / 6.72*5	6.37 / 6.14	7.69 / 6.65	7.05 / 7.12	7.94 / 6.82	
9. The parent banged the child against the wall while shaking him by the shoulders. (The child suffered a concussion.)	6.39 / 7.44	5.21 / 6.22	6.96 / 7.11	7.31 / 8.06	5.60 / 7.75	
10. The parent struck the child with a wooden stick. (The child suffered a concussion.)	4.59 / 7.90	4.47 / 6.73	5.06 / 7.90	4.21 / 8.23	5.00 / 8.42	
11. The parents usually punish their child by spanking him with a leather strap (leaving red marks on the child's skin.)	4.07 / 5.37	3.19 / 4.62	4.04 / 4.94	4.91 / 6.15	3.75 / 5.26	NO AGREEMENT
12. The parents usually punish their child by spanking him with the hand (leaving red marks on the child's skin.)	1.62 / 3.18	1.35 / 2.68	2.00 / 4.19	1.63 / 3.21	1.24 / 2.50	NO AGREEMENT
Fostering Delinquency (5.60)						
13. The parents make their child steal small articles out of the supermarket. (The child was caught stealing.)	6.78 / 6.55*	6.41 / 6.42	6.75 / 7.00	6.95 / 6.38	7.00 / 6.41	
14. The parents make their child take stolen merchandise to a store that sells it illegally. (Their child knows this.)	6.40 / 6.43	5.50 / 5.35	6.18 / 6.53	6.86 / 6.56	6.86 / 7.59	
15. The parents allow an uncle to store stolen merchandise in their house. (Their child knows this.)	3.21 / 4.28	2.63 / 4.13	3.32 / 4.50	3.15 / 3.80	3.78 / 5.58	NO AGREEMENT
Emotional Mistreatment (5.46)						
16. The parents have kept their child locked in since birth. They feed and bathe the child and provide basic physical care. (The child is underdeveloped.)	8.31 / 8.36	8.06 / 7.48	8.37 / 8.45	8.46 / 8.58	8.29 / 8.71	

See end of table (p. 122) for footnotes.

TABLE 3–2. Continued

Vignettes[2]	Overall Rating[3]	Group Ratings			
		Lawyers	Pediatricians	Social Workers	Police
17. The parents dress their son in girl's clothing, sometimes putting makeup on him. They have kept long curls on him. (The child fights with other children.)	5.85 6.01	5.02 4.78	5.15 5.94	6.74 6.63	6.22 6.18
18. A child is severely emotionally disturbed. The parents refuse to accept treatment for themselves or for their child. OR A child is severely emotionally disturbed. The parents have allowed the child to undergo treatment but refuse to cooperate themselves.	6.30 4.55*	5.22 3.77	5.74 4.82 NO AGREEMENT	7.60 4.85	6.17 4.47
19. A child has severe behavior problems. The parents refuse to accept treatment for themselves or for their child. OR A child has severe behavior problems. The parents have allowed the child to undergo treatment but refuse to cooperate themselves.	5.74 4.35*	4.39 4.05	5.82 3.61	6.25 5.35	5.77 4.17
20. The parents are constantly screaming at their child, calling him foul names. (The child does not play with other children.)	4.57 5.28	3.83 4.04	4.64 5.67	5.19 5.62	4.38 5.29
21. The parents ignore their child most of the time, seldom talking with him or listening to him. (The child continually fights with other children.)	4.67 4.62*	3.42 3.74	4.69 4.92	5.57 5.43	4.23 3.62

22.	The parents dress their daughter in boy's clothing and keep her hair cropped short like a boy's. (The child fights with other children.)	4.59 / 4.66	3.30 / 3.73	4.93 / 4.27	4.84 / 5.59	4.75 / 5.18
23.	The parents constantly compare their child with his younger sibling, sometimes implying that the child is not really their own. (The child continually fights with other children.)	4.59 / 4.52*	3.79 / 3.08	4.65 / 5.03	5.71 / 4.94	2.88 / 4.56
	Nutritional Neglect (5.21)					
24.	The parents regularly fail to feed their child for periods of at least 24 hours. (The child was hospitalized for 6 weeks for being seriously underweight.)	6.87 / 7.59	5.50 / 6.75	7.15 / 7.76	7.26 / 7.79	7.08 / 8.08
25.	The parents feed only milk to their child. (The child has an iron deficiency.)	6.09 / 5.49*	4.48 / 4.85	6.03 / 4.20	6.86 / 6.84	6.59 / 5.24
26.	The parents brought their child to the hospital three times for being underweight. Each time the child gained weight during his hospital stay. (On return home, he again lost weight.)	5.37 / 5.75	3.62 / 4.30	5.97 / 5.86	5.65 / 6.88	5.90 / 5.26
27.	The parents fail to prepare regular meals for their child. The child often has to fix his own supper. (The child has an iron deficiency.)	3.72 / 4.67	2.54 / 3.87	3.58 / 4.74	4.20 / 4.91	4.82 / 4.95
28.	The parents always insist that their child clean his plate, which they keep full of food. (Doctors have warned that the child's health will suffer if he continues to eat so much.)	2.44 / 4.32	2.19 / 3.24	2.59 / 3.97	2.48 / 5.72	2.42 / 3.36
	Medical Neglect (5.09)					
29.	The parents ignored the fact that their child was obviously ill, crying constantly and not eating. (When they finally brought the child to a hospital, he was found to be seriously dehydrated.)	6.62 / 6.99	5.28 / 6.05	6.44 / 6.40	7.71 / 7.85	6.61 / 7.16

TABLE 3–2. Continued

Vignettes[2]	Overall Rating[3]	Group Ratings			
		Lawyers	Pediatricians	Social Workers	Police
30. The parents ignored their child's complaint of an earache and chronic ear drainage. (The child was found to have a serious infection and damage to the inner ear.)	5.75 6.39	4.92 5.38	5.46 5.71	6.45 7.22	5.94 6.83
31. The parents have repeatedly failed to keep medical appointments for their child. (Their child has a congenital heart defect.)	4.31 6.73	3.76 6.21	3.97 5.17	5.32 7.52	4.11 7.90
32. The parents do not provide any health care for their child. (The child complains of physical ailments.)	5.08 5.65	4.42 5.19	4.62 5.26	6.00 5.63	5.28 6.82
33. The parents have not given their child medication prescribed by a physician. (Their child has a throat infection.)	4.56 4.61	4.32 4.00	3.09 4.56	5.43 4.73	5.07 5.09
34. The parents have not taken their child to a dentist. (The child has difficulty eating.)	2.63 5.21	2.31 4.16	2.76 4.52	2.52 5.96	3.35 5.76
35. The parents have failed to obtain an eye examination for their child. (The child complains of not being able to see things at a distance.)	2.74 4.26	2.19 3.17	2.03 4.93	3.70 4.17	3.05 4.60
Supervision (5.09)					
36. The parents regularly left their child alone outside the house after dark often as late as midnight. (Neighbors have spotted the child wandering five blocks away from home.)	6.07 6.35	4.27 4.96	5.82 5.88	7.03 7.16	6.65 7.11

37. The parents regularly left their child alone inside the house after dark. Often they did not return until midnight. (On one occasion the child started a small fire.)

    5.75   3.88   6.39   6.33   5.95
    6.52   5.16   5.79   7.64   7.17

38. The parents regularly left their child alone inside the house during the day. Often they did not return until almost dark. (On one occasion the child started a small fire.)

    5.13   4.32   5.26   5.44   5.53
    6.16   4.43   6.17   6.91   6.89

39. On one occasion, the parents left their child alone all night.

OR

    The parents regularly left their child alone all night.

    4.72   3.31   4.37   5.58   5.75
    6.41   5.18   5.89   7.33   6.83

40. The parents regularly left their child alone outside the house during the day until almost dark. (Neighbors have spotted the child wandering five blocks from home.)

    4.12   3.19   4.38   4.42   4.47
    5.04   4.27   4.96   5.33   5.33

41. The parents regularly left their child with their neighbors, without knowing who would assume responsibility and be in charge. (The child wandered five blocks away from home.)

    4.41   3.32   4.17   5.34   4.50
    4.49   3.56   4.84   4.61   5.24

42. On several different occasions, the parents left their child with a grandmother for periods of time up to ten days without providing any means of contacting them. (The child became ill.)

    3.10   2.57   3.66   2.90   3.14
    3.41   2.42   3.68   3.86   3.32

Alcohol/Drugs (4.75)

43. The parents always allow their child to stay around when they have friends over to experiment with cocaine. (The child asks to take drugs.)

    5.82   4.89   5.07   6.12   7.77
    6.54   5.36   6.57   6.74   7.71

117

TABLE 3–2. Continued

Vignettes[2]	Overall Rating[3]	Group Ratings			
		Lawyers	Pediatricians	Social Workers	Police
44. Both parents are drug addicts. (The mother gave birth to a baby who was congenitally addicted.)	5.66 6.44	3.97 5.42	5.96 5.67	5.96 7.38	7.35 7.14
45. A parent experimented with cocaine while alone taking care of the child. (The child swallowed a small box of laxatives.)	5.04 5.82	3.88 4.73	5.23 5.28	5.19 6.23	6.13 7.73
46. The parents use marijuana occasionally, but the father's brother, who is an addict, visits their home often and has used cocaine in front of their child. (The child asks to take some of the drug.)	5.05 5.12	4.30 3.93	5.16 4.38	4.90 5.49	6.13 7.37
47. A parent became very drunk while alone taking care of the child. (The child drank some whiskey and became intoxicated.)	4.30 5.26	2.81 3.68	4.97 5.58	4.28 5.90	5.12 6.18
48. A parent got very high smoking marijuana while alone taking care of the child. (The child took a drag of marijuana.)	4.27 4.98	2.62 3.91	4.48 4.12	4.30 5.14	6.57 6.85
49. The parents always allow their child to stay around when they have friends over to smoke marijuana. (On one occasion, the child took a drag of marijuana.)	4.03 4.85	3.12 3.52	3.30 4.36	4.50 4.63	5.64 7.36
50. The parents always allow their child to stay around when they have drinking parties. (The child has gotten intoxicated.)	3.07 5.06	2.61 3.75	3.47 5.64	2.67 5.21	3.82 5.77
51. The parents leave bottles of whiskey around the house in places where the child can get to them. (The child drank some and became intoxicated.)	3.72 4.40	2.41 3.03	4.26 4.84	4.08 4.80	3.88 4.89

52.	The parents let the child sip out of their glasses when they are drinking whiskey. (The child has gotten intoxicated.)	3.08	4.65	1.93	3.74	3.00	5.00	3.64	4.61	3.67	5.23
53.	The parents are moderate drinkers, but the father's brother, who is an alcoholic, visits their home often, drinking constantly in front of their child. (On one occasion, he allowed the child to get intoxicated.)	2.58	4.42	2.24	3.60	2.71	4.85	2.69	4.17	2.65	4.92

Cleanliness (4.74)

54.	The parents usually leave their child on a filthy, sodden mattress. (The child has infected sores on his body.)	4.92	6.72	3.73	5.83	5.00	5.73	5.36	7.23	5.70	8.00
55.	The parents do not wash their child at all. (The child's arms and legs are covered with encrusted sores.)	4.48	6.48	3.93	5.86	3.97	5.71	5.10	6.90	4.47	7.88
56.	The parents do not wash their child's hair nor bathe the child for weeks at a time. (He has impetigo in several places.)	4.31	5.70	3.62	5.06	3.76	4.88	4.89	6.32	4.76	6.86
57.	The parents make no effort to keep their child clean. (The child's hair is matted with bits of old food.)	4.06	5.04	3.28	4.43	3.78	4.07	4.45	5.50	4.90	5.86
58.	The parents do not see to it that their child brushes his teeth. (The child's teeth have a green film around the gums.)	2.20	3.56	1.89	3.10	2.09	3.58	2.43	3.52	2.22	4.64

Educational Neglect (4.06)

59.	The parents frequently keep their child out of school. (The child is failing in school.)	4.44	4.73	4.23	4.74	4.50	4.96	4.64	4.69	4.23	4.36
60.	The parents know that their child often is truant. But they don't do anything about it. (The child is failing in school.)	4.21	4.70	3.69	4.40	4.18	4.83	4.55	5.05	4.47	4.16

119

TABLE 3-2. Continued

Vignettes[2]	Overall Rating[3]	Group Ratings			
		Lawyers	Pediatricians	Social Workers	Police
61. The parents frequently let their school age child stay home from school for no good reason. (The child is failing in school.)	3.99 4.43	3.39 4.00	4.18 4.97	4.38 4.23	3.26 4.89
62. The parents never see to it that their children do any homework. They let them watch TV all evening. (One child is failing in school.)	2.66 3.57	2.56 2.61	2.76 3.74 NO AGREEMENT	2.68 4.23	2.56 3.41
Parental Sexual Mores (3.47)					
63. The parents permit a relative who is a prostitute to bring customers to their house. (The child knows this.)	5.18 5.02*	5.27 4.35	4.73 4.43 NO AGREEMENT	5.33 5.45	5.47 6.24
64. The parents have intercourse where the child can see. (The child knows this.)	5.18 4.90*	3.00 3.70	4.42 4.31	6.02 5.85	6.81 6.09
65. A divorced mother, who has custody of her child, is a prostitute. (Her child knows this.)	3.00 3.79	2.52 2.75	3.09 3.69	2.80 3.69	4.00 5.68
66. A divorced mother, who has custody of her child, brings home different men often. (Her child knows about her sexual relations.)	2.89 3.84	2.24 2.96	3.27 3.67 NO AGREEMENT	2.97 3.98	2.82 5.06
67. A divorced mother, who has custody of her child, is a lesbian. (Her child knows this.)	2.40 2.87	1.65 2.17	2.21 2.41	2.33 2.49	4.15 5.00
68. A divorced father, who has custody of his child, is a homosexual. (His child knows this.)	2.39 2.63	1.61 1.77	2.80 2.58	2.21 2.42	2.33 5.31

	Col 1	Col 2	Col 3	Col 4	Col 5
69. A divorced mother, who has custody of her child, has a steady boyfriend with whom she has intercourse often. (Her child knows this.)	1.71 / 2.63	1.53 / 2.08	2.38 / 2.63	1.53 / 2.31	1.50 / 3.89
Clothing (3.11)					
70. The parents do not see to it that their child has clean clothing. (Food stains and dirt are splattered all over the child's clothes.)	3.02 / 3.50	2.35 / 2.63	3.13 / 3.94	3.32 / 3.81	2.92 / 3.59
71. The parents always let their child run around the house and yard without any clothes on. (The child has a bad cold.)	2.97 / 3.63	2.09 / 3.03	2.43 / 2.58	3.24 / 4.16	4.47 / 5.43
72. The parents seldom notice how their child is dressed. (The child has frequently been out playing in very cold weather without a coat or sweater.)	2.50 / 3.03	2.14 / 2.38	2.38 / 3.54	2.73 / 3.03	2.50 / 3.20
Housing (3.07)					
73. The parents live with their child in an old house. Two windows in the living room where the child plays have been broken for some time, and the glass has very jagged edges. (The child cut his hand on the jagged edges, requiring three stitches.)	3.76 / 4.52	3.08 / 3.50	3.20 / 4.07	3.90 / 5.11	5.38 / 4.57
74. The parents live with their child in a hotel apartment. There are no adequate cooking facilities. (The child is malnourished.)	2.09 / 5.36	1.36 / 4.15	2.00 / 5.17	2.36 / 6.00	2.42 / 6.44
75. The parents live with their child in a small rented house. No one ever straightens up. (Decaying garbage, rats, and cockroaches are everywhere.)	1.93 / 5.33	1.40 / 4.13	2.00 / 4.18	2.04 / 6.59	2.39 / 6.93
76. The parents live with their child in a skid row neighborhood. Derelicts sleep in the doorway of the building in which they live. (One of the derelicts accosted the child.)	2.59 / 4.01	2.17 / 3.27	2.55 / 3.36	2.76 / 5.10	2.95 / 3.67

TABLE 3-2. Continued

Vignettes[2]	Overall Rating[3]	Group Ratings			
		Lawyers	Pediatricians	Social Workers	Police
77. The parents live in an apartment with their two children. They have few furnishings, a bed where the parents sleep, and two mattresses where each of the children sleeps.	1.67 2.41	1.41 1.76	1.52 1.85	1.67 3.28	2.25 2.18
OR					
The parents live in an apartment with their two children. They have very few furnishings. The four of them all sleep together in a double bed.					
78. The parents live with their child in a small two-room apartment. The three of them have lived there for several months.	1.35 1.83	1.00 1.37	1.79 1.79	1.25 2.27	1.35 1.55
OR					
The parents live with their four children in a small two-room apartment. The six of them have lived there for several months.					

[1] Underlining indicates groups who agreed—that is, indicated no significant difference in ratings based on the Newman–Kuels test.
[2] The statements in parentheses added to the stem vignettes and the statements following the word "or" are the vignettes *with* consequences.
[3] The first number is the mean rating *without* consequence. The second is the mean rating *with* consequence.
[4] The number in parentheses is the overall category rating.
[5] The asterisk (*) indicates a decrease in rating with the addition of a consequence.

volving sexual abuse, alcohol/drugs, and physical abuse. These may be areas where police tend to make judgments first on the basis of the act and then modify that judgment as more information is provided. The role of specific professional knowledge in judgments of the content of the added consequence was most clearly demonstrated in the ratings of the pediatricians with respect to consequences specifying medical conditions. Thus ratings of the seriousness of the statement "The parents feed only milk to their child" went down significantly with the addition of the information "The child has an iron deficiency." Similarly items dealing with the parent's failure to wash the child and keep him/her clean received lower ratings from the pediatricians when the added consequence was, "The child has impetigo."

Another kind of medical situation in which pediatricians differed in their ratings was that where the parent failed to obtain medical care for the child. Table 3–3 shows the ratings by each profession of vignettes with and without consequences dealing with parental failure to obtain medical care for the child. In vignettes 31, 33, and 35 there was a statistically significant interaction effect—that is, the effect caused by the interplay of professional medical knowledge and vignette content. In these cases the differences between the pediatricians' ratings with and without consequences deviated greatly from the differences in ratings by the other professions.[6] A particular item that called forth discrepancies in seriousness ratings between the pediatricians and others was: "The parents have repeatedly failed to keep medical appointments for their child." When the "consequence" "the child has a congenital heart defect" (V 31) was added, pediatricians' ratings were considerably lower than those of the other groups, suggesting that "a congenital heart defect" sounds more serious to the lay person than to the pediatrician. Another area of discrepancy centered on not giving a child prescribed medicine when the child was suffering a throat infection. It appeared that pediatricians were not particularly concerned about following a prescribed medical regimen unless failure to do so resulted in a more serious medical problem, whereas nonmedical personnel saw both as about equally harmful. Thus, professional expertise among pediatricians did influence

[6] In vignette 35, social workers varied very little in their ratings of the vignette with and without consequence. Although this can contribute mathematically to a significant interaction effect, it was primarily interpreted on the basis that social workers did not perceive any difference between the two incidents through a lack of expertise in the area.

TABLE 3-3. Medical Care: Ratings by Four Groups of Professionals

VIGNETTE[1]	GROUP RATINGS[2]			
	Lawyers	Pediatricians	Social Workers	Police
29 Ignored obviously ill child (child found to be dehydrated)	5.28 6.05 (+.77)	6.44 6.40 (−.04)	7.71 7.85 (+.14)	6.61 7.16 (+.55)
30 Ignored child's complaint of earache/drainage (child found to have serious inner ear damage/infection)	4.92 5.38 (+.56)	5.46 5.71 (+.25)	6.45 7.22 (+.77)	5.94 6.83 (+.89)
31 Failed to keep medical appointments (child has congenital heart defect)*[3]	3.76 6.21 (+2.45)	3.97 5.17 (+1.20)	5.32 7.52 (+2.20)	4.11 7.90 (+3.79)
32 No health care for child (child complains of physical ailments)	4.42 5.19 (+.77)	4.62 5.26 (+.64)	6.00 5.63 (−.37)	5.28 6.82 (+1.54)
33 Did not give child medicine prescribed by physician (child has throat infection)*	4.32 4.00 (−.32)	3.09 4.56 (+1.47)	5.43 4.73 (−.70)	5.07 5.09 (+.02)
34 No dental care (child has difficulty eating)	2.31 4.16 (+1.85)	2.76 4.52 (+1.76)	2.52 5.96 (+3.44)	3.35 5.76 (+2.41)
35 Failed to obtain eye exam for child (child cannot see at distance)*	2.19 3.17 (+1.98)	2.03 4.93 (+2.90)	3.70 4.17 (+.47)	3.05 4.60 (+1.55)

[1] The complete wording of each vignette was presented in table 3–2. Vignette numbers correspond to those in table 3–2.

[2] Ratings listed are means. The first number is without consequence, the second with consequence and the third the difference between them.

[3] The asterisk (*) indicates significant interaction effect, as measured by analysis of variance.

their ratings, with and without consequences, but this was an exception to the general pattern; the addition of consequence served to increase the ratings of the vignette by the entire population.

Except where already noted, the relative ranking of a vignette's seriousness did not change with the addition of a consequence. For these reasons we decided that the measure that would best characterize opinions about specific incidents was one that incorporated the rating of the incident with and without consequence, the mean of the two ratings. In subsequent analyses, this mean rating was used as the basic unit.

Perceptions of seriousness of specific incidents: To further examine the question of professional agreement on the seriousness of acts of mistreatment, all four professional groups were compared on all 78 vignettes. It would appear that there was virtually no consensus about the seriousness of the incidents of mistreatment. Statistically significant differences were found among the professionals on all but 9 of the incidents; there was complete agreement in only 12 percent of the vignettes. However, simply looking at the differences across all four groups obscured the actual degree of agreement that existed among particular professions. An additional statistical method was applied, the Newman–Keuls method,[7] to ferret out for each incident the particular *combinations* of professional groups that did in fact significantly agree with one another, and those that deviated from them in their ratings (Winer, 1971: p. 442).

When this was done the picture changed considerably. Table 3–2 illustrates patterns of agreement between particular professions; agreement between at least two of the professions was the rule rather than the exception. Overall, the police and the social workers were the ones most often in agreement (73 percent of the time), and both tended to rate incidents as more serious than did either the pediatricians or the lawyers. The lawyers were the group most often in disagreement with all others (about 45 percent of the time), and they definitely tended to rate the incidents as less

---

[7] Analysis-of-variance designs test significant differences across groups. Only one group need be different for significance to occur. In order to test for differences between all possible pairs of means one of the techniques that can be used is the Newman–Kuels procedure. Other similar procedures are the Scheffe, Tukey, and Duncan methods. The Newman–Kuels method was selected because it was neither as conservative as the Scheffe method nor as liberal as the Duncan method in minimizing type 1 error—that is, rejecting the null hypotheses when in fact it is true. (See B. J. Winer 1971, pp. 196–201 for this discussion.)

serious. The pediatricians' overall ratings tended to fall in the middle, their average ratings came closest to the average for all four groups, and they were much more often in agreement with police and social workers than were the lawyers (pediatricians, 40 percent and lawyers, 13 percent). When the lawyers' ratings were not totally in disagreement with those of all others, for the most part they were in agreement only with the pediatricians, not with the social workers or the police (27 percent of the time). Although this is the *general* pattern, it by no means is uniform across all incidents. The best understanding of these professionals' agreements and disagreements is obtained through careful scrutiny of the nature of the incidents themselves. Who agreed with whom—and who disagreed—was clearly related to the nature of the mistreatment and of the interaction with the knowledge and functions of the different professions. Furthermore, some kinds of mistreatment generated much more disagreement than did others, both among different professions and within the same profession.

Mistreatment incidents tend to aggregate around three general areas: those concerned with parental role failure in the physical care of the child, those concerned with caretaker responsibilities other than the physical, and those involving assaults that transcend child care responsibilities. Those acts that can be placed in the physical-care category include nutritional neglect, medical neglect, poor supervision, and inattention to cleanliness, clothing, and housing. Nonphysical caretaker acts include fostering delinquency, emotional mistreatment, alcohol and drugs, parental sexual mores, and educational neglect. The third category includes physical and sexual abuse. These three areas are useful in examining who agreed with whom and around what issues. In the discussion of the results, attention is given to agreement as to the absolute seriousness of incidents as well as to the relative seriousness of incidents within a given category or situation.[8*] For the most part there was much more agreement about relative than absolute seriousness.

Agreement patterns on matters of physical care: With regard to the 33 vignettes in the area of physical care, social workers and police were most often in agreement in their views of the seriousness of the incidents.[9] In fact, disagreement occurred only four

[8] [See opposite page for asterisked note and illustration.]
[9] See V24–V42, V54–V58, and V70–V78 in table 3–2 (nutritional neglect, medical neglect, supervision, cleanliness, clothing, and housing).

times. These two professions agreed completely in their ratings of incidents concerned with medical care, supervision, cleanliness, and clothing of children.

Lawyers and pediatricians were in agreement 50 percent of the time. They were in complete agreement in the area of cleanliness and in least agreement regarding nutritional issues. Moreover, incidents concerning the cleanliness and the medical care of children tended to polarize the professions—social workers and police versus pediatricians and lawyers. In the area of cleanliness, the lawyers and pediatricians were in agreement on every item, always rating these items as significantly less serious than did the other two professional groups.

Among the cleanliness items, the one rated least serious by all professions was "The parents do not see to it that their child brushes his teeth. The child's teeth have a green film around the gums." The other items all dealt with cleanliness of the body and hair, save for one, the item that was rated as most serious: "The parents leave their child on a filthy, sodden mattress. The child has infected sores on his body." Although the lawyers and the pediatricians were in total agreement with each other, always rating these cleanliness items as significantly less serious than did the other two professional groups, it is notable that the pediatricians' ratings

[8]* Absolute seriousness ratings are those compared only on the numerical values given each incident or group of incidents. Relative seriousness ratings are those compared on a ranking basis—that is, those items that are considered high or low in relationship to other items even though their numerical values may differ. For example, a vignette or category of vignettes may be rated 8 by one respondent and 7 by another; however, each may be the highest absolute rating given by that respondent, making that circumstance the most serious comparatively. Graphically, it means:

Seriousness Rating

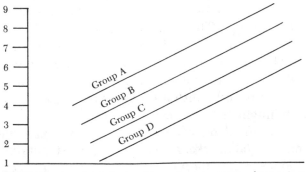

Child Mistreatment Acts (ordered by seriousness rating — least serious to most serious)

were always lower still than those of the lawyers when they had information about the consequences of the act. These differences in
perceptions about the harmfulness to children of poor hygiene may
indeed be factually based. Being dirty may be socially harmful, but
it is not likely to cause physical damage, or at least very serious
physical damage. Hence social valuations are likely to enter into
the evaluation of dirtiness. Additionally, however, the greater likelihood that police and social workers will actually see children in
their work who are in the conditions of the child described in the
cleanliness vignettes (V54–V58) might also influence their higher
ratings. The visual image of a child lying on a "filthy, sodden mattress" may be more vivid for the social workers and the police, since
they are the only ones whose work calls for them to go into the
homes of families accused of mistreating their children.

The items dealing with medical care (V29–V35) were the other
set that brought forth unanimity between the police and social
workers and unanimous disagreement with the others. With
respect to medical care the lawyers and the pediatricians were in
significant agreement in 3 out of the 7 vignettes, and the lawyers
tended to rate the items lower than did the pediatricians. The
relative ratings of seriousness of the items among the three nonmedical professions were quite close, largely attributable, as we
have said, to the pediatricians' seeing the consequences of inadequate medical care stated in the vignettes as less serious than the
nonmedical professionals. Hence, in comparing the combined
ratings of each vignette with and without consequences, the difference in the consequence rating depressed the overall, or mean,
ratings of the physicians.

The situations relating to eye and dental care were the least
serious ones to all groups. Pediatricians rated as least serious the
item "The parents have not taken their child to a dentist. The child
has difficulty eating." The other professions rated as least serious
the item "The parents have failed to obtain an eye examination for
their child. The child complains of not being able to see things at a
distance." It would, of course, have been interesting had there
been some dentists and ophthalmologists among the respondents to
see how they might have ranked these items!

A number of incidents generated a three-way agreement among
pediatricians, social workers, and police, most notable when the
incidents concerned supervision and nutrition. The incidents
describing situations in which the child was left alone and unsuper-

vised provoked more disagreement between the lawyers and the other professionals than did any other type of incident. Typically, social workers, police, and pediatricians were in significant agreement as to the seriousness of these matters. All four groups, however, were generally in agreement as to the *relative* seriousness of the incidents described within the category of supervision: worse to be left alone outside than inside the home, and worse at night than during the day. And it was better to be left with some caretaker, however unreliable, than to be left alone. The divergence of lawyers in their opinions about the seriousness of leaving a child alone is reflective of the public stance taken by many of them, and rests on the distinction between situations of potential harm as opposed to actual harm to children. In these vignettes, nothing actually happened to the child. In one set of consequences the child "is found wandering five blocks away" and in the other the child "on one occasion started a small fire." Hence a different dimension is tapped here along which disagreement might arise. Rather than disagreement over the seriousness of actual harm done, such as described in the medical care vignettes, the issue is one of potential versus actual harm. On this issue the lawyers seem to have parted company with all others.

The next group of incidents that generated high agreement among pediatricians, social workers, and police were those dealing with nutritional care of children. There was less agreement between pediatricians and lawyers around issues of nutritional neglect than for any other category of mistreatment. Interestingly, the lawyers and police, seldom in agreement, did agree on one of these nutritional vignettes: "The parents always insist that their child clean his plate, which they heap full of food. Pediatricians have warned that the child's health will suffer if he continues to eat so much" (V28). While pediatricians gave this a higher seriousness rating than did the lawyers or police, this was not nearly so high as the social workers'. Overfeeding seemed to be of particular concern to social workers. In general, the various degrees of underfeeding were seen similarly by all but the lawyers.

One item (V26) included among these nutritional ones did not concern common underfeeding or overfeeding but what is termed the "failure to thrive" syndrome. The vignette read, "The parents brought their child to the hospital three times for being underweight. On return home he again lost weight." This vignette depicts the definition used in many hospitals in making the diagnosis "failure to thrive"—children gain while in the hospital and lose after they return home. In such cases, simple undernutrition is not thought to be the cause; rather, the failure to thrive is believed to result from psychosocial or emotional deprivation, since the children when in an adequate emotional environment resume a normal rate of growth. The lawyers rated this vignette significantly lower than the other three professions. The significant agreement among the other three professions on the vignette may reflect their familiarity with the "failure to thrive" syndrome, a matter for which protective action may be sought (Evans et al. 1972). Overall the rating was 25th in seriousness among the 78 vignettes.

Two final areas of physical care concern clothing and housing. Both types of items were generally rated as not very serious. As for the clothing items, one dealt with cleanliness and the other two the adequacy—none or not enough—of clothing. The vignette "The parents seldom notice how their child is dressed. The child is frequently out playing in very cold weather without a coat or sweater" is one of the very few in which all four groups were in complete agreement, none ranking this as very serious. Lawyers and pediatricians were in agreement about the child "running around the house and yard without any clothes," and lawyers rated the item on dirty clothes significantly less serious than did the other three groups. These matters about clothing elicited more agreement than other acts and probably represent a threshold for all as to whether they actually do constitute mistreatment.

Unlike the vignettes concerning basic physical care, those concerned with shelter or housing provoked a varied pattern of agreement and disagreement, especially between the police and social workers. Social workers generally rated these items as more serious than the other groups. The vignettes dealt with unsafe housing ("broken windows with jagged edges in the living room"), inadequate cooking facilities, overcrowding, and cleanliness ("decaying garbage, rats and cockroaches are everywhere"). One dealt with an undesirable neighborhood, skid row, where "derelicts sleep in the doorway of the building." All professionals' ratings on these vignettes were generally low. The level of disagreement and the generally low ratings probably reflect the marginality of the whole matter of housing as one constituting mistreatment. An important consideration might well be the extent to which inadequate housing was viewed as a matter attributable to poverty and hence beyond the control of the parents.

Thus far we have considered acts of mistreatment or potential mistreatment that concern basic physical care of children—feeding, clothing, cleanliness, health, protection or supervision, and housing or shelter. Perceptions of the seriousness of these acts in relation to children's welfare were almost unanimous among police and social workers, while pediatricians and lawyers agreed half of the time. Frequently, though not invariably, pediatricians were in agreement with social workers and police, and lawyers almost invariably disagreed with them, always seeing such things as significantly less serious. In summary, in spite of this lack of consensus among the respondents as to the valuations put on any given incident, there was substantial agreement among subgroupings of professionals both as to the relative and the absolute seriousness of acts within any given area of physical child care.

Agreement patterns in nonphysical domains: Incidents that transcend basic physical care include parental responsibilities toward children in the educational, emotional, and moral realms. Moral considerations involve parental behavior not directly related to the parental role, their sexual mores, criminal activity, and their use of drugs and alcohol.[10]

Although American parents are not expected to educate their children, they are generally expected to see that their children get to school. The vignettes dealing with this parental responsibility described a truant child, parents who deliberately kept their child out of school, and those who were lax about seeing to it that their children went to school regularly. The consequence noted for each was "The child is failing in school." These educational matters generated more agreement than did any others. It may be that the police, who generally rated most incidents as relatively more serious than the other professionals, tended to see these matters as somewhat less serious or that education for children is a value perceived in the same way by everyone. One vignette, however, generated total disagreement as to the seriousness of its nature: "The parents never see to it that their children do any homework. They let them watch TV all evening" (V62). The priority of the great American tradition of educating children over the great American amusement is controversial even among these professionals!

The emotional treatment of children has been the focus of more

10 These include V13–V23, V43–V53, and V59–V69 in table 3–2.

explicit controversy than any other category or behavior. As might
be expected, then, the vignettes describing emotional mistreatment
generated a complex array of agreement and disagreement patterns
among the four occupational groups. One vignette was intended to
capture extreme and somewhat bizarre treatment, the kind of incident that is rare but attracts enormous public attention when it is
discovered: "The parents have kept their child locked in since
birth. They feed and bathe the child and provide basic physical
care" (V16). This act of emotional mistreatment was rated as more
serious than any other in the category of emotional mistreatment
by all the professionals, and the third most serious act of mistreatment among all seventy-eight incidents described. Even in this very
serious incident the characteristically low rating style of the
lawyers prevailed: their rating of the act was statistically
significantly lower than the other three professional groups,
although their relative rating for this vignette was the same as the
total sample (the most serious in the category and the third most
serious for all vignettes). This must be interpreted, however, as
more reflective of the lawyers' rating style than as a meaningful rejection of the seriousness of the nature of the mistreatment.

The patterning of the ratings of the other acts of emotional
mistreatment reflects particular professional competencies and interests, not simply rating style. Two vignettes described situations
where the child was clothed and groomed to look like a member of
the opposite sex (V17, V22). Notably, all professionals saw dressing
a boy like a girl as substantially more serious than dressing a girl
like a boy. Only police and social workers agreed in their ratings of
each of the two vignettes and rated them higher than the other
two. Two vignettes were intended to capture perceptions of seriousness about parents' failure to obtain treatment for "a severely
emotionally disturbed child" and a child with a "severe behavior
problem" (V18, V19). There was no agreement among the professionals with respect to the child described as "emotionally disturbed"—perhaps reflecting an inconsistency of understanding
across these professions about what "emotionally disturbed" as contrasted with "severe behavior problems" means—but there was in
the case of "severe behavior problems." For example, while the difference between the lowest and highest overall mean rating for
"emotionally disturbed" (4.62–6.31) and the difference between
the lowest and highest overall mean rating for "severe behavior
problems" (4.18–5.86) were similar, the professions rated along the

whole continuum with respect to "emotionally disturbed," and their ratings were polarized in this range in the case of "severe behavior problems." Lawyers and doctors agreed, while police and social workers agreed. "Severe behavior problems" probably comes closer to describing the types of cases handled by the police, for example, and may account for the police's agreement as to seriousness with social workers, who are frequently involved in similar cases, while this involvement might not hold across these professions for the concept of "emotionally disturbed."

Earlier in this chapter we noted the confusion one group of professionals found between the concepts of "emotional neglect" and "emotionally disturbed." They resolved the confusion by defining emotional neglect as a situation identical to that in our vignette, an emotionally disturbed child whose parents refuse to obtain treatment. Our data here suggest that use of the term "emotionally disturbed" is not likely to be a satisfactory resolution of the definitional problems. At least in terms of seriousness, there is no indication that the term has a shared meaning among any of these professionals.

Finally, three vignettes were intended to depict very specific kinds of parental behavior that in themselves might or might not be considered as emotionally harmful. These included "The parents are constantly screaming at their child, calling him foul names," "The parents ignore their child most of the time, seldom talking with him or listening to him," and "The parents constantly compare their child with his younger sibling, sometimes implying that the child is not really their own." In all these incidents the social workers and the pediatricians were in agreement as to the seriousness of these actions, while lawyers and police agreed in two instances and in all three instances rated these vignettes as less serious compared with the ratings of the other professions. Both by training and by professional function pediatricians and social workers are much more likely to view such actions as diagnostic cues to more pervasive emotional mistreatment. The lawyers and police, on the other hand, are not so readily charged professionally with conceptualizing or diagnosing segments of parental behavior into a general category of emotional mistreatment. While these complex differences in ratings may be explained, the commonly noted explicit controversy about emotional mistreatment is borne out in the ratings by these professionals.

Socially deviant behavior in the parent not specific to the

parental role has also been the object of controversy. These aspects of parental behavior included the use of drugs and alcohol, criminal behavior (specifically, stealing), and sexual behavior. The consequence described for both the parental use of drugs and alcohol and stealing involved the child. With respect to the parents' sexual behavior, no additional information was given save for "the child knows of this."

The items that dealt with stealing were intended to capture a long-recognized dimension of mistreatment: contributing to the delinquency of a minor. Stealing itself is not controversial, as it is uniformly against the law in all states as well as against the commandment "Thou shalt not steal." In this set of vignettes the relationship of the adult in question to the child was varied. In two vignettes the culprits were the parents, in the others an uncle. For the vignette "The parents make the child steal small articles out of the supermarket," there was unanimity of rating by all professionals. In "The parents make their child take stolen merchandise to a store that sells it illegally," only the lawyers rated the vignette significantly lower than did the others. When it came to a third party as the culprit, "The parents allow an uncle to store stolen merchandise in their house," there was total disagreement among all professionals. Lawyers and social workers rated the occurrence as less serious than did pediatricians or police. Obviously, when parents involve their children in what is generally accepted as criminal behavior, these professionals concur in the seriousness of the acts. When the criminal behavior is not directly that of the parents but of others in the child's environment, the professionals diverge significantly in their opinions, reflecting both the imputation of responsibility on the part of the parents and the extent to which the general milieu of children's lives, apart from the parent-child relationship, may be considered harmful to them.

Like stealing, drug and alcohol usage engendered comparatively more agreement than did other types of mistreatment. The items themselves were designed so that the kind of drug in question was varied: cocaine, marijuana, and alcohol. On almost every item at least three professional groups were in complete agreement as to the seriousness of the event, and one of the three overlapped with the remaining professional group. There were a few instances where the police were not in agreement with the others, and these all resulted from their higher rating of seriousness of incidents involving marijuana. Lawyers deviated significantly on three of the vignettes, all of which involved their lower rating of seriousness of incidents pertaining to the use of alcohol. At the time the research was conducted, simple possession of marijuana was still illegal in California, as was that of cocaine, but of course not of alcohol. This fact may have accounted for the apparent distinctions made by the lawyers and the police. The fact that both drug and alcohol use as well as stealing can conflict with the law, as well as possibly having noxious effects on the child, may mean they are considered as serious along two dimensions and account for the relatively high agreement among the four groups of professionals on these matters.

The sexual behavior of parents, while an early preoccupation in mistreatment legislation, is now controversial as grounds for designating mistreatment (V63–V69), as was evident in our findings. The police accounted for a good deal of the overall disagreement, rating all these matters as more serious than did the others. Two vignettes generated total disagreement: "The parents permit a relative who is a prostitute to bring customers to their house" (V63) and "A divorced mother, who has custody of her children, brings home different men often" (V66). Apart from the police the three other professions were in significant agreement as to the seriousness for the child of the statement: "Mother is a prostitute" (with no mention of activity going on in the home). The other two items in this group dealt with the parents' sexual preference, one describing the father as a homosexual and the other, the mother as a lesbian. A vignette that provided the rare occurrence where only the lawyers and social workers were in agreement as to the lesser seriousness of the situation was: "A divorced mother, who has custody of her child, has a steady boyfriend with whom she has intercourse often. Her child knows this."

Overall, the patterning of strong agreement between social workers and police does not hold up with respect to caretaker responsibilities in domains other than the physical. The three-way agreement pattern among pediatricians, police, and social workers was very common: of the 35 vignettes in this domain, in fact, 67 percent were rated in that fashion. The lawyers' disagreement with the other professions was thus quite pronounced. Departures from this pattern are largely attributable to the high ratings of social workers in the area of emotional mistreatment and of police in matters of sexual mores.

Agreement Patterns on Matters of
Physical Injury and Sexual Molestation

One might expect the strongest agreement among professionals to be in the categories of sexual molestation and physical injury of children (see V1–V12). However, this was not the case. The disagreement was mainly about the seriousness of the individual actions within each category. In the policy statements reviewed, all agreed that some actions involving physical injury or sexual molestation constituted sanctionable parental deviance. But the issue of degree of seriousness—the threshold of mistreatment—is controversial, and this is borne out by the data.

The items dealing with sexual activity between parent and child ranged from actual penetration to manual manipulation of the genitals, to verbal suggestion of sexual relations and the exhibition of pornographic pictures. (The items themselves made no reference to the gender of the parent or of the child, so this was not a variable.) The lack of expected agreement resulted in part from the fact that police tended to rate the items extremely high, generally higher than did social workers, who in turn followed their usual pattern of rating these acts as more serious than did either lawyers or doctors. All professionals agreed in their relative ranking of the seriousness of these various sexual acts, except that doctors and social workers rated showing a child pornographic material as more serious than fondling of the child's genitals, unlike the police and the lawyers. In fact, the doctors' rating with regard to fondling of the child's genitals was lower than their rating of most incidents of medical neglect.

Of the items dealing with physical injury of the child, two concerned burns, one with a cigarette on the buttocks, the other through immersion in a tub of hot water, and others involved physical assault with the fist, shaking and banging the child against the wall, and hitting with a stick, a leather strap, and the open hand. The consequences for the burn incidents were "The child suffered second-degree burns." For assault with the fist, "The child suffered a cut lip and a black eye." The assault with a stick and the banging against the wall were said to result in a "concussion." Hitting with a "leather strap" and "spanking with the hand" both had the consequence of leaving red marks on the child's skin (V6–V12).

Agreement between two or more professions occurred in five of the seven vignettes describing a physical injury, while in the remaining two there was complete disagreement. Of the five where there was some agreement, two vignettes elicited total agreement. These concerned assault with a stick and assault with the fist. Among all 78 vignettes, 4 of the 7 physical-injury incidents were among the 10 actions judged most serious by the combined ratings of all the professions. In fact, the action judged most serious of all 78 vignettes was burning a child with a cigarette.

Some differences occurred across the professions. For example, lawyers, in their characteristic manner, selected slightly lower numerical values for their rating but still rated these items as very serious relative to all other items. Pediatricians deviated from the other professions in rating the occurrences as less serious when the consequences were added. To pediatricians, the actions themselves apparently had the potential for inflicting harm greater than the injury specified in the consequences.

The two acts of physical assault where no agreement occurred were also judged as less serious than other acts of physical injury. These actions clearly occupy the margin between acceptable physical punishment and child abuse. These were "The parents punish their child by spanking him with a leather strap (leaving red marks on the child's skin)" and "The parents usually punish their child by spanking him with the hand (leaving red marks on the skin)." Physicians rated both acts as more serious than did any of the other groups, and police rated spanking with the hand as less serious than did the other professions. What is also notable here is the general rank ordering of the instances of spanking in relation to all other acts of mistreatment. Spanking with the hand received the 4th lowest mean rating of seriousness of any of the 78 acts (lower were 2 housing items and "Mother has steady boyfriend"). This would clearly suggest that while professionals disagree as to the seriousness of corporal punishment, they all regard it as generally acceptable, at least relative to all other acts of mistreatment that they examined.

The general patterns of agreement on specific incidents: Throughout the foregoing discussion some general patterns of agreement emerged with regard to individual incidents of mistreatment. Table 3–4 indicates that on such individual incidents, the pairs of professions most likely to agree with each other are social workers with police and pediatricians with lawyers. Such paired agreement, in both cases, is strongest in regard to physical care. The dominant trio of those agreeing were pediatricians, social

TABLE 3-4.   Patterns of Agreement among Professional Groups*

COMBINATIONS OF PROFESSIONS	(33) PHYSICAL CARE	(33) PARENTAL RESPONSIBILITY	(12) PHYSICAL/ SEXUAL
SPo	17	5	3
LPe	14	4	3
PeS	1	2	—
LPo	1	2	—
LS	—	2	—
PePo	—	—	—
PeSPo	10	12	2
LPeS	—	7	1
LSPo	—	—	1
LPePo	—	—	—
LPeSPo	2	5	2
No agreement	—	5	2

* These figures reflect the number of times that *only* this combination agreed (e.g., if PeSPo (pediatricians/social workers/police) agree, they are not double-counted in PeS, PePo, or SPo).

workers, and police, and secondly lawyers, pediatricians, and social workers. It is interesting to note that pediatricians and police were *never* in paired agreement and agreed only when there was another profession in agreement with them, namely social workers. The common agreement between police and social workers and the rarer instances of agreement only between pediatricians and social workers or lawyers and police are probably reflective of similarities in certain professional orientations and duties.

Personal Characteristics of Professionals and Their Perceptions of Seriousness

Although it is clear from the foregoing that one's profession is significantly related to one's perceptions of seriousness, investigation of the personal characteristics of the respondents was warranted to determine whether they also influenced the patterns of agreement or disagreement. Two particular characteristics are germane: the sex of the respondents and their own experience with child rearing.

Because of the rigid roles assigned to men and women in child rearing in our society, in matters so integral to those roles as acts of mistreatment the sex of the respondent might be expected to influence perception of the seriousness of these acts. Women, at least until very recently, have been expected to carry out the major burdens of child care and have been socialized into such a role.

Furthermore, among the sex-linked stereotypes that abound are those related to sentimentality among women and tough-mindedness among men. We look first, then, at the relationship between sex of the professionals and their ratings of seriousness.

As might be expected, the distribution of men and women across professions was anything but uniform. Of the social workers, 82 percent were women, while among the others an almost reverse proportion existed: 28 percent of the pediatricians, 20 percent of the police, and 17 percent of the lawyers. It is most difficult, therefore, to separate out the effects of professional identity from that of the gender of the respondent. The question was pursued in two ways. First, the two sexes' responses were compared on all 78 vignettes. Next, examination was made of the effects of the respondents' gender compared with the respondent's profession.

There were significant differences attributable to the sex of respondents on 36 percent of the vignettes (28 vignettes). However, these differences were not all evenly distributed across the different types of mistreatment (see table 3–5). Rather, those related to basic physical care—medical care, nutrition, supervision, housing, and cleanliness—by far predominated among the types of mistreatment that reflected sex differences in ratings (17 out of 28). Among these 28 vignettes, women always rated them significantly more serious than men. Of the remaining vignettes in the mistreatment categories—fostering delinquency, educational neglect, and clothing—there were no significant differences by sex. Since the matters dealt with in the vignettes that showed differences by sex tended to concern basic "mothering functions," one might conclude that socialization to the mothering role did influence the ratings. However, three facts mitigate this explanation of the ratings. First, for all of the vignettes showing a rating difference by sex, the mean ratings of males, of females, and of social workers were compared, as shown in table 3–5. This was necessary since 93 of the 113 social workers were women, and the issue of occupational effect or sex effect is at issue. In almost every instance the social workers' ratings (a mean of both female and male workers' scores) were higher (more serious) than those of either only men or only women. Furthermore, it must be remembered that in the physical-care domain these kinds of mistreatment—nutritional neglect, medical neglect, supervision, cleanliness, clothing, and housing—were the ones rated by police and social workers with nearly 100 percent agreement, although women constituted only 20 percent of the police re-

TABLE 3-5. Ratings of Significant Effects of Sex and Child Rearing Experience of Respondents

| VIGNETTE[1] | SIGNIFICANT DIFFERENCES WITH REGARD TO:[2] | | | | |
| | Sex | | Social Workers | Child Rearing Experience[3] | |
	Male	Female		Without	With
Sexual Abuse[4]					
1. On one occasion the parent and child engaged in sexual intercourse.	8.06[5] (1.49)[6]	8.47 (1.23)	8.31 (1.37)		
3. The parent repeatedly suggested to the child that they have sexual relations.	6.79 (2.26)	7.40 (2.00)	7.49 (2.01)		
Physical Abuse					
7. The parent immersed the child in a tub of hot water.				7.27 (2.34)	8.29 (2.09)
9. The parent banged the child against the wall while shaking him by the shoulders.	6.47 (2.29)	7.52*[7] (2.04)	7.77 (1.78)		
11. The parents usually punish their child by spanking him with a leather strap.	4.35 (2.54)	5.30 (2.47)	5.58 (2.47)		
Emotional Mistreatment					
17. The parents dress their son in girl's clothing.	5.53 (2.31)	6.43* (2.21)	6.69 (2.10)		
18. A child is severely emotionally disturbed. The parents refuse to accept treatment for themselves or for their child.	5.01 (2.10)	6.20* (2.01)	6.31 (2.21)		
19. A child has severe behavior problems. The parents refuse to accept treatment for themselves or for their child.	4.54 (2.11)	5.64 (2.20)	5.86 (2.11)		
21. The parents ignore their child most of the time.	4.38 (2.35)	4.99* (2.20)	5.49 (2.21)		

23. The parents constantly compare their child with his younger sibling.	4.16 (2.27)	5.06 (2.36)	5.32 (2.19)	
Nutritional Neglect				
24. The parents regularly fail to feed their child for periods of at least 24 hours.	7.04 (2.06)	7.54 (1.61)	7.52 (1.60)	
25. The parents feed only milk to their child.	5.33 (2.43)	6.41* (2.25)	6.85 (1.95)	
26. The parents brought their child to the hospital three times for being underweight.	5.28 (2.57)	5.89 (2.45)	6.18 (2.34)	
28. The parents always insist that their child clean his plate, which they heap full of food.	2.97 (1.94)	3.77 (2.34)	3.95 (2.44)	
Medical Neglect				
29. The parents ignored the fact that their child was obviously ill, crying constantly, and not eating.	6.33 (2.26)	7.42* (2.00)	7.79 (2.01)	
30. The parents ignore their child's complaint of an earache and chronic ear drainage.	5.62 (2.04)	6.71 (1.91)	6.87 (1.83)	
31. The parents have repeatedly failed to keep medical appointments for their child.	4.47 (2.13)	4.71* (2.40)	6.72 (2.15)	
33. The parents have not given their child medication prescribed by a physician.			4.84 (2.53)	6.47 (2.12)
34. The parents have not taken their child to a dentist.			3.99 (2.50)	3.85 (2.21)
Supervision				
36. The parents regularly left their child alone outside the house after dark.	5.78 (2.20)	6.77* (2.01)	7.09 (1.88)	
37. The parents regularly left their child alone in the house after dark.	5.68 (2.32)	6.68 (2.04)	6.89 (1.94)	

See end of table (p. 143) for footnotes.

TABLE 3-5. Continued

VIGNETTE[1]	SIGNIFICANT DIFFERENCES WITH REGARD TO:[2]				
	Sex		Social Workers	Child Rearing Experience[3]	
	Male	Female		Without	With
39. On one occasion, the parents left their child alone all night.	5.14 (2.56)	6.15* (2.35)	6.52 (2.32)		
Alcohol/Drugs					
43. The parents always allow their child to stay around when they have friends over to experiment with cocaine.				5.93 (2.53)	6.47 (2.12)
45. The parent experimented with cocaine while alone taking care of the child.			4.00 (2.37)	4.93 (2.42)	5.78 (2.32)
47. A parent became very drunk while alone taking care of the child.	4.24 (2.24)	3.95 (2.34)			
51. The parents leave bottles of whiskey around the house in places where the child can get to them.	3.78 (2.13)	4.45 (2.38)	4.48 (2.39)		
Cleanliness					
54. The parents usually leave their child on a filthy, sodden mattress.	5.60 (2.24)	6.01 (2.22)	6.23 (2.17)		
56. The parents do not wash their child's hair nor bathe him for weeks at a time.	4.77 (2.19)	5.31 (2.50)	5.54 (2.29)	5.27 (2.20)	4.84 (2.33)
58. The parents do not see to it that their child brushes his teeth.				3.25 (2.25)	2.46 (1.72)
Parental Sexual Mores					
64. The parents have intercourse where the child can see them.	4.61 (2.51)	5.62* (2.33)	5.95 (2.15)		

67. A divorced mother, who has custody of her child, is a lesbian.

	2.02 (1.72)	3.04 (2.54)

Housing

73. The parents live with their child in an old house. Two windows have been broken for some time and the glass has very jagged edges. — 3.87 (2.19) | 4.46 (2.34) | 5.49 (2.21)

75. The parents live with their child in a small rented house. No one ever straightens up. — 3.44 (2.46) | 3.83* (2.76) | 4.24 (2.93)

76. The parents live with their child in a skid row neighborhood. — 3.02 (2.22) | 3.78* (2.43) | 4.04 (2.54)

77. The parents live in an apartment with their two children. They have few furnishings, a bed where the parents sleep and two mattresses where the children sleep. — 1.92 (1.35) | 2.25* (1.81) | 2.54 (1.96)

---

[1] Vignettes listed are only those where significant differences in either sex or child rearing were noted.

[2] F-test statistic used to test significant differences. Significance is P < .05.

[3] Experience with own child or raising of a child.

[4] Vignette numbers correspond to vignette numbers in table 3–2.

[5] Overall mean ratings of vignette without and with consequence.

[6] Standard deviation in parentheses.

[7] Asterisk (*) indicates statistical significance (P < .05) between females excluding social workers and all social workers.

spondents. Finally, there was no statistically significant difference between females and police in 19 of the 28 acts of mistreatment in table 3–5. We examined the females' ratings, excluding social workers, to those of social workers. We found significant differences in 13 of the 28 vignettes, thus leaving 15 remaining that could be attributed to sex. Thus, while the sex of the respondents was linked to their rating of seriousness in 15 of the vignettes, no overall pattern could be detected related to stereotypic expectations of men or of women. Rather, professional function contributed much more to overall differences in perceptions of seriousness.

The other personal characteristic examined was child rearing experience. The question asked was: "Are you now raising or have you ever raised a child?" Child-rearing experience, like sex, was not evenly distributed across professions: 80 percent of the police had parenting experience, 69 percent of the social workers, 52 percent of the pediatricians, and 49 percent of the lawyers. As with sex, the effects of child-rearing experience were tested first by looking at the total vignette ratings and then at the interaction with ratings of statements with and without consequences. Only 8 vignettes (listed in table 3–5) showed any significant difference by child rearing experience, and the seriousness of the rating was higher half the time. Interaction effects with the statement of consequences were found in only 7 of the possible 78 instances. Many childless practitioners have doubtless heard the comment, from client parents as well as from others, "If you only had children of your own, you would understand and not be so hard on me." The information gathered on these professionals suggests that that is a vain hope. Compared with the impact of professional roles, parental experience—like sex—has virtually no effect on the ratings of seriousness. Further, it is noted that lawyers, the professional group with the least child rearing experience, most often perceived all acts as less serious, while the groups with the most experience, the police—with social workers—most often saw mistreatment as more serious.

Establishing Categories of Mistreatment and Assessing Their Relative Seriousness

We have demonstrated that patterns of agreement and disagreement exist among different professionals with respect to perceptions of the seriousness of specific incidents of mistreatment. Furthermore, these patterns reflect professional functions and are not linked to personal characteristics.

The next question we addressed concerned the extent to which these professionals shared perceptions of the ingredients of different types of mistreatment. Here we sought to establish whether various specific incidents were seen to have underlying commonalities. The incidents themselves had been hypothesized to belong to 13 different categories, categories derived from those delineated in the literature, but no empirical test had ever been made as to whether the categories were distinct from one another, and whether the assumed connotations of the category names were actually useful in fitting specific incidents into a given category. In a very practical sense the testing of the professionals' views about underlying commonalities is a basic necessity. Both laws and professional guidelines are in effect directives for making judgments about specific situations. Unless professionals are able to agree on which situations belong to a given classification and share the meaning of those classifications, the laws and the guidelines are not useful. Indeed, shared meaning is a prerequisite of shared communication, even if the communication involves disagreement. Issues of agreement and disagreement about the seriousness of different types of mistreatment make sense only if the types themselves have a common meaning. Apart from the practical implications, from a research standpoint it was first necessary to establish the validity of the categories and the justification for grouping specific incidents. Only then could questions about the relative seriousness of different kinds of mistreatment be addressed.

A principal-components factor analysis was the statistical method employed to determine the commonalities conceptualized by the respondents.[11] This analysis resulted in the development of 9 categories of mistreatment (see table A–1 in appendix for listing of derived categories). In general the items that had been hypothesized as falling into common categories were amazingly similar to

[11] Factor analysis is a statistical technique with many uses, among which is an aid in developing taxonomies. It is a procedure that extracts all the sets of intercorrelated variables called "factors." Factor analysis permits substitution of a defined set of variables (here 9 factors) for an initial set of variables (here 78 variables) with little loss of information. There are as many factors as there are sets of uncorrelated variables. Of the various types of factor analyses, principal-components factor analysis with Varimax rotation was selected because it is the most straightforward method of transforming a set of variables into another set of composite variables or principal components that are uncorrelated to each other. Furthermore, the principal-components method requires the fewest assumptions about underlying structures of the data. The Varimax rotation is used because it clarifies factors by rotating until the loadings on each factor have a maximum variance. Factor loadings (correlation of variable with factor) of .400 or more was used as the criterion for inclusion on a factor. For further discussion see Harry Harmon, *Modern Factor Analysis* (Chicago: The University of Chicago Press, 1967); a less technical treatment is given by R. J. Rummel, *Understanding Factor Analysis* (Evanston: Northwestern University Press, 1970).

those evolved through factor analysis of the respondents' ratings. Seven of the original 13 categories remained virtually intact with the exception of one or two items.

All the vignettes in the derived educational category were identical to those in the hypothesized educational category, and we retained the category name, education. Of the 11 items dealing with drug and alcoholism, one item did not correlate with any of the other items in the derived category, or with items in any other category: alcohol/drugs, "Both parents are drug addicts. The child is congenitally addicted." The matter of the congenital addiction of babies due to their mothers' drug usage as grounds for mistreatment is a controversial one. It also is qualitatively different from drug usage around and by an older child. Hence it is reasonable that these professionals would see the matter as quite separate from all other drug/alcohol-related acts.

All the vignettes depicting physical injury of the child remained intact save for one: "The parents usually punish their child by spanking him with the hand, leaving red marks on the skin." This item was clearly unrelated to other types of physical injury and to the other acts of mistreatment because it did not fit these professionals' view of what constituted physical injury and hence was not viewed as mistreatment.

The incidents of emotional mistreatment, while they generated considerable disagreement among the professionals as to their seriousness, were perceived as having an underlying commonality except for the most extreme situation, where the child was described as having been locked in since birth. Just as it is a rare occurrence in reality, this kind of bizarre situation was not perceived as having a commonality with the other incidents of emotional mistreatment, or any other kind of mistreatment.

The vignettes dealing with the sexual mores of parents and those describing sexual molestation of the child were perceived by the professionals as falling into the same two different categories as had been hypothesized, sexual abuse and parental sexual mores. There was one exception: the vignette "The parents have intercourse where the child can see them" had originally been grouped with vignettes relating to a parent's sexual behavior with persons other than the child. The professionals' ratings of this situation, however, are more highly correlated with those incidents dealing with sexual molestation. Conceivably the act was seen as one intentionally stimulating to the child rather than behavior involving the child only indirectly; hence it shared a common thread with others dealing with sexual stimulation of children.

Finally, the items concerned with supervision grouped in an almost identical fashion to the original conception, and hence were labeled as supervision. There were two exceptions. Leaving the child with a grandmother, without contact, for several weeks, was not perceived in the same way as were the others dealing with supervision of children. Nor did it correlate with any other kinds of mistreatment. The best explanation for this is that leaving a child with a relative is seen as qualitatively different from leaving children alone or with an unrelated person. Again the question is raised as to whether this type of action was seen as mistreatment at all. One vignette previously conceived not as a matter of supervision but as one of the provision of adequate housing did fall into the group dealing with supervision. This was "The parents live with their child in an old house. Two windows in the living room where the child plays have been broken for some time, and the glass has very jagged edges. The child cut his hand on the jagged edges, requiring three stitches." This situation does focus on protection for the child, and it is reasonable that it would have commonality with other situations of leaving a child alone and unprotected. The other housing situations dealt much more with the unsavoriness of the physical environment rather than its dangerousness. This vignette was also judged to be much more serious than any other mentioning housing as the focus for mistreatment.

Two of the 3 vignettes dealing with criminal behavior of parents were highly correlated, while the third, specifying the culprit as "an uncle" rather than the parents, was not. Here again there is a question of whether mistreatment exists when circumstances are peripheral to parental behavior, indicating that, on matters at the borderline, mistreatment may not be at issue. Criminal behavior—in this case, stealing—notably was perceived as quite distinct from parental sexual behavior that for the most part was not illegal, though to some morally reprehensible.[12] Because of the added consequences in these vignettes of involving the child in the act of stealing, we labeled the category "fostering delinquency."

The final category that emerged from the analysis of the profes-

[12] There are 4 additional vignettes that loaded highly enough on this factor to be included; however they are not conceptually relevant to this category and were deleted. It is possible that it was just a spurious relationship, not uncommon in correlational techniques (see vignettes 2, 4, 5, and 10 of deleted vignettes in table A–1).

sional ratings actually represents a combination of the originally
hypothesized categories. All clearly have an underlying dimension
of basic physical care of children. These situations have already
been discussed as the kinds that evoked the most agreement among
police and social workers, and the most disagreement between
these two groups and the lawyers. This category—which we called
"failure-to-provide"—involves parental omissions with respect to
basic medical care, feeding, cleanliness, clothing, and shelter or
housing. All the vignettes originally designated as "medical
neglect" and "cleanliness" were correlated with others in this
category, and with no other. Some items originally grouped as
"clothing" and "housing" also correlated here. However in both
"clothing" and "housing" the additional vignettes from the
hypothesized categories simply failed to correlate with any others
and were deleted. These additional vignettes appear not to have
been perceived in the same way, possibly because it is questionable
whether they constitute mistreatment. The two housing items that
did group on "failure-to-provide" were those dealing with inadequate cooking facilities and inadequate housekeeping. The three
housing-related vignettes that were not included in any category
were concerned with overcrowding and with an unsavory neighborhood. Most likely the descriptions given in these vignettes
evoked images of poverty beyond the parents' control and hence
more ambivalence as to the appropriateness of considering such
situations along with other, more willful acts of mistreatment.
These 3 housing vignettes provoked more disagreement among all
four professionals than did most, and their correlations with other
vignettes was ambiguous. They are thus not included in the final
categories derived and may be considered as very marginal matters
with respect to mistreatment, without any clear recognition of ill
effects on children.

Similarly, of the 3 vignettes depicting inadequate clothing, only
one grouped with those dealing with basic physical care, a vignette
describing dirty clothes. This was doubtless perceived as having a
commonality with the other items about cleanliness. Those describing a child about the home with no clothes or with inadequate
clothing did not conceptually fit with any category. The rationale
is similar to the one offered in regard to housing—the whole area of
clothing just may not be considered within the domains of child
care that concern mistreatment.

The vignettes depicting various deficiencies in feeding a child

were not seen as having a common dimension save for 2, one dealing with feeding a child irregularly and one with overfeeding. The
other vignettes did not correlate in any conceptually consistent
fashion. One described a child fed only on milk and, like the item
depicting the child being locked in since birth, may have an element of rarity that does not fit with more common types of feeding
deficiencies. The other was in fact a description of the "failure to
thrive" syndrome. The child is depicted as having been brought to
a hospital for underweight and then gaining weight in the hospital.
Though dealing with nutrition, this condition is in reality of a
qualitatively different nature—since even in actual cases, there is
no medical certainty that the reason for the condition is invariably
a failure of the parent to feed the child—and in a sense is in a
category by itself.

To summarize, then, 9 categories of mistreatment were empirically developed out of the original 13 hypothesized groups of
vignettes. For the most part these generated categories were almost
identical to the parent categories. The major exception was a category—failure to provide—that combined five elemental aspects of
physical child care. Presumably these professionals did not make
fine distinctions among the various subcategories of physical care
but rather saw them as having the commonality "physical care."
These acts parallel those usually considered to be "physical
neglect."

Thirteen of the 78 vignettes either failed to correlate with or be
conceptually related to any of the 9 categories. These dealt with bizarre or very unusual behavior, or situations very marginal in their
impact on children's welfare, ones ordinarily reflective of circumstances of poverty or conceptually unrelated to the category with
which they were correlated, suggesting a spurious relationship.

The extent to which professionals' ratings reflected a recognition of common underlying themes in these diverse acts of mistreatment is very important. First, it demonstrates the extent to which
they make fine discriminations not only as to the seriousness of individual acts but also, and this is very important, as to the nature
of the acts themselves. Equally important, they share these perceptions of underlying commonalities. In short, professionals may
disagree about the seriousness of individual events, but they
definitely agree on the type of event being seen. This fact
strengthens the argument that the differences among them are
related to their professional roles and ideologies rather than to

idiosyncratic personal characteristics or esoteric opinions about the ingredients of child care. The surmise that is made in the literature—that unconscious factors may deter professional recognition of situations of mistreatment—would not be supported by these data. On the contrary, the respondents appeared to be quite well aware of the nuances in different types of mistreatment and matters of degree within the different types, a fact that precludes any assertion that they are denying or unconsciously blinded to details.

Professional Agreement about the
Relative Seriousness of
Different Categories of Mistreatment

Having established that these four groups of professionals share perceptions of underlying commonalities within the different kinds of mistreatment described, as well as the distinctions among the different types, the next question to be addressed is "Do they agree on the relative seriousness of harm to children among the various categories of mistreatment?" The data are presented in both tabular and graphic form (table 3–6 and figure 3–1). The tabular presentation is the most useful in observing the relative seriousness of the different kinds of mistreatment, the graphic for viewing overall professional comparisons. In table 3–6 the mean ratings for each professional group in each of the 9 categories of mistreatment are presented. There is a very high level of agreement, albeit with some deviations from the overall pattern. All four professions perceive the same 3 types of mistreatment as more serious than any others. These 3 are: physical abuse, sexual abuse, and fostering delinquency. Pediatricians' ratings of fostering delinquency is higher than their ratings of sexual abuse, and police ratings of sexual abuse were higher than those of physical injury. The rank ordering of the other 6 categories among the lawyers, pediatricians, and social workers is similar. Although there is some slight deviation among them, it is quite insubstantial, because for any given profession the mean ratings of some categories were almost identical (for example, pediatricians' ratings of emotional neglect and supervision were, respectively, 4.98 and 5.00).

The perceptions of the relative seriousness of these types of mistreatment among the police were somewhat different. They rated educational neglect as the least serious, while others rated parental sexual mores as the least serious. The police also rated the category failure to provide as the 6th most serious, while pediatri-

TABLE 3-6. Professional Agreement on Categories of Mistreatment[1]

CATEGORY	OVERALL RATING[2]	PROFESSION			
		Lawyers	Pediatricians	Social Workers	Police
Physical abuse	6.89	6.08	6.95	7.22	7.21
Sexual abuse	6.67	5.92	6.13	7.05	7.70
Fostering delinquency	6.55	5.74	6.62	6.68	6.95
Supervision	5.19	4.01	5.00	5.81	5.81
Emotional mistreatment	5.05	4.06	4.98	5.79	4.95
Alcohol/drugs	4.62	3.53	4.63	4.80	5.80
Failure-to-provide	4.23	3.38	4.16	5.06	5.04
Education	4.06	3.70	4.23	4.24	3.90
Parental mores	3.21	2.52	3.18	3.14	4.47

[1] Underlining indicates groups who agreed.

[2] The ratings were derived by taking the weighted average of all items in the category. For example, all ratings of the professions were derived in the following way: the sum of the individual ratings for each item was added to the sum of all other individual ratings for all the items, then divided by the total number of ratings for all items.

cians and lawyers rated it 8th, or next to least serious. Similarly the police gave a lower ranking to the category of emotional neglect than did the other groups. Except for these distinctions, these professionals do agree as to the relative seriousness of different kinds of child mistreatment, just as they agree on the relative seriousness of most individual acts within each category.[13]

Table 3-6 also offers summary information as to the level of agreement about the absolute ratings of seriousness of each category. This information, of course, reflects what has already been observed with respect to the individual vignettes.

These general observations can be made: Lawyers' ratings of the seriousness of all categories were lower than any other profession, significantly so in all but three categories. On the other hand, police and social workers' ratings of seriousness were greater than the other two professions. They also were most often in significant agreement with one another as to the overall seriousness of each type of mistreatment. The exceptions resulted from the police's perceptions of the greater seriousness of matters of parents' sexual behavior and the use of drugs and alcohol.

The disparity among the professions in their absolute ratings of

[13] To ensure that there was no statistical difference in the rankings between professions, a Kruskel–Wallis one-way analysis of variance was performed. This showed no significant difference between the rankings of the professionals. See Sidney Siegel, *Non Parametric Statistics* (New York: McGraw-Hill, 1956), pp. 184–193.

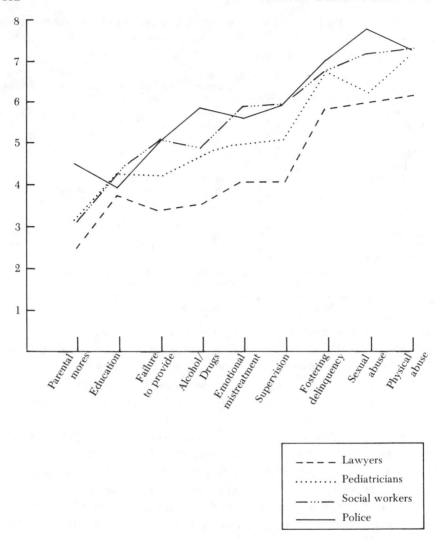

FIGURE 3–1. Professional Agreement on Categories of Mistreatment

seriousness is very clear from the chart. However, the curves of the ratings of each of the professions show some interesting similarities as well as differences. While the social workers and police are both distinguished by their high ratings, the shape of the social workers' rating is as much like the lawyers', as is the pediatricians'. The peaks and valleys in the social workers and lawyers curves are alike save for two categories where they are quite disparate: the relatively higher rating of seriousness of failure to provide is in contrast to the much lower ones of the lawyers; conversely the lawyers' ratings of alcohol/drugs depart from the relative lower ratings on this category by the social workers'. But the distributions of these two groups' ratings on all other categories is similar.

In contrast, the social workers and the police show discrepancies in their curves in several areas, particularly in the realm of emotional mistreatment, with social workers perceiving such mistreatment as relatively much more serious than did police, and of course the reverse situation with respect to parental sexual mores, alcohol/drugs, and sexual abuse.

The pediatricians have a curve that appears at some points like the social workers' and at others like the lawyers'; however, the tendency is to look more like the lawyers' curve. Their lower ratings of sexual abuse distinguish them from all three of the other groups, and their relatively high ratings of fostering delinquency is similar only to that of the police. The elevated ratings of pediatricians and lawyers on educational neglect may reflect the fact that their educational level is higher than that of the other two, and hence may reflect a higher value on education itself, their own prestige deriving as it does from their high level of professional education. The pediatricians' perceptions of sexual abuse may reflect the fact that very little is actually known about the harmful effects of sexual abuse, though pediatricians may know the physical harm to be relatively rare.

The similarity of the generally higher absolute ratings given by police and social workers suggest the duality in the police role in child mistreatment. This is both a social service function and a law enforcement one. In chapter 2, discrepant views about the role of the police in handling mistreatment were noted. These data do suggest that the dissimilarities between law enforcement and social service orientations may have been unduly stressed, and in part are more stereotypic than based on reality. It is possible that the police in this study, especially in the specialized Child Abuse Unit, may share a social service orientation that police in other communities do not. As they have been described by attorneys Sussman and Cohen (1975): "The Los Angeles City Child Abuse Unit is unique. A cross between social service and law enforcement agency, it has the powers of law enforcement combined with the sensitivity for the causes and character of child abuse" (p. 194).

The particular functions these professionals perform are reflected in their ratings. The generally higher ratings of the police and social workers are related to their distinct professional roles in the handling of mistreatment, roles that provide them with different kinds of experiences and different obligations. Since they are the ones who perform the initial investigation of complaints of mistreatment, they have the most direct experience with the whole gamut of situations, particularly those matters that can only be observed at first hand, within the home. As the primary gatekeepers, they bear a special burden through their investigatory functions. If they should decide not to pursue a complaint of mistreatment, then that situation would not be processed further into the system. This responsibility was expressed very clearly by one of the officers in the special child abuse unit. During consultation in the early part of the research, this officer looked over the vignettes and stated: "I could put them all in the ninth category [the most serious] because I would investigate all of them." From the perspective of this primary gatekeeper, the reference point of "seriousness to the welfare of the child" is necessarily linked to the particular burden of screening cases into or out of the system. "Seriousness" therefore can take on the connotation of "serious" or "potentially serious" enough to warrant investigation, even though the outcomes of investigation would vary as to the extremity of measure to be taken.

Pediatricians are also in a quasi-investigatory role because of their reporting responsibility. However, they are mandated to report only matters of physical injury, though they may seek intervention from the police and social workers in other matters. Their primary area of expertise, however, is the physical well-being of children, and many of these categories transcend the physical realm. Thus the consistency of ratings among them is not like that of the police and social workers, whose investigative work brings them into contact with the full range of types of mistreatment.

Those areas where the social workers and police failed to agree also reflect different professional orientations and roles. Social workers by both training and conviction are particularly attuned to emotional and psychological matters. Social-work leaders in child protection have pioneered the movement to include emotional mistreatment within the purview of protective agencies. Quite expectedly, then, they would perceive emotional mistreatment as more serious than others did, including the police. The social workers in this study have different options open to them with respect to disposition in that the agency within which they work can provide services on a voluntary basis, without court intervention; thus they may be less influenced than the police by criteria used by the courts in designating mistreatment. The police do not have primary access to noncourt types of intervention, but they do perform a function that the social workers do not: as peace officers they are charged with arresting those who have broken the law, no matter how unpopular or controversial that law might be at any given time. Thus, with respect to the use of marijuana and cocaine, or prostitution and homosexuality, the police orientation is likely to be different from that of social workers or the other professions. They alone have the function of apprehending those who have broken the law. While social workers might view such matters solely from the perspective of the parent-child relationship, the police role mandates an additional burden. This difference very probably played a part in their perception of the greater seriousness of situations involving drugs and alcohol, and the sexual behavior of the parents.

The generally low ratings of lawyers might be explained in part by their difference in professional functions: they represent both prosecutors and defenders of mistreatment perpetrators. The work of the prosecutors is not limited to child mistreatment. Hence, in their frame of reference, the incidents described in these vignettes—if they are crimes at all—are considerably less serious for the most part than others with which they deal, such as homicide, rape, and robbery. Furthermore, many of the types of mistreatment described are not subject to the criminal laws they enforce. On the other hand those attorneys whose experience and responsibility have been the defense of parents most likely would view incidents of mistreatment on the less serious side of the spectrum, as they are charged with defense of their clients' actions.

While these factors of sampling may have served generally to lower the lawyers' ratings, they are probably not the only explanation of the discrepancy between them and the other professionals. Members of the legal profession have been in the forefront of the movement to restrict definitions of mistreatment. It can come as no surprise that they would be the ones to perceive of mistreatment as less serious than the others. The criteria for demarcating harm by the JJSP/S is reflected in the lawyers' ratings. They, along with others, see as most serious those categories that the JJSP/S clearly includes among the harms defining an endangered child: physical abuse, sexual abuse, and fostering delinquency. They deviated

widely on the category of supervision, a category that involved potential harm rather than actual harm. With the social workers and
pediatricians, they saw as least harmful matters pertaining to the
parents' sexual mores, matters totally excluded by the JJSP/S.
Finally, the lawyers deviated most from police and social workers
on the failure to provide category, incidents of neglect that would
not meet the stringent standard of physical harm as grounds for
legal intrusion. All these findings imply that the lawyers in this
study, while agreeing with the other professions as to the relative
harmfulness of the categories of mistreatment, might well have a
lower threshold on the continuum as to where the line should be
drawn in demarcating situations of mistreatment.

Hence, while we find agreement in relative terms, the importance of differences in the absolute ratings cannot be ignored.
Social workers saw emotional mistreatment as less serious than
three other kinds of mistreatment, as did the other professions. But
their higher absolute rating, compared with the others', certainly
could be anticipated from the statements of leaders in the social-
work profession. Because the findings of the study do reflect the
controversies explicit in the field, their importance concerns both
the disagreement in the absolute ratings as well as the agreement in
the relative ones. Both are influenced by professional functions and
orientations to the problems, and not by idiosyncratic or psychodynamic factors. These professionals agree on what they see—the
areas of disagreement are based on valid arguments, albeit value-
based ones. We shall have more to say on potential resolutions of
the areas of disagreement in chapter 6. We turn now to examination of the views of the lay population, and the degree of agreement and disagreement that exists among them and between them
and the professionals.

CHAPTER 4

The Community Views Child Mistreatment

SITUATIONS OF MISTREATMENT begin in the community, are first identified there, and then are brought to the attention of professionals. While professionals play key roles in defining cases of mistreatment, members of the general population play equally significant roles. The laws proscribing mistreatment and outlining its control are made by legislators responsible to the populace, and the services provided by the professionals are tax-supported. Identification of mistreatment—successful case finding—is to a great extent dependent upon initial recognition by lay people close to the situation. Finally, of course, professionals identify and label adults as mistreating, adults who are members of the general population. Whether from the standpoint of accountability for tax-supported services, reliance on community members for identification, or imposition of the mistreating label on private citizens, community members are integrally involved in the processes of defining mistreatment. Any social definition of mistreatment is inadequate if it does not include the general population's perceptions of mistreatment. What are these perceptions, and what is the degree of agreement about them among subpopulations in the community? To what extent do members of the community share professionals' opinions about the absolute and relative seriousness of different kinds of mistreatment? These are the issues addressed by the research reported in this chapter. At the time the research was conducted, no systematic investigation had been made of these questions. However, there has been considerable speculation as to different community perceptions of mistreatment, especially among different social classes and ethnic groups. We begin with a review of that material.

SOCIOCULTURAL PLURALISM AND CHILD MISTREATMENT

At the heart of the controversies over what should and should not be considered mistreatment warranting state intrusion into family life is concern that such intrusion may simply constitute the imposition of the values of one segment of the community on other segments with different values. Professionals are seen as imposing their views on the populace at large, or at best upholding the values only of middle-class whites, those most like themselves, but not those of lower socioeconomic and other ethnic statuses. In the JJSP/S one reason that is given for the establishment of stringent criteria for restricting the options open to judges and social workers is: "Extensive intervention carries a substantial risk of intervening to 'save' children of poor parents and/or minority cultures" (p. 37). Class differences between judicial and social-work definers and those they label as mistreating have also been observed by Sanford Katz, and he notes as well the middle-class biases of most legislators, biases reflected in the neglect laws: "Since judges and legislators are generally drawn from the middle-class environment, it should not be surprising that laws and their interpretations about parents and children reflect prevailing middle-class mores" (Katz 1971, p. 5).

Definitions of mistreatment are vulnerable to subjective value judgments partly because we do not know enough about child rearing and child development to make objective judgments about what is harmful to children. Both legal and social-work commentaries demonstrate cognizance of the idea that variant child rearing practices among different social class and cultural groups cannot be interpreted as detrimental to children just because they are different. One of the general principles underlying the JJSP/S specifically refers to the importance of "protecting cultural differences" in establishing standards for coercive intervention.

> Given the cultural pluralism and diversity of child rearing practices in our society, it is essential that any system authorizing coercive state involvement in child rearing fully take these differences into account. Moreover, failure to recognize that chil-

dren can develop adequately in a range of environments and with different types of parenting may lead to intervention that disturbs a healthful situation for the child [JJSP 1977, p. 44].[1]

Respect for cultural diversity has been expressed within social work as well as law. The Child Welfare League of America's Standards for Child Protective Services are referred to in chapter 3. In that report's discussion of the establishment of community standards of child care, explicit recognition was given to group diversity:

> Community standards for child care reflect changing public attitudes and different views among different groups regarding what is essential for the child and what jeopardizes his well-being and future development. What may be considered neglect or abuse in one community, or for one group of children, may not be so considered in another. The point at which individuals in a community may take action, and the situations which are tolerated, will often differ from community to community, and within communities [CWLA 1970, p. 8].

In spite of controversy over the value-laden dimensions of the definitions of mistreatment and the expressed desires to respect cultural differences, very little is actually known about the specifics of the assumed differences themselves, including differences in child rearing behaviors and attitudes toward parenting. Yet, despite the lack of research-based information about such differences, the speculation is considerable. Such speculation is generated by information from the broader arena of child development research and from specific information about the incidence rates of reports of mistreatment among various social groups.

Social class differences in child rearing practices and attitudes have not been ignored by child development researchers and others, but they are of limited use in attempting to assess differences in deviant parenting. First of all, most of the research has been concerned with differences in normative behavior, not with aspects of parenting that might be harmful to children. The quest has been to establish a link between social class status and the ways

---

[1] The JJSP itself was criticized by professionals from several ethnic groups as being potentially biased, its committee memberships made up largely of white males. In 1973 a Minority Group Advisory Committee was established, and several members of that group subsequently joined the commission guiding the entire project as well as the drafting committee. Leon Chestang, a Black professor of social work then at the University of Chicago, served as consultant to the committee that drafted the standards relating to child abuse and neglect.

in which normal child rearing tasks are carried out. Bottle feeding versus breast feeding, for example, was an early preoccupation, as was toilet training. Matters of cognitive stimulation have been of more recent concern. For example, observational techniques have been utilized to study class differences in mothers' language patterns in speaking to their children, and their general capacities to be teachers to them. Here again the quest has been to identify maternal behavior that enhances optimal development, rather than grossly injurious behavior such as might be considered as mistreatment. Parental attitudes toward child rearing have been the preoccupation of many, but the validity of this work, especially with reference to the link between differences in attitudes and in actual behavior, has been questioned.

Furthermore, work based on direct observation, as well as that derived from interviews and/or questionnaires, has been criticized for the failure to account for situational variations. The assumption that parents or children possess general traits such as acceptance or aggressiveness is challenged as being unresponsive to the variations in behavior that situational contexts must influence. For example, the severity of punishment surely must vary with the nature of the infraction, where it occurs, at home or in public, and the success or failure of milder punishments to stem the offensive child behavior. This deficit is particularly true of techniques that depend on parents' reports of their practices, reports that must rest on some kind of subjective averaging by them to describe their typical behavior (Martin 1975, pp. 469–70). Two further limitations are the fact that the majority of the studies have focused on very young children and are limited to mother-child interaction, with fathers being ignored. Mistreatment involves children of all ages, and fathers as well as mothers.

But these methodological limitations are not the only ones in child development research that render it a shaky foundation on which to base supposition about social status links to mistreatment. The most glaring omission in the child development research, one that precludes any ready assumptions about cultural differences, has been that of families other than white parents and children, and especially those with language preferences other than English. Thus, while social-class dimensions of normal child rearing have been studied with respect to differences among white people, the information is of limited utility in understanding differences even among them regarding mistreatment—deviant child rearing—and it is not at all helpful in understanding such attitudes among those who are not white or not English-speaking.

There is one piece of work that deals with social class orientations to basic child care standards, including some aspects of marginal care that overlap "neglect." While limited to only a part of the total spectrum of mistreatment, it is directly germane to the questions being pursued here. In a study conducted not long after our research, Polansky and Williams (1978) investigated differences in attitudes toward standards of child care between white working-class and middle-class mothers. They adapted the Childhood Level of Living Scale, referred to in chapter 1, for measuring middle- and lower-income white mothers' attitudes toward physical care and cognitive/emotional development of children. Some examples of statements in the scale are "Mother mentions use of TV to teach child," "Clothing usually appears to be hand-me-downs," "The child is often pushed aside when he shows need for love."

Respondents were asked to grade each of the 214 items on a scale ranging from "should be reported to legal authorities" to "excellent care." The scale does not deal with physical or sexual abuse, and since it is intended to capture information about especially good care, it contains items that are not likely to be considered as mistreatment by anyone as well as many that might be. From their work with one sample of fifty-seven working-class mothers in Camden, New Jersey, and another of fifty-eight middle-class mothers in Philadelphia, Polansky and Williams reported "startling" similarities in the ratings of all the mothers. They concluded that "despite the differences in education and socioeconomic status among these mothers, they are *very* homogeneous in their evaluations of basic elements in child care" (Polansky and Williams 1978, p. 11). Hence their research would refute any ready assumptions about a greater acceptability of inadequate care in a given social class group.

With respect to attitudes toward physical abuse, there is some germane research that focused on the use of corporal punishment. The use of corporal punishment cannot justifiably be equated with physical abuse. Though to some any physical assault on children might be considered as abusive, this stance does not appear to be the norm. Indeed, as recently as 1977, the U.S. Supreme Court ruled that corporal punishment in schools was permissible on the basis of the common-law precedent of disciplinary corporal punishment in public schools (*Ingraham* v. *Wright*, 97 S. Ct. 1401, 1977).

As we saw in the last chapter, professionals did not see spanking a child and leaving red marks as very serious at all; in fact, they saw it as qualitatively different from other more serious physical assaults. Thus, in describing research focused on the acceptability and use of corporal punishment as potentially linked to child abuse, a cautionary note must be made. Questions about the acceptability of various *degrees* of severity of punishment must be raised, for they are really the same questions that surround the issues of demarcating "normal punishment" from "child abuse." Cultural differences in the use of corporal punishment cannot justifiably be translated into evidence of cultural differences in the acceptance of "child abuse." It might seem logical that more frequent use of corporal punishment increases the risk of injury to children—intentional or unintentional—but this link is yet to be demonstrated. Complex factors such as the degree of parental control over their own behavior may be quite as important determinants as the frequency of punishment.

Until very recently it was generally accepted that the use of physical punishment in disciplining children was more common among lower than higher social classes. In a comprehensive review of related research, Bronfenbrenner in 1958 concluded that "physical punishment was most frequently used by working-class parents, while those of the middle class were more likely to employ 'love-oriented' discipline techniques." Although some of the work has been criticized on methodological grounds, particularly the deficiencies of interview data as opposed to direct observation, the consistency and the magnitude of the differences (hence their importance) has not been challenged until recently. Howard Erlanger reviewed the available studies on the subject published between 1936 and 1970 and concluded that the association between social class and corporal punishment was at best tenuous (1974). Among the nine studies he reviewed, only five demonstrated a statistically significant association between lower socioeconomic status and physical punishment. Some studies actually reported that such punishment was *less* common among lower- than middle-class families. These studies were limited to particular cities, and only one included Black parents (Davis and Havingshurst 1946).

In 1968 a national survey conducted for the National Commission on the Causes and Prevention of Violence sampled 941 white and 195 Black adults. Questions put to the respondents concerned their experiences with being spanked by their own parents as well as consideration of various situations in which they would approve of spanking a child. The respondents' families of origin were designated as "middle" or "working class" by the respondents themselves. Frequent childhood experience with spanking was more common among the "working-class" groups, and more common among Blacks than whites, about a 10 percent difference in each instance. The greatest difference, however, was between middle-class and working-class Blacks: 29 percent of the former and 44 percent of the latter reported "frequent" spankings. In no combined class/racial group was "frequent" spanking reporting by as much as 50 percent of the respondents (Erlanger 1975, p. 155).

In examining their own tolerance for spanking, respondents were grouped by education and race. Acceptance of spanking was found to be related to both factors. There were very few respondents in any grouping that did not approve of spanking under any circumstances—but those most intolerant of spanking were college-educated Black adults and whites with only a grade school education! The group that was most accepting of spanking under a range of circumstances was composed of Blacks with only a grade school education, but the difference between this group and all other groups was not as great as the difference between them and college-educated Blacks (Erlanger 1975, p. 156).

The data from this survey as well as from previous studies indicate some relationship between punishment techniques and social class and ethnic identification, but it is far from a simple one to understand. With respect to sociocultural factors and punishment, Erlanger concluded that the relationship is "probably not strong enough to be of great theoretical or practical significance" (p. 154). If such an ambiguous situation maintains with so straightforward a matter as the use of corporal punishment, it is unlikely that there is clear evidence regarding the pattern of sociocultural differences in more complex matters of child rearing, such as emotional nurturance and moral development.

Although Erlanger's reviews cast doubt on the strength of the available data, an even more important criticism must be made of the kind of application that is made of it. Differences between groups cannot be used as a measure of characteristics of either group. Depending on the size of the samples, statistically significant differences can be found between groups when 10 percent more of one group does or says something than another. Stress on the 10 percent difference obscures the fact that 60 percent of one group and 70 percent of the other possess the characteristic in question. Clearly what is most characteristic of both groups in such a circumstance is that which is most common in each. Hence the 10 percent difference obscures not only the similarities between the groups but, more important, also the modal characteristics within groups. The data referred to from the National Commission illustrate this point: though there were class and ethnic differences, with respect to the frequency of spanking, the majority (over 50 percent) of both Blacks and whites, and of those within all income strata of either group, had not been "frequently spanked." Erlanger took note of this inappropriate use of data, whether the data themselves be weak or strong:

> Most statements on the relationship between social status (class or race) and techniques of punishment imply the existence of a *strong relationship* between those variables. At a minimum, spanking is thought to be a much more frequent occurrence in lower class and black families than in middle and upper class white families. But often something more fundamental is implied by these statements, and social groups are *characterized* as to methods of punishment [Erlanger 1975, p. 151].

Yet it is precisely this kind of thinking that is used in trying to explain class and race differences observed among reported incidents of mistreatment. Information about the relative incidence of reported mistreatment among various social classes has sparked considerable speculation that at least some forms of mistreatment may be more acceptable to persons in certain classes. The accumulated facts do indicate that among reported cases of mistreatment, families at the lower end of the socioeconomic spectrum are overrepresented. The facts concerning disproportionate representation of those of ethnic minority status are less clear.[2] These studies

---

[2] In estimating over- or underrepresentation of any segment of the population in a problem-identified group, a major methodological hazard is selection of inappropriate comparison statistics. Blacks, for example, may constitute 20 percent of the total population. However, in some cities they may constitute 40 percent. Thus a national statistic cannot validly serve as a basis for selected parts of the country. Further, Blacks are overrepresented in the lower socioeconomic strata.

all used different definitions of the kinds of mistreatment under scrutiny and varying indices of social status. Hence they do not constitute a body of work with comparable findings. Yet, the consistency of the findings lends some support to the popular notion that the incidence of various kinds of mistreatment is greater among the lower classes. But how *much* greater is a very controversial question.

Cohen, Mulford, and Philbrick (1967) gathered data on the 959 neglectful families seen in a single year by the Children's Protective Services of the Massachusetts SPCC. They found that parents of lower social status were overrepresented relative to their numbers in the population as a whole. Over 75 percent of their sample earned $100 a week or less; 67.2 percent never graduated from high school. A similar finding was reported by Simons, Downs, Hurster, and Archer (1966) based on 313 cases taken from the New York City child abuse registry, and also by Allen, Kosciolek, Bensel, and Raile (1969) in their study of thirty-three abused children and their families seen in hospitals. In a related matter, Simons, Downs, Hurster, and Archer (1966) found that Black and Puerto Rican families—who tended to fall in the lower socioeconomic categories—were overrepresented among reported abusers in New York. Additionally, this relationship between high incidence of mistreatment and low social status has been often posited by reviewers of the general literature—empirical and impressionistic—on substandard parental behavior (Silver 1968; Wright 1970).

The most comprehensive quantitative epidemiologic study was conducted by David Gil (1970), who carried out the first exhaustive analysis of data from the then newly enacted child abuse reporting laws across the nation. In selecting the reports for inclusion in his study, Gil used a more precise and restrictive definition of child abuse than the others: the willful infliction of physical injury. From his analyses, Gil concluded that the families reported were drawn disproportionately from the poor and poorly educated and from ethnic minorities (Black and Puerto Rican). Sixty-five

---

Hence, in making comparisons with the general population on a problem known already to draw disproportionately from the lower strata, their difference must be controlled for in making estimates of disproportionate representation. None of the studies cited controlled for either variable—that is, the comparison of the problem group with the proportion of low-income Blacks in the population where the study took place.

percent had less than a high school education, and 65 percent had annual incomes of less than $7,000 a year. (This was about 22 percent more families with such low incomes than were found among all U.S. families in 1969.) Gil further interpreted the data as yielding an overrepresentation of Black children, 21 percent of his overall sample as compared with only 15 percent of all children in the population.

Serious questions can be raised as to whether the general population was the appropriate comparison group, since in urban areas Black children make up a considerably larger proportion of the population, and no stratification by income was performed. Even with these drawbacks, Gil's data still remain the most comprehensive on the incidence of physical abuse as he defined it.

Perhaps as important as the study itself for our purposes is the interpretation he placed on the data and the controversies it has generated. Some have rejected the study out of hand as not reflective of true incidence, since it is based only on reported cases. The middle and upper classes are said to be shielded from reporting and from public intrusion by biases in the reporting mechanisms as well as factors in their lives, including the reluctance of private physicians (more likely to be used by the higher social classes) to report cases of abuse among their patients. Furthermore, the isolated, single-family dwelling pattern of the middle and upper classes has been thought to decrease the potential for detection of abuse by friends and neighbors. It is further speculated that community agencies may be more reluctant to intervene into the lives of such families (Parke and Collmer 1975; Gabarino 1977; Kempe and Helfer 1972). Certainly no one, least of all Gil, denies that cases of physical abuse are observed and reported at all social class levels. The controversy centers on the meaning of the relatively higher incidence among the lower classes.

Among those who do accept the higher incidence of reported cases as an accurate reflection of what actually goes on, different interpretations have been offered. These interpretations are necessarily speculative; the only available facts are the reporting rates themselves. One interpretation, not disavowed by Gil, is that the stresses of poverty, especially when compounded with those of racial discrimination, are likely to precipitate social-psychological reactions that lead to physical mistreatment of children. Similar explanations are offered for the occurrence of other forms of mistreatment apart from physical injury (Young 1964; Giovannoni and

Billingsley 1970; Gelles 1973). Such formulations do not necessarily postulate that members of the lower classes and of ethnic minorities necessarily find such mistreatment acceptable, but rather that more of their members are likely to be driven to such mistreatment through environmental pressures.

With respect to physical injury, Gil postulated that especially among nonwhites, dynamics may operate that would imply acceptability. While he does not use the term, he essentially describes a culture of violence as a cause of child abuse, not unlike the culture-of-violence concept used to explain adult crime (Wolfgang and Ferracuti 1967). Gil (1974) perceived a general predisposition to violence against children in society as a whole and believed that an important manifestation of that tendency is the widespread use of physical punishment as a means of disciplining children. Physical punishment, in turn, is seen as laying the groundwork for the use and acceptance in society of the more violent acts of child abuse. That is, an atmosphere is created within which abuse is tolerated or overlooked.

Although he fully acknowledges that these higher rates are probably caused in part by the particular problems of poverty and discrimination faced by such families, Gil nevertheless goes beyond such a structural explanation to maintain that the evidence points to differences in child rearing philosophy among these groups. In explaining his findings and using them to support his contention of a cultural predisposition among the poor toward child abuse, Gil refers to research on social-class differences in the use of corporal versus noncorporal punishment (p. 127): "Studies of child-rearing patterns have found a strong association between low socioeconomic status and the use of physical means in disciplining children." Actually, Gil cites only one study, that conducted by Miller and Swanson in 1953. Indeed, they did find a strong association in that study between working-class status and preference for corporal punishment (52 percent of working class and only 11 percent of middle class) (Miller and Swanson 1960). However, as Erlanger points out, this study had by far the most extreme results of any such study conducted over a forty-year period (Erlanger 1975, p. 157). Gil goes on to state, though giving no reference to the source, "It has also been observed that the uninhibited acting out of aggressive impulses is more likely to occur in poor and working-class families than in middle-class families" (p. 127). The inescapable conclusion is that lower-class and minority parents hold to philosophies that are somehow more accepting of violence against children.

Furthermore, Gil perceived an extra difference in the case of minority parents. In explaining his findings of higher abuse rates for Blacks and other nonwhites, he maintained that low educational and income achievement are not the only reasons for this phenomenon, but that "specific cultural patterns" are, if anything, even more important in this regard. While Gil acknowledges that some of the overrepresentation of Black and Puerto Rican children in his sample seemed to be "a function of discriminating attitudes and practices on the part of reporting sources," he goes on to seek a further explanation within these ethnic groups themselves: "Since different ethnic groups may differ in child-rearing practices, the possibility cannot be ruled out that such differences between whites and nonwhites could be a contributory factor. . . . Ethnically linked differences in using physical force in child-rearing may reflect the violence experienced by nonwhite minorities over many generations in American society" (pp. 106–7). The logic, therefore, of the existence of a subculture of violence among the poor and nonwhite—or, as Gil saw it, a subculture of superviolence amidst a more generalized culture of violence—is that these groups simply are more accepting of the physical mistreatment of children.

Of course, the concept of a subculture of violence as the cause of child abuse and neglect has been disputed by others in the field. In this vein, Parke and Collmer (1975) cited Gil's own study of public knowledge and opinions about abuse (1967), in which he found little or no class difference among response rates to a question on how individuals thought they would react upon learning of an incident of abuse in their neighborhood. They concluded: "There is no evidence to support the view that lower class adults are indifferent to the occurrence of child abuse or are more likely to condone abuse than adults from higher social classes" (Parke and Collmer 1975, p. 526).

Although speculation abounds about sociocultural differences in perceptions of child mistreatment, the available facts are few and the interpretations highly controversial. One factor must be underscored: Mistreatment that is socially defined is designated as deviant. Discussions about differences in child rearing practices and in reported incidences of mistreatment tend to eclipse similarities and commonalities that the facts themselves belie. Though something may occur *more often* among one group than another, the relative difference does not mean that the occurrence is *typical* of that group. Such occurrences may still be considered deviant, and highly deviant, in both a social and a statistical sense. Certainly, the magnitude of differences does have implications for *how* much more or less deviant an occurrence might be, but that is still a relative judgment, not an absolute one. The presence of deviance and deviant individuals in any group does not necessarily imply that the deviance is condoned by other members of the group. With respect to child mistreatment, before any judgments can be made about the cultural contributions to its occurrence, considerably more needs to be known about culturally linked attitudes toward the acts of mistreatment themselves. Similarly, before it can be assumed that professionals are imposing their values on various subsegments of the populations, much more needs to be known about the actual value differences. Here it is crucial to note again that no group is homogeneous. Perpetrators of mistreatment may have values that clash with those of professionals. But these same values may also clash with other lay people in their own social status—for example, the individuals who initiated the investigation into the situation.

As we approached the task of investigating community members' opinions about mistreatment, there was no definitive previous work to suggest what the results might be. Not only was relevant research limited, but the findings conflicted, and the interpretations of those findings were highly controversial. The lack of empirical evidence in the area of community perceptions with regard to child mistreatment is not altogether surprising. This is a topic that elicits an emotionally charged response from many individuals. Nevertheless, some rather negative implications arise from this lack of empirical evidence. For example, case-management techniques are often founded upon assumptions concerning the nature of community perceptions. Child-mistreatment statutes on a statewide level have been based, at least in part, upon generally held beliefs about the seriousness of various abusive and neglectful acts. Similarly, the myriad of local, state, and national social-action programs designed to ameliorate the problems associated with child mistreatment are based on commonly held beliefs about community perceptions of this social problem. And controversies over appropriate definitions and professional intrusion are likewise based on assumptions about differences in child rearing attitudes and behavior among subgroups—assumptions, as we have seen, that have few data to support them. This opinion survey was intended to overcome some of the deficits in this important arena.

Research Procedures

The basic vignettes presented to the professionals were used in the study of community opinions, with variations in structuring: the age of the child was randomly varied (three, seven, or thirteen years or no mention), along with information about the occupation of the parents, variously described as having one of the following occupations, representing four socioeconomic levels: (1) doctor, lawyer, professor; (2) accountant, teacher, programmer; (3) bookkeeper, welder, bank teller; (4) clerk, laundry worker, machine operator. Additional options varied randomly with these were "welfare recipient" or no occupation mentioned at all. As with the professionals, the variation of consequence or no consequence for the child was maintained.

An example of how a vignette would read that had all information included—age of child, occupation of parent, and a consequence—is: "The parent banged the seven-year-old child's head against the wall. The child suffered a concussion. The parent is a bookkeeper." The computer program developed for constructing the vignettes provided for random selection of each of the additional variables in each vignette produced. As had been done with the vignette construction for the professionals in each computer-produced packet of 60 vignettes, random selection procedures ensured that no stem vignette appeared with its counterpart mentioning a consequence. In certain vignettes where a particular age level would be inappropriate, it was not included for possible selection—for instance, "three years old" would be inappropriate for the vignette about keeping a child out of school. As with the professionals, the first four vignettes were the same in every packet. Each packet of vignettes was thus made up of 64 vignettes, the first four the same ones in all packets. The remaining 60 contained 47 randomly selected stems out of the total 78, to which was added an age for the child and an occupation for the parent. An additional 13 stems always had added age seven for the child and contained no mention of the parents' occupation. Exactly half the vignettes had a consequence for the child stated, and half did not.

The purpose of including the age of the child and the occupation of the parent was to see if this kind of information would alter the respondent's perception of the seriousness of the events. There is some speculation that extraneous factors, especially the socio-economic status of parents, influence judgments about the seriousness of mistreatment. According to this line of reasoning, perceptions of mistreatment are beclouded by prejudices regarding factors not integral to the mistreatment itself.

The instructions given to the respondents for rating the vignettes were similar to those given to the professionals, and the criterion of "seriousness" for the child was identical.

> I would like to begin by asking you to rate a stack of cards that have a short statement about specific parent-child situations. (Hands first card to respondent. Allows respondent to read fully. Hands respondent board.)
>
> As you see, there are a series of envelopes on this board. The envelopes are numbered from one (1) to nine (9). These numbers represent a 9-point scale of seriousness. The numbers between 1 and 9 represent varying degrees of seriousness between least and most. For example, if you feel an act was only moderately serious, you might rate it a 4, 5, or 6. If you feel it is less serious, but not least, you might rate it 2 or 3, or if you feel it was more serious, but not most, you might rate it 7 or 8. Please rate the card you have just read on this scale according to how serious you feel the act is for the well-being of the child. Use 9 for the most serious acts and 1 for the least serious acts. Remember, this is only your opinion of the seriousness of the act; there are no right or wrong answers.

If the respondent expressed difficulty with a particular card, interviewers were instructed to tell them to do their best. Following the administration of the vignettes an interview was held with each respondent. The questions asked in this interview were based on those contained in the 1967 national opinion survey by David Gil and John Noble (1967). The questions were specifically focused on child abuse, defined as: "when an adult physically injures a child, not by accident, but by anger or deliberately."

One purpose of the Gil and Noble study was to estimate from the sample respondents an incidence rate of child abuse. Our intention here was simply to ascertain the level of knowledge about child abuse among respondents and how they thought it should be handled.

Respondents were asked if they had heard about child abuse, in general and with reference to a specific incident; how they thought both the perpetrator and the child victim should be handled; and whether they thought anyone or they themselves might abuse a child. These questions were asked after the respondents had completed rating the vignettes.

Respondents were given the option of reading the vignettes in Spanish or English and of being interviewed in either language. The interviews were carried out in the respondents' homes by trained survey-research interviewers. The sample was selected from the Los Angeles Metropolitan area, utilizing the most current census data. Households were selected through a multistage, stratified probability sampling procedure. In order to meet the specifications of stratification, a particular respondent was selected from each household. The obtained sample included 1,065 respondents, of whom 85 responded in Spanish and the rest in English. The ethnic breakdown was as follows: Black 129 (12 percent); Hispanic (both English- and Spanish-speaking combined), 177 (17 percent); white, 687 (65 percent); and "other" ethnic groups (7 percent), mainly Asian and Native American. Of all respondents, 43 percent were male and 57 percent female. The median age was thirty-five. Over half (58 percent) had no minor children living in the household, and of those that did have children living with them, the great majority had no more than two. Socioeconomic characteristics were related to ethnicity, with whites having had a higher mean education, income, and occupational status than respondents in the other ethnic groups. (Table 4–1 gives an overview of the sociodemographic characteristics of this sample.)

COMMUNITY RATINGS OF SPECIFIC INCIDENTS

Effects of Age of Child and
Occupational Status of Parents

Very little is known about the relative importance of factors that may influence an individual's perception of acts of child mistreatment. In this study three types of variables were possible in each vignette: age of child, occupation of the parent-perpetrator, and the presentation (or nonpresentation) of a consequence of the action. The addition of information about the consequence had a strong and uniform effect on the ratings—in 65 percent of the vignettes the difference was statistically significant.

Like the professionals, community respondents almost invariably rated incidents as more serious when given information about

TABLE 4–1.   Demographic Characteristics of the Community Sample

DEMOGRAPHIC CHARACTERISTICS	ETHNIC GROUP			
	White N = 687	*Black* N = 129	*Hispanic* N = 177	*Total** N = 1065
Sex				
Male	41.9%	38.0%	47.5%	42.5%
Female	58.1	62.0	52.5	57.5
Education				
Grade school	6.7	12.4	31.6	10.9
Some high school	11.8	20.2	20.9	14.0
High school grad	30.8	28.7	27.1	29.5
Some college	30.0	31.0	13.1	26.4
College grad	10.2	7.7	4.5	9.7
Postgrad	10.5	0.0	2.8	9.5
Age				
17–25	17.1	16.8	29.9	19.2
26–32	24.0	19.2	20.9	19.4
33–44	13.7	28.0	22.0	20.7
45–59	15.1	22.4	20.3	21.8
60 +	30.1	13.6	6.9	18.9
Religion				
Protestant	52.0	82.9	11.3	47.5
Catholic	19.4	6.2	83.1	29.4
Jewish	9.5	1.6	0.6	6.7
Other	2.7	1.6	—	2.9
None	16.4	7.7	5.0	13.5
Marital Status				
Never married	18.8	17.8	22.0	19.4
Married	57.3	45.0	58.2	56.3
Divorced	9.8	16.3	11.9	10.9
Separated	2.3	9.3	3.4	3.5
Widowed	11.8	11.6	4.5	9.9
Total Family Income				
Less than $5,000	17.3	28.6	18.6	17.4
$5,000–$9,999	18.4	33.9	29.4	20.8
$10,000–$16,999	20.9	20.5	28.8	20.8
$17,000–$24,999	22.5	14.3	12.4	17.8
$25,000 and over	20.5	2.7	7.9	15.2
No Response	0.4	0.0	2.9	8.0
Occupational Levels				
Professional, technical	16.2	7.0	7.3	14.0
Manager, office	10.2	3.9	1.7	7.7
Sales	4.8	0.8	3.4	4.0
Clerical	13.8	16.4	11.3	13.7
Crafts, foreman	5.8	3.1	6.8	5.5
Operative	5.7	15.6	22.0	9.5
Not in labor force	37.6	42.2	35.0	36.8
Other	5.9	11.0	12.5	8.8

TABLE 4–1.   Continued

Demographic Characteristics	Ethnic Group			
	White N = 687	Black N = 129	Hispanic N = 177	Total* N = 1065
Number of Children				
0	66.3	42.6	36.2	57.6
1	12.2	23.3	19.2	14.7
2	13.7	14.0	20.9	15.5
3	5.5	8.5	13.6	7.1
4 +	2.3	11.6	10.1	5.1

* The total includes 72 "other" responses. These responses were made up of Asian Americans, Native Americans, and other groups who identified themselves as other than the three groups given here.

the consequences for the child. In fact, the ratings of all but 9 vignettes increased with the addition of a consequence. In the 9 vignettes where the addition of a consequence decreased the ratings, the "consequence" either referred to the child's behavior (for example, "continually fighting with other children") or was not really a "consequence" but rather a statement that "the child knows this."

With respect to the age of the child-victim and the occupation of the perpetrator, the picture was less clear. The ambiguity resulted primarily from the number of possible variations within the combinations of each of these variables. To obtain at least a preliminary overview as to what effect these variables might have on the ratings of the vignettes, an analysis of variance was undertaken to measure differences across ages and across occupational levels. To the extent that interpretation of such confounding variables is possible, it appeared that occupational levels made almost no difference in ratings; in fewer than 5 percent of the vignettes was there a statistically significant difference. (Chance alone could produce statistical significance at the .05 level for 5 percent of the vignettes.) On the other hand, variation in the age of the child made some difference, but this was suggested in only 25 percent of the ratings. The problem of the interaction effects of these variables with consequence further obscures any firm conclusions with regard to these three variables. However, the strength of the effect of the addition or deletion of consequence in the professionals' study when coupled with the high degree of statistically significant differences found in the community study attests to the importance of the consequences of actions. The effects on ratings of the addition of a consequence are more clearly borne out than the effects of information about the age of the child and/or the occupation of the parent.[3] Therefore, common speculation that perceptions of mistreatment are influenced by attitudes toward parents unrelated to the mistreatment itself was not supported by the data in this study. Whatever the effects of these considerations, they were overridden by the consequence of the act and the nature of the act itself. The perceived seriousness of the nature of the mistreatment and the seriousness of the consequence of that mistreatment for the child were paramount in the judgments made about the incidents.

Ethnic Differences in Ratings of Specific Incidents

Compared with any of the professional groups, the ratings of seriousness by community members were extremely high. In fact, although 9 levels of seriousness were given as options in making the ratings, the overall mean rating on 85 percent of the vignettes was 6 or more, indicating that these respondents were for the most part rating on a scale from 6 to 9 rather than 1 to 9. The fine distinctions of degrees of seriousness made by all the professionals were not apparent among this lay population (table 4–2 lists the community ratings).

The literature reviewed earlier is scant when it comes to the lay population's opinions about different kinds of mistreatment. However, what does exist, at least with respect to the physical injury of children and the use of corporal punishment, suggests that people of lower social status and nonwhite ethnic background are more tolerant of mistreatment and likely to have a higher threshold for considering actions as mistreatment. From the standpoint of socioeconomic indicators—education, income, or ethnic status (Black,

[3] In the substudy of this project, with an additional 301 respondents, Garrett and Rossi also found that the perpetrator's occupation had no significant effect on seriousness ratings, while age of the child and consequence of the action did have a significant effect. However, the amount of variance contributed by knowledge of the age of the child was very slight, while consequence was the largest explanatory vignette component. They state, "Of greatest significance in determining seriousness judgments is the act itself and its consequences. However, ratings are also affected by the age of the child described in the vignette and the statements describing both the child and the adult involved in the incident. Furthermore, assessments are independent of considerations of the sex of the participants and the social status of the household in which the event is said to occur" (p. 15). See Karen Ann Garrett and Peter H. Rossi, "Judging the Seriousness of Child Abuse," *Medical Anthropology*, Winter 1978, part 3: pp. 1–48.

TABLE 4-2. Ratings of Vignettes by Ethnicity of Community Sample[1]

Vignette[2]	Overall Rating[3,4,5]	White	Black	Hispanic Overall	HISPANIC	
					English Speaking	Spanish Speaking
Sexual Abuse	(8.06)					
Sexual intercourse on one occasion.	8.73 H-1 (0.93)	8.70 (0.91)	8.70 (1.30)	8.80 (0.73)	8.72 (0.82)	8.88 (0.64)
Mutual masturbation on one occasion.	8.28 H-5 (1.49)	8.16 (1.65)	8.47 (1.17)	8.54 (1.09)	8.33 (1.38)	8.80 (0.51)
Suggested child have sexual relationship.	8.22 H-6 (1.57)	8.19 (1.57)	7.98 (2.01)	8.61 (1.00)	8.39 (1.27)	8.85 (0.50)
Fondled genital area once.	7.81 (1.84)	7.65 (1.90)	7.91 (1.85)	8.38 (1.31)	8.20 (1.43)	8.59 (1.13)
Showed child pornographic pictures repeatedly.	7.71 (1.79)	7.58 (1.89)	7.85 (1.62)	8.18 (1.34)	8.08 (1.51)	8.29 (1.13)
Physical Abuse	(7.07)					
Burned with cigarette on buttocks and chest.	8.63 H-2 (0.98)	8.61 (1.00)	8.54 (1.16)	8.68 (0.96)	8.78 (0.79)	8.59 (1.08)
Child immersed in tub of hot water.	8.32 H-4 (1.49)	8.22 (1.61)	8.57 (1.12)	8.53 (1.26)	8.45 (1.37)	8.62 (1.12)
Child hit in face with fist.	7.77 (1.75)	7.61 (1.85)	8.03 (1.62)	8.29 (1.18)	7.99 (1.39)	8.61 (0.80)
Banged child against wall.	7.65 (1.93)	7.40 (2.08)	8.24 (1.42)	8.27 (1.42)	7.96 (1.75)	8.61 (0.80)
Struck child with wooden stick.	7.19 (2.32)	6.96 (2.45)	7.64 (2.16)	7.80 (1.84)	7.26 (2.11)	8.56 (0.99)
Punish by spanking with leather strap.	6.42 (2.50)	6.25 (2.49)	5.91 (2.89)	7.32 (2.11)	7.18 (2.23)	7.46 (1.97)

Punish by spanking with hand, usually.	4.35 L–2 (2.76)	4.00 (2.68)	4.92 (2.96)	5.24 (2.74)	4.82 (2.77)	5.71 (2.64)
Fostering Delinquency	7.79		NO AGREEMENT			
Parents make their child steal.	8.07 H–8 (1.48)	7.96 (1.53)	8.26 (1.64)	8.33 (1.13)	8.09 (1.35)	8.59 (0.74)
Make child take stolen merchandise to store.	8.00 H–10 (1.52)	7.90 (1.59)	8.33 (1.45)	8.29 (1.08)	8.00 (1.31)	8.64 (0.58)
Allow uncle to store stolen goods.	7.00 (2.10)	6.69 (2.18)	7.60 (1.86)	7.64 (1.86)	7.50 (2.14)	7.77 (1.54)
Emotional Mistreatment	7.65		NO AGREEMENT			
Child locked in room since birth.	8.41 H–3 (1.36)	8.46 (1.28)	8.19 (1.77)	8.41 (1.37)	8.43 (1.45)	8.39 (1.29)
Child severely emotionally disturbed, refused treatment.	7.39 (1.83)	7.25 (1.90)	7.73 (1.63)	7.64 (1.69)	7.72 (1.65)	7.57 (1.74)
Dress boy like girl.	7.28 (2.03)	7.13 (2.10)	7.98 (1.76)	7.56 (1.70)	7.74 (1.59)	7.36 (1.80)
Constantly screaming at child, calling him foul names.	7.03 (1.93)	6.84 (1.95)	7.49 (1.94)	7.45 (1.75)	7.33 (1.88)	7.58 (1.61)
Severe behavior problems, refused treatment for parent and child.	6.98 (1.93)	6.77 (2.00)	7.48 (1.77)	7.51 (1.50)	7.59 (1.36)	7.42 (1.64)
Compare child with sibling, sometimes implying not theirs.	6.85 (2.11)	6.66 (2.11)	7.31 (2.19)	7.23 (1.96)	7.49 (1.80)	6.89 (2.12)

See end of table (p. 183) for footnotes.

TABLE 4-2. Continued

Vignette[2]	Overall Rating[3,4,5]	White	Black	Hispanic Overall	HISPANIC	
					English Speaking	Spanish Speaking
Ignore child, seldom talking or listening.	6.67 (2.07)	6.50 (2.08)	7.41 (1.76)	6.98 (1.99)	6.86 (2.08)	7.12 (1.88)
Dress daughter in boy's clothing.	6.17 (2.41)	5.92 (2.46)	7.04 (2.17)	6.55 (2.15)	6.52 (2.30)	6.59 (1.98)
			NO AGREEMENT			
Nutritional Neglect	6.69					
Regularly fail to feed child for 24 hours.	7.87 (1.75)	7.76 (1.84)	8.23 (1.57)	8.08 (1.48)	8.05 (1.56)	8.12 (1.40)
Parents feed child only milk.	7.29 (1.99)	7.25 (1.97)	8.14 (1.54)	7.18 (2.05)	7.21 (2.12)	7.14 (1.97)
Parents brought child to hospital three times for underweight.	6.32 (2.41)	5.96 (2.45)	7.40 (2.06)	6.93 (2.19)	6.86 (2.33)	6.98 (2.10)
Fail to prepare regular meals.	6.31 (2.40)	6.03 (2.41)	7.10 (2.32)	6.97 (2.15)	6.88 (2.22)	7.07 (2.07)
Parents always insist child clean plate.	5.76 L-7 (2.54)	5.46 (2.58)	6.54 (2.50)	6.33 (2.31)	6.41 (2.41)	6.25 (2.20)
Medical Neglect	6.98					
Ignored obviously ill child.	7.71 (1.69)	7.56 (1.76)	8.16 (1.27)	7.93 (1.62)	7.85 (1.63)	8.01 (1.61)
Ignored complaint of earache/drainage.	7.65 (1.68)	7.48 (1.77)	8.19 (1.31)	7.85 (1.50)	7.70 (1.58)	8.02 (1.41)
			NO AGREEMENT			
No health care provided.	7.36 (1.77)	7.13 (1.85)	8.05 (1.43)	7.88 (1.42)	7.82 (1.40)	7.95 (1.47)

178

Repeatedly failed to keep medical appointments.	7.10 (2.19)	6.90 (2.33)	7.88 (1.45)	7.51 (1.82)	7.49 (1.95)	7.52 (1.72)
Not given medication prescribed by doctor.	6.95 (2.12)	6.74 (2.13)	7.60 (1.97)	7.54 (1.82)	7.51 (1.81)	7.58 (1.83)
Failed to obtain eye examination.	6.29 (2.44)	5.96 (2.46)	7.28 (2.10)	6.96 (2.24)	6.63 (2.34)	7.32 (2.08)
No dental care.	6.07 (2.43)	5.82 (2.44)	6.58 (2.55)	6.62 (2.27)	6.48 (2.42)	6.78 (2.09)
Supervision	(7.15)					
Regularly left child after dark, often as late as midnight.	7.74 (1.69)	7.55 (1.81)	8.39 (1.28)	8.12 (1.29)	8.21 (1.43)	8.02 (1.12)
Regularly left child alone in house during day; often not return until dark.	7.54 (1.85)	7.33 (1.98)	8.40 (1.00)	7.80 (1.52)	7.80 (1.58)	7.80 (1.45)
			NO AGREEMENT			
Left child alone all night once.	7.28 (2.02)	7.00 (2.19)	8.08 (1.31)	7.81 (1.45)	7.63 (1.58)	7.95 (1.32)
Left child alone inside house after dark, often not return until midnight.	7.27 (2.09)	7.04 (2.22)	7.91 (1.75)	7.73 (1.70)	7.52 (1.97)	7.95 (1.32)
Left child alone outside until dark regularly.	7.01 (2.12)	6.70 (2.21)	7.67 (1.90)	7.75 (1.54)	7.72 (1.67)	7.78 (1.39)
Regularly left child with neighbors; no one in charge.	6.67 (2.22)	6.32 (2.29)	7.58 (1.92)	7.40 (1.79)	7.37 (1.92)	7.42 (1.64)
Left with grandmother for long periods, several times.	5.97 (2.53)	5.68 (2.54)	6.94 (2.34)	6.41 (2.48)	6.18 (2.45)	6.83 (2.54)

TABLE 4-2. Continued

Vignette[2]	Overall Rating[3,4,5]	White	Black	Hispanic Overall	HISPANIC English Speaking	Spanish Speaking
Drugs/Alcohol	(7.00)					
Parents are addicts.	8.13 *H-7* (1.59)	8.05 (1.62)	8.37 (1.73)	8.37 (1.24)	8.22 (1.51)	8.56 (0.78)
Allow child at cocaine parties.	8.02 *H-9* (1.67)	7.84 (1.80)	8.54 (0.99)	8.37 (1.38)	8.17 (1.60)	8.59 (1.07)
Parent experiments with cocaine.	7.82 (1.90)	7.70 (1.95)	8.00 (1.95)	8.09 (1.66)	7.65 (1.95)	8.44 (1.33)
Father's brother addict and around often.	7.60 (1.98)	7.40 (2.08)	8.03 (1.68)	8.19 (1.47)	7.96 (1.89)	8.45 (0.69)
Parents always allow child to stay at marijuana parties.	7.08 (2.36)	6.74 (2.51)	7.74 (1.93)	7.89 (1.73)	7.53 (2.14)	8.28 (1.01)
Parent high on marijuana while alone with child.	7.01 (2.37)	6.66 (2.49)	7.56 (1.96)	7.92 (1.78)	7.48 (2.19)	8.39 (1.00)
Parent became very drunk while alone with child.	6.89 (2.17)	6.58 (2.24)	7.53 (1.79)	7.58 (1.81)	7.41 (1.92)	7.75 (1.68)
Parents leave bottle of whiskey around.	6.57 (2.36)	6.26 (2.44)	7.22 (2.06)	7.33 (1.90)	7.14 (2.02)	7.54 (1.76)
Let child sip whiskey out of their glass.	6.56 (2.39)	6.21 (2.46)	7.20 (2.18)	7.49 (1.79)	7.24 (2.08)	7.76 (1.36)
Let child stay around at whiskey parties.	6.46 (2.29)	6.15 (2.34)	7.23 (1.98)	7.08 (2.10)	6.78 (2.43)	7.40 (1.62)
Father's brother around drinking.	6.29 (2.34)	5.96 (2.48)	6.97 (1.87)	7.08 (1.83)	6.85 (2.01)	7.36 (1.59)

180

Cleanliness	(6.58)					
Parents usually leave child on filthy, sodden mattress.	7.44 (1.87)	7.28 (1.88)	7.86 (1.91)	7.82 (1.67)	7.61 (1.83)	8.11 (1.39)
Parents don't wash child's hair or bathe for weeks at a time.	7.17 (2.07)	6.96 (2.16)	7.98 (1.44)	7.58 (1.80)	7.57 (1.75)	7.59 (1.85)
			NO AGREEMENT			
Parents don't wash child at all.	6.99 (2.32)	6.84 (2.36)	7.48 (2.21)	7.45 (1.87)	7.41 (1.97)	7.49 (1.80)
Make no effort to keep child clean.	6.38 (2.32)	6.13 (2.33)	7.21 (2.16)	6.86 (2.16)	6.57 (2.37)	7.18 (1.87)
Parents don't see that child brushes teeth.	5.54 L–5 (2.50)	5.19 (2.46)	6.51 (2.38)	6.28 (2.39)	5.87 (2.50)	6.72 (2.19)
Educational Neglect	(6.51)					
Parents know child is truant often.	6.85 (1.92)	6.59 (1.99)	7.45 (1.80)	7.47 (1.47)	7.40 (1.52)	7.54 (1.42)
Let child stay home from school.	6.50 (2.14)	6.17 (2.23)	7.33 (1.89)	7.25 (1.50)	6.98 (1.49)	7.65 (1.45)
Frequently keep child out of school.	6.48 (2.23)	6.11 (2.29)	7.61 (1.74)	7.11 (1.96)	7.10 (2.08)	7.12 (1.87)
Never make child do homework.	6.21 (2.22)	5.86 (2.23)	7.24 (1.92)	6.99 (1.86)	6.72 (2.05)	7.29 (1.59)
Parental Sexual Mores	(6.46)					
Parents permit relative (prostitute) to bring customers.	7.96 (1.52)	7.78 (1.72)	8.34 (1.17)	8.15 (1.11)	7.93 (1.24)	8.47 (0.84)
Parents have intercourse where child sees.	7.61 (1.97)	7.38 (2.09)	8.16 (1.73)	8.11 (1.47)	8.00 (1.62)	8.24 (1.29)

TABLE 4-2. Continued

Vignette[2]	Overall Rating[3,4,5]	White	Black	Hispanic Overall	HISPANIC	
					English Speaking	Spanish Speaking
Divorced mother often brings home different men.	6.71 (2.42)	6.37 (2.43)	7.43 (2.35)	7.85 (1.71)	8.14 (1.31)	7.55 (2.04)
Mother is a prostitute.	6.33 (2.56)	6.10 (2.63)	7.14 (2.41)	6.95 (2.04)	6.67 (2.37)	7.29 (1.53)
Father is a homosexual.	5.98 (2.79)	5.54 (2.80)	6.42 (2.66)	7.42 (2.28)	6.22 (2.83)	8.38 (1.01)
Mother is a lesbian.	5.81 L-8 (2.77)	5.42 (2.81)	6.21 (2.77)	6.94 (2.35)	6.33 (2.59)	7.62 (1.86)
Intercourse with steady boyfriend often.	5.66 L-6 (2.85)	5.29 (2.86)	NO AGREEMENT 5.96 (3.05) NO AGREEMENT	6.75 (2.48)	6.13 (2.81)	7.41 (1.87)
Clothing	(5.73)					
Always let child run around without clothes.	6.03 (2.49)	5.60 (2.49)	6.84 (2.34)	7.03 (2.23)	6.79 (2.20)	7.30 (2.25)
Parents do not see child has clean clothes.	5.81 L-9 (2.44)	5.41 (2.42)	6.88 (2.36)	6.64 (2.22)	6.26 (2.36)	7.05 (1.99)
Parents seldom notice what child is wearing.	5.23 L-4 (2.47)	4.86 (2.43)	6.38 (2.36)	5.82 (2.29)	5.61 (2.43)	6.05 (2.14)
Housing	(5.85)					
Live in skid row neighborhood.	6.48 (2.47)	6.16 (2.60)	7.52 (1.84)	6.90 (2.24)	6.79 (2.46)	7.02 (1.98)

182

			NO AGREEMENT			
Live in old house with broken windows.	6.24 (2.37)	5.90 (2.40)	7.36 (1.99)	6.70 (2.16)	6.42 (2.31)	7.00 (1.96)
			NO AGREEMENT			
Live in house where no one straightens up.	6.05 (2.63)	5.74 (2.69)	6.94 (2.48)	6.68 (2.29)	6.38 (2.41)	7.01 (2.12)
Live in hotel rooms without cooking facilities.	5.86 L-10 (2.52)	5.40 (2.57)	6.72 (2.53)	6.65 (2.13)	6.56 (2.50)	6.76 (1.60)
Parents and children sleep separately.	4.45 L-3 (2.64)	4.07 (2.53)	5.05 (2.87)	5.62 (2.79)	5.07 (2.84)	6.28 (2.64)
Parents and child in two rooms.	3.62 L-1 (2.58)	3.03 (2.58)	5.23 (2.80)	4.56 (2.40)	5.15 (2.43)	4.06 (2.29)

[1] The underlined groups indicate agreement.
[2] Abbreviated version of the vignettes; for complete vignette wording see table 3–2.
[3] The ratings reflect the mean ratings of vignettes without and with consequence. The number in parentheses is the standard deviation of this.
[4] H-1–H-10 = ten highest-rated vignettes.
[5] L-1–L-10 = ten lowest-rated vignettes.

183

white, Spanish-surnamed)—there was nothing in these data to support such notions. In fact, quite the opposite was true. (For intergroup comparisons, the Asian-American and other ethnic groups' ratings were not included in the analyses because of the small number of raters.)

With respect to the absolute ratings of specific vignettes, ethnic differences were very pronounced. In 94 percent of the vignettes the white sample rated the incidents as *less* serious than did either the Black or Hispanic groups; Black respondents rated 58 percent of the vignettes as more serious than did either of the other two groups, and Hispanics rated 40 percent as more serious than did either the Blacks or whites. Overall there was total agreement among all three groups on only 7 vignettes, and total disagreement on 10 vignettes. This very low degree of agreement was due to the lowered ratings of the white respondents. Their ratings were significantly lower on 54 of the 78 vignettes, vignettes where Blacks and Hispanics were in significant agreement. The few vignettes that generated agreement among all three groups tended to be ones rated as more serious, and within categories of mistreatment generally rated as more serious. Two of these concerned sexual abuse, having intercourse with the child and repeatedly suggesting sexual relations; two pertained to physical abuse, both involving burning, and two involved the use of cocaine, the most seriously rated drug. One item involving emotional mistreatment, "The child is emotionally disturbed, parents refuse treatment," obtained unanimity. The items that generated total disagreement—those where Blacks and Hispanics disagreed with each other as well as with whites—had a rather ambiguous pattern, though some might have been anticipated to generate disagreement. "Spanking the child leaving red marks" was one with no agreement, just as it had been with the professionals. Hispanics had the highest rating on spanking. Two vignettes concerning emotional matters generated total disagreement, "dressing a boy like a girl and putting makeup on him" and "ignoring a child, seldom talking or listening to him." Blacks rated both of these as more serious than the other two groups. As a whole the emotional mistreatment items showed a somewhat different rating pattern than most other kinds of vignettes: agreement between Blacks and Hispanics, disagreement between them and whites. Of eight emotional mistreatment vignettes, one showed total agreement, as noted, two total disagreement, and one, "locking the child in a room," was a rare instance where Hispanics were in agreement with whites but not with Blacks. Two items relating to parental sexual mores obtained total disagreement, "mother is a lesbian" and "mother has a steady boyfriend with whom she has intercourse." Like emotional mistreatment, parents' sexual mores had one vignette where Hispanics agreed with whites but not Blacks, the one describing a relative who is a prostitute bringing customers to the home. The other items where there was no agreement among the three ethnic groups all involved types of mistreatment that they had rated as relatively less serious ones. One pertained to medical neglect, ignoring a child's infected ear. Two pertained to housing, living on skid row and having a broken window with jagged edges. One involved cleanliness, seldom bathing the child, and one supervision, leaving the child alone all day inside the house. Interestingly enough, though these vignettes were of the types of lesser seriousness, *within* each type they were the first or second most serious. Perhaps this indicates that while Blacks and Hispanics saw the general types as less serious, the particular incidents hit an upper threshold for Blacks, who always rated them as more serious, but not for Hispanics.

In sum, the absolute ratings of the specific incidents indicated very little agreement between whites and Blacks or Hispanics. The reason for the disagreement was the significantly greater seriousness ratings of the Blacks and Hispanics. Although the Blacks and Hispanics were in agreement 75 percent of the time, perusal of their ratings suggested some possible patterns of difference between them relating to the nature of the mistreatment described. Hispanic respondents almost invariably had rated vignettes depicting sexual abuse, physical injury, and drug/alcohol abuse as more serious than did Blacks. Conversely, Blacks consistently had higher ratings on matters pertaining to nutrition, medical care, supervision, cleanliness, education, clothing, and housing. As we shall see in the next section, dealing with categories of mistreatment as they are perceived by community members, these ethnic-specific valuations on particular kinds of mistreatment proved to be significant.

COMMUNITY PERCEPTIONS OF TYPES OF MISTREATMENT

What do community members, lay people, see to be the underlying commonalities among specific incidents of mistreatment? This is an important question in comprehending what the meaning of mistreatment is to lay people, and consequently for placing in perspective how professionals' views coincide with or diverge from those of the public they serve.

Principal-components factor analysis was used as the method of developing categories from the community members' ratings, as had been done with the professional study. As might be expected from the overall attenuation of ratings on individual vignettes (all ratings were skewed to the more serious ends of the scale), community ratings resulted in fewer distinct categories than the professionals'. Whereas analysis of the professionals' ratings yielded 9 categories of mistreatment, only 5 emerged from analysis of the community ratings.[4]

The major difference was in the less-fine discriminations made among situations relating to the physical and nonphysical domains of general child care responsibilities. From the professionals' ratings, three separate categories were derived from a large number of these kinds of incidents: failure to provide (basic physical care, feeding, medical care, hygiene, and so forth), educational neglect, and emotional mistreatment. These three separate categories did not emerge from analysis of the community ratings of the same incidents. Rather, items dealing with all three domains of child care were found to be related. Altogether, there were 23 items that formed the category we have labeled as "failure to provide"—7 items related to medical care, 3 to feeding, 3 to cleanliness, 5 to emotional treatment, 3 to housing, and 2 to education. One item referred to leaving a child with irresponsible neighbors.

The lay respondents' failure to discriminate between the emo-

---

[4] In the selection of vignette packets, 47 stem vignettes were the same for each respondent (for instance, consequence, age of the child, and occupation of perpetrator were the varying factors). Thirteen of the remaining 31 vignette pairs were randomly selected to complete the packet of 60 vignettes to be used in the research. Because of this method of selection 47 vignettes were rated by all respondents, while a varying number of respondents rated the remaining 31 vignettes. The disparity in respondent sample sizes between the group of 47 and the group of 31 as well as the highly skewed distribution of ratings suggested that the multivariate technique of factor analysis could not be used on all 78 pairs of vignettes as was done with the study of the professions. Thus, the categories derived for the community study are based on ratings for the 47 vignettes, accounting for most missing vignettes and explains the comparatively low categorical ratings on certain areas such as physical abuse. For example, those items not included in the group of 47 were items with very high ratings, such as "The parent immersed the child in a tub of hot water" and "The parent burned the child on the buttocks and the chest with a cigarette." The differences in sample size do not affect the other types of analyses used in this study.

tional and the physical realms may suggest that the controversy among professionals about emotional mistreatment is not one that would be well understood by the general public. They appear to view child-caring responsibilities more wholistically, perhaps as do most parents and children. From children's standpoint, not having different kinds of needs met may hurt in the same way. From parents' standpoint, meeting children's needs is not experienced in any kind of neat hierarchy of responsibilities. This is not to impugn the legitimacy of the distinctions made among the emotional and physical care realms by professionals, for they are making such distinctions for very different kinds of reasons, having to make judgments in their work that lay people are not called upon to make. The lay respondents' ratings do indicate that they see emotional matters in very much the same way as some physical kinds of mistreatment, and thus give no indication of a public willingness *not* to consider emotional matters as a significant area of mistreatment. While the community members may not have distinguished between physical and emotional realms in basic child-caring responsibilities, they clearly did distinguish between these responsibilities and other kinds of deviant parental behavior.

The four categories developed in addition to the broad "failure to provide" were more proximate to those derived from the professionals' ratings. First were items dealing with supervision. All items pertaining to leaving a child alone formed one category, very like the supervision category derived from the professionals. (As just noted, the lay respondents distinguished between leaving a child all alone and leaving him with an irresponsible person, as did the professionals. That item did not correlate with the others in the "supervision" category but rather with those in "failure-to-provide.")

Next, a category concerning incidents of physical abuse emerged as distinct, as did one of sexual abuse. As in the professionals' ratings, the item "parents have intercourse where child can see them" was correlated with sexual abuse items, not as originally hypothesized as "parents' sexual mores." Finally, a category was developed that consisted essentially of strongly related items pertaining to drug and alcohol abuse by the parents and two items pertaining to the mother's sexual behavior ("mother is a lesbian" and "mother has a steady boyfriend with whom she has intercourse often"). Table 4–3 gives a comparison between categories developed from the professionals' and community's ratings.

TABLE 4-3.   Comparison of Professional- and Community-Generated Categories

PROFESSIONALS	COMMUNITY
Physical abuse——————————————————————Physical abuse	
Sexual abuse————————————————————————Sexual abuse	
Failure-to-provide	
Emotional mistreatment————————————————Failure-to-provide	
Educational neglect	
Supervision—————————————————————————Supervision	
Parental sexual mores	
Drugs/alcohol——————————————————————Drugs/sex	
Fostering delinquency— — — — — — — — — — (Not included as a category*)	

* Vignettes that formed this category were not included in the factor analyses from which the categories for the community were developed.

Most of the categories of mistreatment derived from the professionals' and the community's ratings bore a strong substantive relationship. Both groups made distinctions as to degrees of seriousness within types of mistreatment. But professionals distinguished the degrees of seriousness along a wider spectrum of incidents and yet considered them to belong qualitatively to different kinds of mistreatment.

One explanation for this difference may lie in the fact that professionals, especially police and social workers, are daily exposed in their work to a wide spectrum of mistreatment. Lay people, on the other hand, when faced with the need to make judgments about a variety of acts, come to the task with very irregular and uneven degrees of direct experience with such acts.

To summarize, then, data on the development of categories of mistreatment among lay persons' ratings indicate that they do distinguish among different types of mistreatment, albeit not so finely as do professionals. There is a clear distinction among these types of mistreatment: physical injury, sexual abuse, inadequate supervision, and drug use. And clearly delineated from these matters of parental care was a general category related to physical, emotional, and educational aspects of child rearing, failure to provide. Further, lay people made distinctions of degrees of seriousness within and among the various types of mistreatment.

Having established the categories of mistreatment perceived in common by community respondents, we move now to an examination of the relationships between the particular social characteristics of the sample and differences in their perceptions of kinds of mistreatment.

ETHNIC AND SOCIAL CLASS DIFFERENCES
IN ATTITUDES TOWARD MISTREATMENT

Discussion of ethnic differences frequently generates controversy as to whether such differences are valid reflections of cultural variation or simply artifacts of social class differences, since people from different ethnic groups are not distributed equally across social class strata. In this community sample, both Blacks and Hispanics had considerably lower incomes and educational levels than did whites, and as we have already shown their ratings were much more alike than like the whites. In our analyses we looked first at differences in perceptions of mistreatment by conventional social-class indicators of education and income. Next we examined differences *among* the three ethnic groups, with educational and income levels held constant. Finally we examined the interaction between social class and sex and attitudes toward mistreatment *within* each ethnic group separately.

The Role of Education and Income

The considerable amount of attention paid to the relationship of social class and child mistreatment in the literature reviewed earlier in this chapter suggests a greater frequency of abuse and neglect among lower socioeconomic families, and from this is implied greater acceptability of mistreatment among them. The findings of this research contraindicate that view. Rather than view mistreatment more permissively, the individuals of lower socioeconomic status in this study generally saw mistreatment as more serious than did those of higher socioeconomic status. Tables 4–4 and 4–5 give the mean category ratings for different educational and income levels within the population. Table 4–4 illustrates the mean ratings for each category generated by community ratings for each educational level. *Without exception*, educational achievement is inversely related to degree of seriousness—*the more highly educated the respondents, the lower their seriousness ratings.* However, it is interesting to look at the relative rankings of categories within an educational level. Among those without a college degree there was unanimity about the relative seriousness of all categories. However, among those with a college degree physical abuse was perceived to be relatively more serious than, say, parents' sexual mores and drug usage. This was not the case among the less well educated.

Table 4–5 depicts the mean ratings of the community's cate-

TABLE 4-4.   Mean Category Ratings by Education of Respondents

CATEGORY	OVERALL RATING	EDUCATIONAL LEVEL*			
		Below High School	High School	Some College	College
Sexual abuse	(7.83)	8.13	8.01	7.79	7.24
Supervision	(7.39)	7.78	7.66	7.16	6.76
Drugs/sex	(7.30)	7.45	6.90	6.37	5.57
Failure-to-provide	(6.61)	7.03	6.84	6.41	6.00
Physical abuse	(6.55)	7.01	6.64	6.33	6.03

* Below High School includes no schooling at all up to some high school education, but without diploma; High School includes those with a diploma; Some College includes those who attended college but did not receive a degree; and College includes those with a Bachelor's or higher degree.

gories across income groups. The picture is not so clear as it was for the educational groups, but the trend is similar: *the higher the income level of the respondents, the lower their seriousness ratings.* Table 4-5 shows that the $17,000 + group rated lower than did those with less income in every case except with regard to sexual abuse. In that case the highest and the lowest income groups agreed. All the income groups had similar views as to the relative rankings of the mistreatment categories: sexual abuse was perceived as the most serious category, regardless of the educational or income level of the respondent.

These data indicate that the educational and income levels of individuals was related to their perceptions of the seriousness of mistreatment but not in the direction that is commonly postulated. It was the less well educated and those with lower incomes who perceived all kinds of mistreatment as more serious than did the more affluent and better educated. However, the relative seriousness of different kinds of mistreatment was perceived with very high agreement across all social class strata except for the perception of greater seriousness of physical injury by the college-educated, more serious than sexual and drug transgressions on the part of parents. This probably reflects some differences in social values attributable to higher education, specifically a somewhat greater tolerance of moral deviation than is characteristic of the less well educated. The strongest influence of socioeconomic status, then, was in the perception of the absolute seriousness of mistreatment rather than the relative seriousness of different kinds of acts.

Ethnicity and Social Class

Since less educated persons and those with less income perceived mistreatment as more serious, as did Black and Hispanic

TABLE 4-5. Mean Category Ratings by Income of Respondents

CATEGORY	OVERALL RATING	INCOME GROUP				
		Less than $5,000	$5,000–$9,999	$10,000–$16,999	$17,000–$24,999	Over $25,000
Sexual abuse	(7.83)	7.71	7.93	7.98	7.85	7.75
Supervision	(7.39)	7.46	7.60	7.49	7.40	6.92
Drugs/sex	(7.30)	6.85	6.93	6.77	6.44	6.07
Failure-to-provide	(6.61)	6.77	6.85	6.79	6.49	6.14
Physical abuse	(6.55)	6.89	6.75	6.72	6.29	5.94

people, who tended to be less affluent and less educated, it was quite possible that the ethnic differences simply reflected social-class differences. The question we then posed was "Within a given educational or income grouping, could ethnic differences still be observed?" In almost every instance the answer was "yes." The continuing effects of ethnicity are clearest within educational groupings. Ethnic differences were found in the seriousness ratings for almost all mistreatment categories and within almost all educational levels. For the failure-to-provide category within all educational levels, Black respondents' ratings were significantly higher than were all others. The same was true for the supervision category, except for those with some high school. Hispanics rated the drug/sex category as significantly more serious than did others within all educational groups. The same was true with respect to physical injury, save for those with some college. The only category where ethnicity seemed to have little impact was that of sexual abuse. Hispanics in the extremes of the educational spectrum (grade school or college) rated the sexual abuse matters as significantly more serious than did others. In the other educational groupings, ethnicity was not a significant factor in distinguishing seriousness ratings.

Within the various income groupings the pattern was not quite so consistent but was very similar. For the extreme ends of income (the less-than-$5,000 and $17,000 + groups), the same results occurred. However, there were categories where ethnicity did not play a role, such as sexual abuse. Supervision was viewed similarly by the "working poor" (earning about $5,000–$10,000); that is, there was a consensus across ethnic groups about issues related to supervision. With respect to physical injury, among those earning under $17,000, ethnicity made a difference, while among those over $17,000 there was agreement across ethnic groups about the seriousness of physical injury.

In sum, the combined data show that while social class was a major variable that influenced perceptions of seriousness, ethnicity had an overriding influence with respect to perceptions of most kinds of mistreatment. We now look at the ways in which social class factors and sex of respondents within each of these ethnic groups influenced attitudes.

Differences within Ethnic Groups

In the beginning of this chapter we noted that a common phrase used in speculation about child rearing attitudes and mistreatment is "the poor and ethnic minorities," a phrase that ignores the facts that the "poor" are not all alike, nor are all ethnic minorities. The data that follow underscore these facts. Not only were differences in attitudes found among the various ethnic groups, but the relationships between other characteristics—social class and gender—and opinions about mistreatment were different within each of the ethnic groups.

We have already noted that the Black and the Hispanic respondents perceived all incidents as more serious than did the white respondents. However, differences in the perception of the *relative* seriousness of different kinds of mistreatment were revealed between the Black and the Hispanic groups. Here the effects of ethnic differences were pronounced. The Black respondents perceived the categories of failure to provide and supervision as more serious than did the Hispanics and as more serious than parental moral behavior or physical injury (see table 4–6). The Hispanics, on the other hand, perceived the categories of sexual abuse, physical injury, and drugs/sex issues as more serious than did the Blacks, and as more serious than the incidents encompassed by failure to provide. These data indicate that the cultural dimension is a very complex one and that understanding of the complexity can only be obscured by viewing differences from the dichotomous stance white versus nonwhite. The major difference between the white and "nonwhite" respondents in this study was the perception of lesser seriousness among the whites. The speculation that "minority groups" are more tolerant is not borne out by these data. What seems to be the more accurate view is that both Blacks and Hispanics are very concerned about child mistreatment. The cultural variations between them are reflected in an even *greater* concern about *particular* kinds of mistreatment, a concern embedded in a more generalized one about all mistreatment.

These ethnic differences are further emphasized in the data that follow with respect to the influence of other characteristics on the perception of mistreatment *within* the ethnic groups. While we have already seen that the overall socioeconomic status of respondents was related to their perceptions of seriousness, these factors do not appear to have had uniform effects within each ethnic group. The differences indicate even more strongly the complexity of the ethnic dimension. Within each ethnic group we examined the relationship between education, income, and sex of the respondents and their seriousness ratings. The data are presented separately for each group.

TABLE 4-6. Mean Category Ratings by Ethnicity of Respondents

CATEGORY	OVERALL RATING	ETHNICITY		
		White	Black	Hispanic
Sexual abuse	7.83	7.70	7.97	8.32
Supervision	7.39	7.16	8.09	7.85
Drugs/sex	7.30	6.35	7.24	7.48
Failure-to-provide	6.61	6.36	7.38	7.12
Physical abuse	6.55	6.31	6.78	7.28

Black respondents: Among the Black respondents there were no statistically significant differences among educational, income, and gender categories in ratings of the seriousness of any category of mistreatment. In relation to the ratings of the other groups, those of the Black respondents clearly were distinguished by ethnicity rather than by the other social characteristics that were measured. The perception of greater seriousness of failure-to-provide and supervision were shared by all in the Black sample. These two facts, then, most characterized the Black respondents: they showed the greatest concern for those kinds of mistreatment, and, unlike the other ethnic groups, demonstrated greater consensus as a group without regard to social class and sex differences among them. These particular kinds of mistreatment are among the ones that commonly are supposed to involve imposition of middle-class white professionals' values on the life styles of minorities, especially low-income ones. This is one reason the JJSP gave for deciding that physical care and supervision that did not result in physical injury should not be subject to court intrusion. As we discuss below, none of our data can be construed as constituting an endorsement of how respondents thought particular kinds of mistreatment should be handled, such as taking court action. However, these data suggest that matters of basic physical and emotional child care and protection are taken very, very seriously by Blacks. Concern for the values of all ethnic groups is a matter for continuing vigilance, to be sure, but such concern does not automatically create understanding of what the particular values of a specific ethnic group might be.

Whites: Within the white sample, the amount of education respondents had did make a significant difference in their perception of seriousness of the incidents in each category: those with less education rated the incidents in each category as more serious than did the better-educated respondents. This finding, of course, runs counter to the popular notion that even among whites less-well-educated people are more tolerant of various kinds of mistreatment, or that treatment considered to be deviant by higher educated people is more acceptable to the poorly educated. There are no comparable data on attitudes toward deviant practices such as those dealt with in these vignettes. However, some parallels can be drawn between the kinds of situations dealt with in two of these categories that would be in accordance with the data here. The 1968 Violence Commission survey reported that less-educated whites were the most rejecting of spanking (Erlanger 1975). This corroborates our finding that physical abuse was perceived as more serious by the less-well-educated. Polansky and Williams' (1978) data on marginal kinds of inadequate parenting would correspond roughly to the kinds of situations described in the vignettes included in the category "failure to provide." They found no difference in attitudes between working-class and middle-class white mothers toward these marginal kinds of neglect, a finding that in itself does not support the popular belief. Hence, while our findings with respect to education and perceptions of seriousness may be surprising to some, they are more consonant with what relevant research findings there are than is the commonly held conception of a reverse situation.

Income also made a significant difference in the ratings in failure-to-provide and physical injury, and in the same direction as education: the lower-income people perceived both types of acts as more serious than did higher-income ones. Income and education are, of course, highly correlated within this white sample; however, income level did not have the same effects over all categories of mistreatment as did education.

Incidents of sexual abuse and drug/sex issues were not rated significantly differently by persons of varying income levels. With respect to both kinds of mistreatment, in addition to educational level, the sex of the respondents was a significant influence. Women rated incidents in both categories as more serious than did men. Both sexual abuse and drug usage tap issues of morality beyond the considerations of the effects on the child (which is not to imply that physical abuse of children is moral!). And it is probably greater moral indignation by women that was expressed here. Societal permissiveness is greater toward men in sexual matters generally, and both drug addiction and alcohol abuse are generally considered less shameful for men than for women. Further, while the vignettes describing acts of sexual abuse did not specify the gender of either the parent or the child, it is more than likely that respondents interpreted the child victim to be a girl rather than a boy. Father-daughter sexual abuse is certainly the more commonly *apprehended* kind of situation. Interestingly enough, women did not rate either physical injury or failure-to-provide any differently than did men. The major differences found between the sexes among the professionals were in ratings of incidents in the failure-to-provide category. (Given the lack of difference between men and women in the community respondents, the differences among the professionals cannot be said to be a reflection of a more general difference between men and women, and strengthen the argument that the differences observed among professionals were due to profession rather than to actual sex-linked attitudes.)

The white sample's ratings of the supervision incidents were affected by all three characteristics—education, income, and sex—again with the women rating these situations where a child is left alone more seriously than men, as did the less well educated and less affluent. That both education and income are related to the perceptions of seriousness of inadequate supervision of children would not corroborate opinions that this aspect of child care reflects a difference in life style among those less well off. Coupled with the data about the perception of very great seriousness of leaving a child unattended evidenced by the Black respondents, these findings underscore the point that among lay persons, especially black and less-well-off whites, leaving a child alone in and of itself is considered as very serious, whether or not anything happens to the child. Once again, the criterion of potential, not just actual, harm was very salient.

In sum, among white respondents, differences in perceptions of seriousness were found among different educational groups with respect to all kinds of mistreatment. That this is not simply a reflection of rating styles among the various educational levels is validated by the fact that other characteristics, particularly sex, influenced ratings with respect to particular categories. The relationship between the nature of the mistreatment and the characteristics of the respondents is particular and not evidence of any uniform generalized response, nor of overall rating style attributable to a particular income group, nor of the differences between men and women.

All Hispanics: The Hispanic respondents in this research offered an excellent opportunity to investigate further the interaction between social class and cultural differences. Given a choice between reading the vignettes and being interviewed in Spanish or in English, 92 of the 177 chose to be interviewed in English and 85 in Spanish. Insofar as language preference can be taken as an indicator of degree of assimilation into the majority culture's mores and values, analyses of the total Hispanic group's ratings of seriousness of incidents of mistreatment can yield insights into the ways in which different cultural values might influence perceptions of mistreatment.

Overall, the Hispanic sample rated as significantly higher than either Blacks or whites the items in the categories of sexual abuse, physical injury, and drugs/sex. They did not see situations of poor supervision or of failure to provide for children as seriously as did the Black sample, but they did rate these categories as significantly more serious than did the whites. When the two Hispanic subsamples were compared on the variable of language preference, the Spanish-speaking rated the categories of sexual abuse, physical injury, and drug/sex significantly higher than did the English-speaking Hispanics. Their ratings on failure-to-provide and supervision were not significantly different.

There is a qualitative difference between the kinds of parental failure implied in these two categories: the categories where there were differences are those that go beyond parental failure to matters that intersect other domains of cultural values—violence, sexuality, and drug use. Thus it is not surprising that within the Hispanic group these same kinds of mistreatment are perceived as even more serious by those who may be much more influenced by their own cultural values than by those of the dominant Anglo culture, having been less assimilated into that culture, as signified by their language preference.

What other factors influence the perceptions of seriousness of mistreatment among the Hispanic groups? The effects of education, income, and sex of respondents were looked at separately within each of the language preference groups. The two groups themselves differed markedly with respect to education and income, but these differences did not negate the effects of their different language preferences.

Spanish-speaking Hispanics: Eighty-five respondents preferred to be interviewed in Spanish, 45 percent of them female and

55 percent male. The education level was attenuated toward the lower end: 54 percent had a sixth-grade education or less, 18 percent some high school, and 28 percent a high school diploma or more. The income distribution was more dispersed than that of education. Among the Spanish-speaking respondents neither sex nor level of education affected the ratings of seriousness. Income level, however, was related to seriousness ratings in all categories of mistreatment save physical injury. The effect was uniform: the lower the income, the greater the perception of seriousness. The fact that no differences were found by sex indicates that the underlying values expressed through the ratings are homogeneous among men and women, unlike the white sample. The highly skewed distribution in education among this group no doubt accounts for the fact that education itself was not related to their seriousness ratings. Further, most were not educated in this country; hence what education they had had was within their own cultural milieu. Level of income, however, was related to their perceptions, and it is not unreasonable to interpret the income differences themselves as at least partial measures of assimilation. Level of income does indicate some upward mobility within the rewards systems of the majority culture. The way in which higher income among Spanish-speaking respondents was related to perceptions of seriousness corroborates that view: those with *higher* income perceived the three categories of mistreatment—sexual abuse, drugs/sex, physical abuse—as *less* serious than did the lower-income persons.

English-speaking Hispanics: The English-speaking Hispanic sample was more heterogeneous with respect to both education and income than was the Spanish-speaking. However, the correlation between income and education was far from perfect, with many of the higher-educated respondents having relatively low incomes. The group was evenly divided between men and women.

Income itself was not related to any of the categories of mistreatment. Sex, however, was an influential factor in all, with women respondents rating all kinds of mistreatment significantly higher than did the men. However, while sex was a contributing factor, with respect to the three categories that Hispanics characteristically rated higher than did other respondents, education was more important in explaining the ratings. For sexual and physical abuse and drug usage, the higher the level of education, the lower the ratings of seriousness. Education did not make a significant difference with respect to failure-to-provide or supervision. Hence, among the English-speaking Hispanics, the pattern of factors related to their opinions of particular types of mistreatment was very much like the pattern that distinguished them from the Spanish-speaking group and the total Hispanic group from Blacks and from whites. The data reveal that Hispanics in general placed high value on matters related to children's welfare; however, these values may be less tenaciously held by those more assimilated into the dominant culture—the better-educated, English-speaking Hispanics.

While overall the lay respondents saw all kinds of mistreatment as very serious, there were differences among different segments of the population. These differences are complex, particularly with respect to the interaction between ethnicity and social class. The data not only belie suppositions about the greater tolerance of mistreatment among certain population groups but also indicate the great injustice that is done to all groups by any kind of generalizations about them.

COMPARING THE COMMUNITY AND THE PROFESSIONALS

As noted earlier, compared with those of any of the professional groups, the ratings of seriousness by the community members were extremely high. This difference should not be taken as an indication that the professionals regard acts of mistreatment as less serious than does the community: rather, because of their professional knowledge and experience, professionals make finer discriminations. But certainly the data do not justify any contention that the community members view any of these acts of mistreatment as less serious than do professionals. Suppositions that professionals are imposing their particular values on the general community are not borne out, at least not from the standpoint that professionals see acts of mistreatment as serious in a way that lay persons do not.

There are indications in the data, however, that there are some differences between the lay populations and the professionals, though not many, in the kinds of things seen as *relatively* more serious. This is particularly true with respect to the physical injury and punishment of children. The vignettes rated as most and least serious by the professionals and by the community members were compared. There was more similarity between the two in the least serious matters than in the most serious ones. Eight of the 10 situations rated as least serious by the professionals were identical to those rated least serious by the community. These were vignettes that described situations of inadequate housing, dirty clothing, not brushing teeth, mother being a lesbian or having a steady boyfriend, and spanking the child. Two vignettes that were among the least serious to professionals but not to the lay sample were "Father is a homosexual" and "Child left for weeks with grandmother." The community rated as less serious than these items two items describing inadequate cooking facilities and overfeeding the child. Substantively, then, matters seen as least serious by both the lay and professional communities were very similar. This can be taken to mean that while the rating styles of the general population differ from those of the professionals in that the latter make fine discriminations, the substantive matters that constitute the threshold of what might be considered as mistreatment—the least serious— was the same for both lay and professional people. Notably, spanking is included in this very marginal area for both professional and lay people.[5]

The situations considered *most* serious, however, did not have this same kind of substantive uniformity. Very extreme situations were rated most serious by both lay and professionals: burning the child with a cigarette, immersion in hot water, keeping the child locked in a room, and incidents of sexual abuse of the child. In addition, professionals rated as among the most serious incidents ones specifying physical harm to the child, through either physical abuse—banging the child against the wall, hitting him with a wooden stick—or severe malnutrition from underfeeding. Among the lay population these kinds of incidents were not considered among the most serious. Rather, matters pertaining to drugs and engaging the child in stealing were seen as more serious. Contrasted to physical injury and malnutrition, drug abuse and stealing by parents are less directly related to the physical well-being of children and are more of an affront to the "common decency." Pro-

---

[5] In fact, spanking of a child, more commonly referred to as corporal punishment, while being the fourth from the bottom of least serious vignettes among the professionals and second from the bottom of least serious vignettes among the community, failed to obtain agreement among subpopulations of professionals or community groups. This fact suggests that while corporal punishment is not seen as an act of mistreatment by anyone, there is clear controversy about its seriousness as an action itself.

fessionals did not equate the seriousness of such morally tinged matters with that of physical harm to children, as did the community sample.

Pursuing the comparison of professionals and community ratings, we moved from analysis of specific incidents to an assessment of the relative seriousness of different types of mistreatment. As discussed previously, the categories developed by the community ratings were those developed from the professional study. To facilitate a more detailed comparison, the categories developed from the professionals' study were utilized. Table 4-7 shows the mean ratings of items in those categories for the community sample and the professional sample.

The data extend the observations already made with respect to the specific vignettes considered most and least serious. The relative ratings of the various categories of mistreatment are fairly similar. Most similar are the relative rankings of categories by the police and lay population. Notably, matters considered least serious by professionals and lay people are those relating to the sexual mores of parents. The three categories rated as most serious are also the same. However, the seriousness rating of physical injury by the community sample is in striking contrast to that by the professionals. Both sexual abuse and engaging child in crime were considered more serious by the lay population and, in fact, considerably more serious than was physical injury. The use of drugs and alcohol by parents ranked fourth among the lay population, ahead of all others pertaining to general child care. This is not to imply that lay people thought physically injuring a child was *not* serious. They did, and very serious. However, it is not the only or

TABLE 4-7. Comparison of Mean Category Ratings of Professional and Community Respondents

Category	Mean Professional Ratings	Mean Community Ratings
Physical abuse	6.89	7.61
Sexual abuse	6.67	7.98
Fostering delinquency	6.55	8.03
Supervision	5.19	7.16
Emotional mistreatment	5.05	6.89
Drugs/alcohol	4.62	6.92
Failure-to-provide	4.23	6.58
Education	4.06	6.53
Parental sexual mores	3.21	6.07

even the most paramount concern with respect to mistreatment. Here we see a discrepancy between the opinions of these community members and the opinion that physical harm is the only real mistreatment. No single criterion such as physical harm can capture the diverse nature of phenomena encompassed by mistreatment, mistreatment considered as noxious to the child's welfare. Among these respondents manifestations of mistreatment other than physical injury were considered even more serious. What may be implied here is a greater acceptance of physical punishment among the lay population than among the professionals. This must be considered a relative matter, for both the lay people and the professionals saw spanking as not very serious at all. But when one considers that among the consequences specified in the physical-injury vignettes were "concussion" and "a cut lip and black eye," the ratings clearly indicate that such physical abuse is just not considered by the general population to be as serious as sexual acts, or even as serious as engaging a child in an act of thievery.[6]

The relative seriousness of poorly supervising and protecting children is borne out of the community ratings as it was with the professionals. This domain of child care was seen as both distinct and serious by the professionals and the lay populations. The uniformly low ratings given these matters by lawyers would not appear to be consonant with the valuations by other professionals or by the community. The *potential* harm suggested by the nature of these vignettes was of concern to the community, more so than some actual harms engendered by lack of cleanliness or poor nutrition. The sexual life style of parents was not deemed to be very serious, in fact it was thought to be the least serious of all. In sum, in their perceptions of the relative seriousness of different kinds of mistreatment, the professionals and lay people were very similar. However, the truly notable exception was an important one: the perception of lesser seriousness of physical injury of children among the lay respondents.

COMMUNITY KNOWLEDGE AND OPINIONS
ABOUT THE HANDLING OF CHILD ABUSE

In the interview that followed the administration of the vignettes, the community respondents were asked several questions

[6] This particular patterning of the three most serious categories is not like any of the professional groups. While police also saw sexual abuse as the most serious, they rated physical injury higher than fostering delinquency. Pediatricians saw

about child abuse. The reference point for these questions was specifically physical injury. The definition used was: "Child abuse is
when an adult physically injures a child, not by accident, but in
anger or deliberately." No questions were asked about other types
of mistreatment, so responses cannot be taken to mean that respondents felt the same way about other kinds of mistreatment. It seems
quite likely, however, that at least for those categories of mistreatment that they thought were less serious than physical injury,
similar responses would have been obtained, but not necessarily for
those kinds of mistreatment considered as more serious. The
assumption here is that they would not likely take more drastic action for less serious matters, but they might for more serious ones.

In analyzing the respondents' answers to these questions, each
was examined in relation to a number of demographic characteristics. We report here on those that were most strongly related to
differences among the answers, when indeed there were such differences. In general we found more ethnic unanimity of response
on these questions than in the ratings of vignettes.

The first question concerned the population's general awareness
of child abuse—had they heard about the general problem within
the last year? There had been publicity given to the problem in the
preceding year, 1975, as that was the year that the educational
programs sponsored by the National Center on Child Abuse and
Neglect had been effected. Consequently, it was not surprising that
most respondents had heard something about the problem. Eighty-
one percent of Black and white respondents had heard of the problem and 71 percent of the Hispanic sample. However, educational
level did influence awareness of the problem. As the educational
level increased, so did the level of awareness, from 67 percent of
those with less than a high school education to 85 percent of those
with a college education. This might indicate that educational programs and media publicity had been more effective in reaching
better-educated and English-speaking people.

The respondents' opinions about how child abuse should be
handled were tapped through three questions: What type of
agency should be responsible? What should be done with an
abuser? and What should be done to protect the child? There was
very little difference in the answers given to these questions by

---

fostering delinquency as more serious than sexual abuse but less serious than
physical injury. Lawyers and social workers rated physical injury and sexual
abuse as more serious than fostering delinquency.

members of different ethnic groups, but there were differences that were related to educational level. The majority of respondents favored a "treatment" rather than a legalistic or punitive response to abuse, and measures to protect the children that were less extreme were favored over removal from the home. However, those with less education were more likely than the higher educated to favor the more punitive and extreme interventions. When asked what kind of agency should be responsible for handling child abuse, 53 percent of the total sample favored a social service agency, and approximately 20 percent favored either a law enforcement or a health agency. But among the less well educated, about one-fourth thought law enforcement should handle child abuse, while only 14 percent of the college-educated did. The favoring of a more punitive over a treatment or social service approach was even more evident in answers to the question as to how abusers should be dealt with. Among those with less than a high school education, one-third thought abusers should be punished. This proportion decreased at each educational level, with only 14 percent of the college graduates preferring punishment over treatment for the abuser. It still must be noted, however, that the majority, over half of the respondents in each educational grouping, did prefer a treatment orientation.

When asked what they thought should be done with abused children, the respondents were given the options of "remove the first time," "remove only as a last resort," and "all right to leave the child at home." Again educational level was related to the most extreme intervention, removal, and in a very similar pattern to the punitive/treatment dimensions in the handling of abusers. Thirty-eight percent of those with less than high school education favored "removal the first time," and the frequency of this endorsement decreased as education increased, with only 18 percent of the college graduates favoring this option.

The relationship of educational level to both the awareness of child abuse and the stringency with which it should be managed is quite consistent with the findings of perception of greater seriousness of all kinds of mistreatment. As the less well educated persons perceived all kinds of mistreatment as more serious, it is only logical that they would more often perceive more stringent kinds of intervention as appropriate. Again it must be noted, however, that the majority of all respondents did favor less punitive and less extreme interventions. But the consistency with the previous findings of a perception of greater seriousness does refute the notion that the poorly educated are in any way more accepting of child abuse.

Finally, two questions were asked that reflected, if not a sympathetic attitude toward abusers, at least an empathetic one. These were: "Do you think that anyone might injure a child?" and "Do you think that you yourself might injure a child?" The responses to these questions were quite interesting. Overall, 75 percent of the respondents thought that anyone might injure a child. However, when the question came closer to home, this proportion was reversed; only 30 percent agreed that they themselves might injure a child. Ethnicity was not related to either answer. Education was not strongly related to the questions of a general propensity to abuse but was clearly related to the way respondents replied to the inquiry about their own potential for abusing a child. As with other questions, the differences were positively correlated—that is, as the level of education rose, the proportion of persons stating that they might abuse also rose. Among those with only a grade school education, 22 percent stated that they might be capable of abuse, and 42 percent of those with a college education recognized such potential. One other characteristic was also related to responses to this question, and that was the respondent's age. Of those in the childbearing years, those most likely to have and/or to be around children, 38 percent acknowledged the possibility of their being abusive, but only 14 percent of those aged sixty or over made such acknowledgment. Day-to-day pressures of living with children, expectedly, did influence the willingness to acknowledge some greater likelihood of being abusive to them at some time.

The greater willingness of the higher-educated to admit to their own potential for being abusive is in keeping with other findings related to the perception of less seriousness of mistreatment and less punitiveness toward abusers. However, this admission may also reflect a more sophisticated knowledge about current thinking among child abuse experts. The higher-educated respondents also had a higher level of awareness of the problems in general, indicating that they, as might be expected, had been more exposed to the current thinking of experts through the media and educational programs. Though some might disagree that anyone has the potential to abuse, most recent publicity about the subject has stressed this point. Virtually all the public information that has been disseminated likewise has stressed the idea that abusers are "sick," themselves victims of abuse as children and in need of treatment, not punishment. Hence, the gestalt of the responses of the higher-educated to all these questions is quite in keeping with the views most commonly expressed by leaders in the field. The extent to which the responses of persons with more education reflect views gleaned through public educational programs is difficult to estimate, but in all likelihood such exposure played a part in their answers and in their seriousness ratings as well. This does not necessarily mean that they falsified their responses, though the wish to give the socially desirable answers most likely did influence them to some extent. Curious as it may seem, while the lower classes are thought to be more accepting of child abuse, this was not borne out in the data in this study at any time; it is the higher classes that display this somewhat greater acceptance, possibly because that is the message most frequently generated in the educational campaigns. These educational differences are all relative ones. Taken in concert, both the findings regarding the community perceptions of seriousness of mistreatment and the general denial of a personal propensity to abuse indicate that the lay population views mistreatment as socially deviant and highly so. Indeed, while they subscribe to a treatment/rehabilitative perspective over a legalistic/punitive one, they definitely see mistreatment as a matter calling for social intervention. Historically, as was demonstrated in chapter 2, the legalistic/punitive approach preceded the gradual evolution of the treatment/rehabilitative one to the management of mistreatment. These data show that public attitudes have evolved in a similar fashion. Yet the stability of these attitudes may be questionable. The general repugnance toward child abuse is illustrated by the unwillingness to imagine any personal propensity to abuse. Hence, attitudes may well be volatile, and the more benign views might quickly give way to very punitive ones in the face of particularly gruesome, cruel situations, the ones most likely to be reported in the media.[7]

CONCLUSIONS

Starting from the premise that child mistreatment is socially defined, we set out to answer questions regarding the degree of

[7] In the beginning of chapter 1 we cited a Tennessee case of a stepfather who had walked a three-year-old to death by exhaustion. Tennessee, especially the city of Nashville, had a very progressive program aimed at preventing placement of abused and neglected children. In response to public outcry over this case (the child had been returned home from foster care), the social service authorities took drastic action, refusing to return any more children home or to allow abused children to remain with abusing parents.

consensus that exists among different populations about the seriousness of different acts of mistreatment. Phenomena that are socially defined can come into being only when there is some degree of consensus among the potential definers. We addressed the matter of consensus in two ways. First, what is the degree of agreement among various subgroups in the general population? Next, what is the degree of agreement between professionals and the lay population?

Overall, we found a high level of agreement among some lay subpopulations, and between professional and lay ones. However, the differences that were found are important.

With respect to the relative seriousness with which different kinds of mistreatment are viewed, we found professionals and the general community to agree on what is most and least serious. Perceived as most serious were acts of sexual abuse, contributing to the delinquency of a minor, and physical injury. Perceived as least serious by all were acts pertaining to the sexual mores of the parents and acts that involved other adults, not children. Between these extremes, other kinds of mistreatment were perceived somewhat differently by professional and lay people. These differences were related not so much to differences in perceptions of degree of seriousness within types of mistreatment as to differences in making distinctions among different kinds of mistreatment. Inadequately supervising children and drug and alcohol abuse were perceived by both professionals and lay people as constituting distinct types of mistreatment, and with about the same degree of seriousness. Other child-caring domains—including routine physical care and emotional, nutritional, and educational provisions—were not distinguished one from another among lay people, as they were among professionals. However, here again, the relative seriousness of these matters was seen by both groups in about the same way: less serious than sexual abuse, physical injury, and contributing to the delinquency of a minor, and more serious than the sexual habits of the parents. One important difference in perceptions of relative seriousness was the fact that the community saw physical injury as less serious than did any professional group. The distinctions, then, between the professionals' and the community's responses gave evidence of differences between them in experience, expertise, and relative exposure to a wide spectrum of acts, rather than divergence in basic values relating to the various domains of child care. Hence the data do not support suspicions that professionals' designation of parental acts as ones of mistreatment or as deviant are based on values unique to them and imposed on, not shared by, the general populace. If anything, the absolute ratings of seriousness of the specific acts of mistreatment would indicate the potential for quite the opposite situation.

If the general population sees all these acts as much more serious impediments to children's welfare than do the professionals, then, of course, professionals may not feel as strongly the devaluation and ascription of deviance to some acts of mistreatment that community members do. Repeated exposure to any situation, of course, is more likely to diffuse rather than increase the reaction to it. The most tenable explanation, however, of observed differences between professional and lay persons is simply that the differences are attributable to experience and expertise. Professionals make finer discriminations among different acts of mistreatment, as their experience no doubt renders them appreciative of more subtle nuances of different effects on children. With respect to particular professions, the police appear to conceive of mistreatment in terms of relative seriousness more as the general population does, and lawyers' perceptions were the least like the lay people's. This is so with respect to the absolute judgments of seriousness, and particularly so with respect to mistreatment that involves leaving children unsupervised. In matters of supervision, there was the greatest divergence between lawyers and other professionals, on the one hand, and between lawyers and the general population sample on the other, both in absolute and in relative terms.

In spite of these differences, there is a high level of agreement among professionals and the general population in their perceptions of child mistreatment, agreement that indicates a very high potential for consensus with respect to the social definitions of mistreatment.

The major question addressed in this chapter concerned the degree of consensus among various subpopulations of the community, particularly those defined along lines of social class and ethnicity. The most widespread speculation has been that persons of "poor and ethnic minority status" do not share the same values related to mistreatment held by the majority and the more affluent. To some extent the data in this study corroborate that view, but in the opposite direction from that expected from popular beliefs. People of lower socioeconomic status and those other than white, regardless of educational level, perceive these matters of child mistreatment almost invariably as more serious. But what is most striking about the data is not the comparison along the usual lines of lower and higher social class, or white versus nonwhite. Rather it is the ethnic differentiation among subpopulations other than whites. Indeed, these data bring into stark relief the gross oversimplification implied in the very term "those of ethnic minority status." Such oversimplification can do nothing but becloud understanding of the differences that might exist and their importance. To be sure, ethnic and racial minorities in this country, as in most, do share a common experience of discrimination and all its ramifications. But discrimination is not the only thing that shapes values, customs, and beliefs. Religion and other historical antecedents of the groups rooted in other cultures also play a part in shaping values, including values related to child care, both benign and deviant. It is differences such as these that were highlighted in the data in this study, particularly with reference to differences in valuations of different areas of mistreatment between the Black sample and the Hispanic sample and even within the Hispanic subsamples of the English and Spanish speakers. The Black respondents showed significantly greater concern over matters pertaining to supervision and protection of children and to failure to fulfill general parenting responsibilities. The Hispanic and especially the Spanish-speaking Hispanic groups showed particular concern over matters of physical injury, sexual abuse, and drug/alcohol abuse. Furthermore, while difference in education and in sex interacted with ethnicity among the three groups of respondents, this interaction did not follow the same pattern, indicating that ethnicity itself must be a continuing concern in attempting to understand what the different valuations are of child-caring practices. Ethnic and cultural differences cannot be dismissed as simply factors reflective of social class differences.

It is tempting indeed to speculate as to why these differences were obtained. However, to yield to that temptation would only add to the mass of speculation that already exists, speculation not based on systematic investigation. Why these different ethnic groups responded as they did is a matter yet to be investigated, and one certainly worthy of further investigation.[8] But the fact remains

[8] There is ongoing work addressed to filling this gap in knowledge about ethnic-specific factors in mistreatment. The National Center on Child Abuse and Neglect has funded ethnic-specific research and demonstration projects. Included among these is an opinion survey of Black populations in three Midwestern cities conducted by the National Urban League, focused on both definitions and means of handling mistreatment.

that they did, and the facts belie any speculation that Black or Hispanic people are any less concerned or more accepting of child mistreatment than are other groups. If in fact the incidence of mistreatment is higher among them, it cannot be attributed to greater tolerance or perception of deviance. Conceivably, the higher incidence rates may simply reflect the one experience they have in common, discrimination, including discrimination in the reporting and apprehension of mistreatment. It is possible, however, that if the higher apprehension rates are valid indicators of the true occurrence of mistreatment in these populations, what is being reflected is not greater tolerance but greater concern about mistreatment. Such concern over the treatment of children could lead to more frequent recourse to societal intervention, for help in abating it and in protecting children. Given the inequality that exists among disadvantaged ethnic groups in access to a variety of interventions, other than official bureaucracies such as the police and public welfare departments, the greater *concern*, not greater *tolerance*, is then likely to be reflected in the statistics of those agencies. The fact that ethnic differences were not found in opinions regarding the management of child abuse indicates that while members of these ethnic groups may be extremely concerned about child mistreatment, the perceived solution is one of help, not punishment. But such help is less likely to be forthcoming to them. In the next chapter we examine how a sample of families exhibiting different kinds of mistreatment were in fact handled and the kinds of interventions that were sought for them.

CHAPTER 5

Definition in Action: Identification and Disposition of Cases

THUS FAR IN OUR EXAMINATION of issues in the definition of mistreatment, we have presented observations based on the opinions of key people in the definitional process, professionals and the community members that they serve. Although there are indications of disagreement among these various definers, there is evidence of substantial agreement on two points. First, both professionals and community people share perceptions of distinct kinds of mistreatment, the underlying commonalities within different types and distinctions among them. Next, there is a high degree of agreement as to the relative seriousness of the different kinds of mistreatment. The data presented thus far are basically attitudinal in nature, and as such may or may not reflect the behavior of these definers in actual cases of mistreatment. Are these distinctions among varying degrees of seriousness of mistreatment actually reflected in what happens to families and children? Are more extreme kinds of intervention sought when there is more serious mistreatment involved and less extreme intervention with less serious kinds?

In answering these questions we draw on data from a study of 949 families who had come to the attention of protective systems in four counties in California from April of 1975 to February of 1976. Of all the cases reported to these county agencies during that time the 949 were randomly selected from among those where the complaint of mistreatment had been substantiated and the case had been processed through to some kind of interventive disposition. The questions we examine are (1) Who participated in the process of defining these families as mistreating? (2) What kinds of mistreatment prompted the action? (3) What was the relationship between the kinds of mistreatment and what happened to the children? (4) Are particular family characteristics associated with particular kinds of mistreatment? and (5) What kinds of help are offered to the families? The information was gathered through a questionnaire filled out by the protective agents responsible for each case. Over the ten-month span of the study (April, 1975, through February, 1976), 144 social workers and 15 probation officers participated in completing the questionnaires.

WHO DEFINES MISTREATMENT?

The first two questions asked were "Who initiated the complaint that brought the family to the attention of protective agents?" and "Who directly brought the case to their attention?"

The process by which cases of mistreatment ultimately are officially designated can be a multistage one. For example, a private citizen may call the police about an incident, and the police, after investigation, may then bring the case to the attention of the social service department. In such a case it is the private citizen who initially made the complaint and thus started the definitional process. The majority of complaints made are not subsequently substantiated. In chapter 3 we made reference to a study of the factors that distinguish complaints that had been substantiated from those that had not (Groeneveld and Giovannoni 1977). In that study it was found that complaints from private individuals were less likely to be sustained than were those from professionals, such as physicians and social agencies. This relatively negative response to community complaints may be reflective of the differences we noted in comparing professionals' and community members' perceptions. If it is true, as we demonstrated, that the lay population sees all kinds of mistreatment as more serious than professionals do, then it is not surprising that situations of mistreatment a lay person regards as serious enough to warrant action are often considered not so serious by the investigating professionals. The research reported here did not cover that aspect of the defining process but was limited to those situations in which the professionals *did* think mistreatment was serious enough to warrant their intervention.

Who were the initial definers in these 949 cases?[1] The largest single source of initial complaints were private individuals— relatives, neighbors, babysitters. Forty-five percent (432) of these situations of mistreatment were first noticed and re- ported by such individuals; no other source accounted for nearly so many of the initial reports. Other sources included medical per- sonnel (12 percent), other personnel in the departments of social services (10 percent), schools (8 percent), law enforcement (6 per- cent), and a variety of social agencies (4 percent). In 13 percent of the cases the original seekers of intervention by the protective agency were parents themselves. Most of these parents were re- questing help with a child they could not manage. In the majority of cases, then, the initial definition of mistreatment arose within the community, among lay people, not professionals, and usually lay people who knew the families involved and very often were related to them or lived near them.

Of these private individuals, about half (212) brought their complaint directly to the protective agencies involved. But a third (142) had sought the aid of the police, who then made the referral to the agencies. Most of the professionals who brought the original complaint, such as school personnel and medical agents, had not sought any other assistance but had gone directly to the protective agency. As might be expected, the police were most likely to have been active in cases involving the more serious kinds of mistreat- ment, such as physical injury and sexual abuse.

The importance of the role of the police in the interface be- tween the community and the protective system can be seen in the data. Only 55 cases (6 percent) were initiated by police. However, 327 cases were brought to the attention of the protective system by the police. In addition to the 142 noted from private individuals, the remainder had been brought to the police's attention through personnel in schools, social agencies, and, in 26 cases, by the care- takers themselves. (Again, most of these were parents distraught over their children's behavior.) Medical sources, physicians, and hospitals had initiated 110, or 12 percent, of the complaints, and in 89 of these had brought the complaint directly, without recourse to police or other intermediaries. In these four counties, then, the key

[1] Data are presented in tabular form in appendix table B–5.

definers of mistreatment were private individuals in initiating the processes of definition, and the police as intermediaries between private individuals, community institutions, and the protective agents.

The data concerning the preponderance of initial complaints arising from private citizens, rather than professionals, can be related to that in the last chapter concerning attitudes of lay people toward mistreatment. First of all the perception of great seriousness of mistreatment evidenced by the community respondents in the opinion survey is borne out here: the lay reporters in these counties obviously saw situations of mistreatment to be serious enough to call in the authorities—police and protective services. With reference to ethnic variation in the perception of mistreatment, we examined the sources of referral of these 949 cases by the ethnicity of the families identified in the complaint. We found no significant differences in the rate of referrals from private individuals in any ethnic group.[2] Although we cannot assume that all the reporters were of the same ethnic group as the families, it is a safe assumption that the majority were. Relatives certainly are of the same ethnic background. And given the housing patterns in these counties, as elsewhere, neighbors tend to be people of both the same ethnic and socioeconomic statuses. We conclude, then, that in the majority of these cases, it was individuals most like the offending families themselves who made the initial designation of deviance expressed through the complaints about mistreatment. Such a conclusion then corroborates the attitudinal data of the opinion survey: mistreatment is perceived as deviant by persons of lower-class as well as middle-class status and by all ethnic groups. The presence of mistreatment does not imply tolerance of mistreatment—these community people were intolerant enough to seek official help.[3]

[2] The ethnic breakdown of the entire 949 cases was as follows: white, 70.6 percent; Black, 14.4 percent; Hispanic, 7.5 percent; other (including Asian and Native American), 7.5 percent. Within each group the proportion of cases initiated by a private individual respectively was 47 percent, 45 percent, 42 percent, and 39 percent.

[3] The rate of complaints generated by private individuals in this study is quite similar to that found among twenty-eight states reporting all their cases to the American Humane Association. In 1976 a total of 99,579 cases were reported. In 43.4 percent of these the referral source had been a private individual. (*National Analysis of Official Child Neglect and Abuse Reporting: An Executive Summary*, American Humane Association, 1978.)

DEFINING MISTREATMENT IN ACTUAL CASES

What was the nature of the mistreatment that brought these families into the protective networks of these counties? We adapted the methods used in the opinion study in answering this question. First of all, the questionnaire included a lengthy checklist of specific incidents and behaviors indicative of mistreatment (table 5–1). For each case the agency workers were instructed to check off all the incidents or behaviors that constituted the reasons for protective action being taken in that family, and to write in any additional ones not on the checklist. The incidents paralleled those in the hypothesized categories of child rearing that had served as the basis for the vignettes in the opinion survey. For example, items under physical injury included "brain damage," "sprain, dislocation"; under nutrition, "known dietary deficiency—e.g., fed regularly only on one food" and "not fed more than once in twenty-four-hour period"; under emotional, items included "child witness to frequent marital conflict" and "openly rejected, siblings obviously preferred."

When the data had been collected, all the behavioral items on the checklist and those written in were presented to all the participating workers, and they were asked to rate the seriousness of each incident. The ratings task was identical to that used with the other professionals and the community; each incident was rated from the standpoint of the seriousness for the child. In this way we were able to establish objective criteria for assessing the seriousness of the mistreatment in each of the 949 cases under study.

There was very high agreement among these protective workers in their ratings of the seriousness of these incidents. Each case was then scored by totaling the means of the workers' ratings of the various incidents or behaviors it included. For example, if in a given case there had been "a bruise," "failure to feed over twenty-four hours," and "open rejection of the child," each of those items checked off in that case was scored according to the mean rating given each incident by the workers. This provided a measure of the absolute seriousness of each kind of incident as well as a measure of the relative seriousness of different incidents of mistreatment.[4]

In establishing what the categories of mistreatment were, the same statistical procedures were used as were used in the opinion

---

[4] A more detailed description of the various scoring procedures used is given in appendix B.

TABLE 5–1. Checklist of Incidents Constituting Complaint of Mistreatment

DERIVED CATEGORY[1]	INITIAL CATEGORY/INCIDENTS	PERCENTAGE OF 949 CASES WITH ITEM CHECKED	WORKERS $\bar{X}$ SERIOUSNESS RATING
	Physical Injuries		
PI	Brain damage	1	8.52
PI	Blinding, damage to the eyes	0.6	8.75
PI	Bone fracture, other than skull fracture		8.25
PI	Broken nose or jaw	0.2	8.19
PI	Broken or missing teeth	0.3	7.13
PI	Bruise, contusion, welt, abrasion	22	7.31
PI	Burn, scalding	3	8.44
PI	Dismemberment	—	—
PI	Freezing, frostbite	—	—
PI	Hemorrhage, hematoma	2	8.31
PI	Internal bleeding	0.5	8.40
PI	Internal injuries	0.7	8.65
EM	Physical injury not sustained, but child in pain or severe discomfort, e.g. tied, locked in	1	7.77
EM	Ruptured eardrum, damage to the ears	0.3	8.22
EM	Skull fracture	1	8.75
EM	Sprain, dislocation	0.4	6.80
*[2]	Suffocation, drowning	1	8.90
PI	Wound, laceration, cut	3	6.97
	Other (please specify)	—	—
	Nutritional State		
FTP	Child(ren) left to feed themselves more than once	13	4.24
PI	Dehydration	1	7.72
*	"Failure to thrive"	5	8.0
FTP	Known dietary deficiency—e.g., child(ren) fed regularly on only one food	5	6.15
FTP	Child(ren) malnourished	6	7.20
FTP	Missed meals a common occurrence (2–3 times a week)	11	5.03
FTP	Child(ren) not fed over 24-hour period, once	1	4.90
FTP	Child(ren) not fed over 24-hour period, more than once	1	5.91
	Other (please specify)	—	—
	Hygiene, Cleanliness, Protection from Elements		
IPE	Clothing dirty	15	2.13
IPE	Clothing ill-fitting, too small or too big	8	2.37
IPE	House dirty, bedclothing soiled or missing	3	3.94

See end of table (p. 220) for footnotes.

TABLE 5–1. Continued

Derived Category[1]	Initial Category/Incidents	Percentage of 949 Cases with Item Checked	Workers X̄ Seriousness Rating
IPE	House messy	21	1.87
FTP	House does not provide shelter from the elements (no heat, broken windows, doors off hinges)	0.5	5.78
IPE	House infested with rats, vermin	0.5	6.08
FTP	Infected sores, diaper rash on child(ren)	4.2	6.25
IPE	Lice/vermin on child(ren)	0.4	5.62
FTP	Child(ren) outdoors without any clothing	1	4.10
FTP	Child(ren) outdoors without sufficient clothing	3	3.27
IPE	Skin dirty	4	2.48
IPE	Spoiled food, garbage inside house	2	4.56
	Other (please specify)	—	—
IPE	Lack space	0.2	3.21
IPE	Poor sanitation	2	4.87
	Supervision, Protection		
*	Child(ren) abandoned/deserted	0.6	8.4
IPE	Child(ren) left in the home of others, without the whereabouts of the responsible caretaker(s) being known, for hours at a time, but not overnight	3	
IPE	Preschool child(ren) left in the home of others without the whereabouts of the responsible caretaker(s) being known, overnight	5	4.52
IPE	Child(ren) left with an uncertain babysitter (one not known before, casual acquaintance, no one specified responsible adult)	4	4.00
FTP	Preschool child(ren) left alone once	2	3.73
FTP	Preschool child(ren) left alone more than once	4	5.62
FTP	School-age child(ren) left alone at night once	1	3.83
FTP	School-age child(ren) left alone at night more than once	2	5.20
	Other (please specify)	—	—
FTP	School-age child(ren) left alone during day	6	3.50
FTP	Poor supervision, caretaker present	7	3.20
IPE	School-age child(ren) left with an uncertain babysitter overnight	2	3.59
FTP	Locked out	6	6.10

TABLE 5–1.   Continued

DERIVED CATEGORY[1]	INITIAL CATEGORY/INCIDENTS	PERCENTAGE OF 949 CASES WITH ITEM CHECKED	WORKERS X SERIOUSNESS RATING
	Medical/Health Care		
*	Child(ren) in need of dental care, in pain, or experiencing difficulty in eating	3	6.1
FTP	Child(ren)'s obvious illness not attended to, need for medical attention substantiated by a physician	8	6.91
FTP	Child(ren)'s obvious illness not attended to, need for medical attention *not* substantiated by a physician	3	6.34
IPE	Teeth dirty, cavities obvious	2	4.46
	Other (please specify)	—	—
IPE	Lacks general medical care	2	5.11
	Drugs, Alcohol		
D/A	Child(ren) given drugs/alcohol by an adult in the household	2	7.35
D/A	Child(ren) took drugs/alcohol due to lack of adult supervision or caution	4	6.46
D/A	Congenital drug addiction	1	7.37
M/L	Drug use by adults in the household	7	5.44
M/L	Drunkenness of adults in the household	17	4.71
	Other (please specify)	—	—
	Moral/Legal		
M/L	Child(ren) involved in illegal behavior by adults in the household	1	6.83
M/L	Child(ren) witness to illegal behavior	2	4.79
M/L	Promiscuous sexual behavior in the household	2	4.83
M/L	Prostitution in the household	—	5.55
	Other (please specify)	—	—
CBP	Caretaker ignores criminal behavior of child	1	5.87
M/L	Deviant sex between caretakers	0.2	6.79
M/L	Illegal activity, child not witness	2	2.71
	Sexual Abuse		
SA	Sexual abuse/molestation of the child(ren) by the responsible caretaker(s)	4	8.67
SA	Sexual abuse/molestation of child(ren) by an adult	2	7.79
	Other (please specify)	—	—

TABLE 5-1.   Continued

Derived Category[1]	Initial Category/Incidents	Percentage of 949 Cases with Item Checked	Workers $\bar{X}$ Seriousness Rating
SA	Molestation by other child	0.3	7.23
	School		
FTP	Child(ren) deliberately kept out of school for days at a time, on more than one occasion	4	5.24
CBP	Child(ren)'s school attendance noted by school authorities to be a problem but not known to be deliberate	7	2.86
	Other (please specify)	—	—
CBP	Absent/tardy	2	3.57
CBP	Poor in studies	0.5	2.90
CBP	Behavior problem, fights at school	1	4.22
FTP	Child not enrolled in school	0.1	4.84
	Emotional/Psychological		
*	Child(ren) forced to work in violation of child labor laws	0.1	5.30
EM	Child(ren) forced to assume inappropriate responsibility in the household	7	4.60
EM	Child(ren) *openly* rejected; siblings obviously preferred	12	6.40
EM	Child(ren) repeatedly called bad or unworthy of caretaker's love, criticized unjustly, unfairly	12	6.33
EM	Child(ren) witness to frequent marital conflict, fighting	9	4.35
EM	Child(ren) passively rejected, ignored	11	6.01
EM	Child(ren) receive(s) little nurturance, love, attention—e.g., being held, read to, talked to	12	6.30
CBP	Child(ren) out of control, known to law enforcement agency, courts	6	5.27
CBP	Child(ren) out of control, caretakers fearful that child(ren) in danger of engaging in illegal activity	6	4.94
CBP	Child(ren)'s behavior beyond control of the caretakers; while no indication of trouble with the law, the child(ren)'s behavior is beyond the tolerance of the caretakers	13	4.92
EM	Child(ren) emotionally disturbed, verified by psychiatric/psychological evaluation	10	6.50

TABLE 5-1.   Continued

DERIVED CATEGORY[1]	INITIAL CATEGORY/INCIDENTS	PERCENTAGE OF 949 CASES WITH ITEM CHECKED	WORKERS $\bar{X}$ SERIOUSNESS RATING
EM	Child suspected of being emotionally disturbed, not verified by psychiatric/ psychological evaluation	13	6.32
	Other (please specify)	—	—
EM	Child severely disciplined	0.1	6.26
EM	Child exposed to physical violence in home	0.1	6.29

[1] FTP = failure-to-provide
  IPE   = inadequate physical environs.
  EM   = emotional mistreatment.
  CBP   = child behavior problem.
  D/A   = drug/alcohol use by child.
  M/L   = moral/legal behavior—parents.
  PI   = physical injury.
  SA   = sexual abuse.
[2] Asterisk (*) indicates not correlated with derived categories.

surveys. A principal-components factor analysis of the ratings of all the incidents was performed, and from the results 8 categories of mistreatment were established. These categories were very similar to those that emerged out of the study of the four professions' opinions. The categories, in rank order of their rated seriousness, were: physical injury, sexual abuse, drugs/alcohol abuse (by the child), emotional neglect, moral/legal transgressions (parent), failure-to-provide, child behavior problem, and inadequate physical environment.

The differences between these categories and those of the other samples (charted in table 5-2) were as follows: Supervision did not emerge as a special category but rather was subsumed under failure-to-provide. Criminality in the parents, fostering delinquency, and the sexual mores of the parents were grouped together rather than in separate categories. Environmental inadequacy, mainly lack of cleanliness, emerged as separate from the more general failure-to-provide. These situations of poor sanitation and housing, it will be recalled, were not part of any category established by the other professionals, suggesting that they simply were not viewed as mistreatment at all. Among the protective workers, although environmental inadequacy was a separate category, it clearly was perceived as the least serious. Finally, the most important dif-

TABLE 5-2. Comparison of Categories across Three Populations

POPULATIONS		
Four Counties	*Professionals*	*Community*
Physical abuse———————Physical abuse———————Physical abuse		
Sexual abuse———————Sexual abuse———————Sexual abuse		
Failure-to-provide———Failure-to-Provide———Failure-to-provide		
Inadequate physical———Supervision——————Supervision		
environs		
Emotional mistreatment—Emotional mistreatment—Drugs/sex		
Moral/legal (parent)———Parental sexual mores		
Fostering delinquency		
Drugs/alcohol———————Drugs/alcohol		
Child behavior problem*--Educational neglect		

* Child Behavior Problem includes truancy and other school difficulties, but is more comprehensive than Educational Neglect.

ference was the establishment of a category that referred to disordered behavior by the child. Some of the items in this category came from the write-ins supplied by the workers, including situations like "fighting at school," "truancy," and "beyond the control of the parents." These kinds of situations were clearly distinct from those that grouped under emotional neglect, all of which referred not to the child's behavior but to the parents'. The new category actually represents an increasing use that is being made of child protective networks, as a recourse for parents who simply cannot handle their children.[5]

[5] Four of the items in this category referred to the child's behavior at school—fighting, poor attendance, tardiness, and academic failure. The other four pertained to delinquency or delinquency-prone behavior, beyond the control of the parents and/or known to the police. We had not included any items like this in the vignettes, not anticipating that such behavior on the part of children might be considered as mistreatment. Indeed, one can question the appropriateness of including it here. Our rationale for inclusion was that these children and their families and their problems were being processed through the protective services systems and using the resources of those systems. There are two reasons why such cases are increasing in protective caseloads. One is that status offenders—children whose "offenses" are not crimes for adults—can no longer be detained against their wills by the courts. However, if adjudicated as "dependent children" or placed voluntarily by their parents, they can be separated from their parents. The other reason for the increase is that voluntary foster home placements cannot be reimbursed with federal monies unless the case is court-adjudicated. Hence counties are motivated to seek such adjudication, even though the parents would gladly voluntarily place the children. Frequently, if possible, in such cases, though the initial motivation for placement might be the child's troublesome behavior, if neglect or abuse also exists, then the case might be court-adjudicated on that basis.

NATURE OF MISTREATMENT

In assessing the nature of the kinds of mistreatment involved in this sample of cases we calculated the numbers of cases in which each kind of mistreatment was a component, and the numbers of cases in which a particular kind of mistreatment was the *only* aspect of mistreatment noted. In response to the question "What was the nature of the mistreatment that brought these families to the point of protective intervention?" the answer is clear. Families where at least two or more different kinds of mistreatment existed were more common than were families exhibiting any particular single type of mistreatment. (In making this computation, we did not include emotional mistreatment even if checked as part of the combinations computed, since 594, or 63 percent, of the cases had this checked. If we had, virtually all cases would involve combinations. (Tabular presentation is given in appendix b, table B-6.) Of the 949 cases, in 459 there existed two or more kinds of mistreatment. Only one-third of the children who had received a physical injury had no other complaint, and at least half of those who were sexually assaulted had also been mistreated in some other way. These very serious kinds of mistreatment were thus very often accompanied by other, less serious ones. Of particular note is the fact that among the more controversial kinds of mistreatment—emotional neglect and immoral activity by parents—there were very few cases in which these were the sole reasons for protective action. Although emotional neglect was a component in over half the cases, in only 5 percent was it the only kind of mistreatment at issue. Similarly, while a third of the cases involved some morally reprehensible behavior on the part of the parents, in fewer than 5 percent was it the only matter at issue. Finally, matters pertaining to the physical care of children (failure to provide and inadequate physical environs), considered as relatively less serious by these workers, were the sole reason for action in only 15 percent of the families. There were almost as many cases where the sole complaint was not that of the parents' failures but rather the disordered behavior of the children (115, or 12 percent), cases where the parents themselves often were seeking assistance.

What significance can be attached to this information with respect to the appropriate standards for definitions of mistreatment and the relationship between perceptions of seriousness and the action taken on the basis of these perceptions? First of all we must again point out that the families in this study constituted a screened population: these were families where it had been determined that some kind of mistreatment had occurred that warranted intervention. The workers who participated were in effect the gatekeepers at the boundary of the protective network. Hence in terms of their own definitional actions, these cases represent those, among all the ones investigated, that were considered serious enough to process into the system. Insofar as this sample of cases is representative, it would appear that the workers defined very few cases as mistreating in which emotional neglect or immoral behavior of the parents was the only kind of mistreatment, and relatively few where it was only failure to provide. Hence, at the first step in the definitional process such cases may well be screened out. Since we do not have information on the kinds of mistreatment initially reported, we cannot say whether fewer of these kinds of mistreatment were brought to the attention of workers or whether the investigating workers tended to decline to take action on such complaints. And if the workers did not take action, it may not always have been because they did not want to take action.[6] While the workers are the primary boundary decision makers, they are not unmindful of the definitional standards being utilized by the courts with which they deal and whose ultimate approval is needed if coercive intervention must be sought. Nonetheless, it would appear that the kind of mistreatment deemed least serious by the other professionals and by the community—immoral behavior of the parents—is only rarely substantiated as a case of mistreatment in and of itself. In the more controversial area of emotional mistreatment, it would appear that, in practice, the controversy is resolved in favor of those who do not perceive it as sufficiently serious to warrant intervention. Disagreements appear to be resolved in the direction of sentiments more representative of lawyers than of social workers or police. This point will become more obvious in the next section, where actual case dispositions are examined in relation to the seriousness of the reported mistreatment.

---

[6] More than one worker told us that there were situations about which they felt very concerned at times but where the parents refused to let them enter their homes or talk to them. They did not pursue these cases because they knew that the judge would not take action in them. The police with whom they worked also knew this and thus were reluctant to use their authority in assisting the worker in gaining access to these homes. Most typically these involved situations of mild neglect and suspected emotional mistreatment.

DEFINITIONS OF MISTREATMENT AND
THE KINDS OF DISPOSITIONS MADE

Does the perceived seriousness of mistreatment affect the dispositions made in families' lives? This is a very crucial point with respect to the definition of mistreatment. Much of the ongoing controversy over what should and should not be regarded as mistreatment stems from value conflicts over what constitutes sufficient grounds for intruding into families' lives.

The dispositions available in these counties were like those available in the rest of the country, although the resources available to carry out any one of the types of dispositions can and do vary considerably from one state to another and one county to another, even in the same state. For example, some counties with few resources may be able to allocate scarce resources only to the most serious cases. Hence in such cases foster placement services may be available, but help to families in their own homes may be restricted (Groeneveld and Giovannoni 1977). There are two dimensions along which dispositions vary: one, whether the children are removed from their parents or not, and the other, the degree of coerciveness involved, whether the disposition is made through the courts or is made through a voluntary arrangement with the families. In these 949 cases the dispositions made were as follows: in 52 percent the children were left with their families and court action was not sought; in 5 percent the children remained at home, but under court supervision; in 18 percent the children were removed through the voluntary arrangement with their parents, and finally, the most extreme disposition, 25 percent were removed by court action. In three of these counties all the protective functions were performed by social workers employed by the department of social services. In one county investigation of cases for court action was performed by probation officers attached to the court and employed by the probation department. All other service functions were performed by social workers in the department of social services, as they were in the other counties. In that county at the time of the study it was the routine practice to refer to probation for investigation cases of physical injury, sexual abuse, and severe malnutrition. When we looked at the relationship between the seriousness of mistreatment and the kinds of dispositions made, we kept this organizational difference in mind, and we analyzed that county's data separately from the other three. It was anticipated that such an organizational difference might affect the definitional processes, and in fact it appeared that it did.

Keeping in mind that the majority of these cases involved multiple kinds of mistreatment, we used a statistical procedure that could capture the effects of such combinations: discriminant function analysis.[7] Basically the question posed was "To what extent did the kinds of mistreatment distinguish between cases receiving one kind of disposition from those receiving another?" Or in other words, "If one knew how the children had been mistreated, how accurately could one classify a given case as to the kind of disposition that had been made?" Two types of dispositions were the focus of the analysis, those representing opposite poles: removal by the courts versus voluntary (noncourt) in-home supervision. These two dispositions do not overlap on either the dimension of court action or removal of children. One would expect the cases involved in each to be the most different and thus the easiest to discriminate between.

In the county where probation did the investigations, only two kinds of mistreatment significantly discriminated between cases where the children had been removed by the court and those where they were allowed to stay home under voluntary supervision. These were the two most serious kinds of mistreatment—physical injury and sexual abuse. If one were to guess that in cases where one or both of these kinds of mistreatment was present, the children had been removed by the courts, the guess would have been correct 65 percent of the time. Knowledge about additional kinds of mistreatment would not have been helpful in discriminating between cases in the two different outcome groups. Among children removed by the courts and those remaining at home, roughly the same propor-

---

[7] Discriminant analysis is a specific type of regression analysis that allows one to distinguish between two or more groups defined by the researcher. To distinguish between the groups, a set of "discriminating variables" is selected on which the groups may be differentiated. Simply, this technique allows one to "discriminate" between groups by measuring differences across a set of variables (see Maurice M. Tatsuoka, *Multivariate Analysis* [New York: Wiley, 1971], for a more complete discussion). In this analysis cases were scored only on the basis of the presence or absence of each kind of mistreatment. Previous analyses had demonstrated that the degree of seriousness of mistreatment *within* types did not distinguish between cases adjudicated by courts and those not sent to court. Those data are discussed and presented in appendix B. Discriminant function analyses like the ones presented here were also performed for a three-way dispositional grouping: (a) court removal, (b) voluntary removal, and (c) in-home supervision. As expected, these were not as successful. Those data are also presented in the appendix B.

tions of each had experienced the same kinds of mistreatment, with the exception of physical injury and sexual abuse. Among the court cases 48 percent had been physically abused, but only 25 percent of those left at home. Twenty-six percent of the court-removed children had been sexually abused, but only half that many, 13 percent, of those not taken to court (see table 5–3A).

In the other three counties the pattern was different: only two kinds of mistreatment did not discriminate between the two outcome groups. These both related to the children's behavior, drug use, and disordered behavior. The presence of all other kinds of mistreatment increased the likelihood that court removal had been sought in the case. In other words, the more kinds of mistreatment involved, the more likely that extreme intervention had been used. In these counties knowledge of the kind of mistreatment involved resulted in the correct classification of 71 percent of the cases. The various kinds of mistreatment were not of equal significance in discriminating between cases in the two outcome groups. Of least significance were the categories of failure-to-provide and inadequate environment. Immoral/illegal behavior of the parents was the most significant, followed by sexual abuse, physical injury, and emotional neglect.

In these three counties for each kind of mistreatment there was a greater proportion of children in the court group who had experienced it than in the noncourt group. For example, 53 percent of the court cases involved failure-to-provide, and 37 percent of the voluntary ones. With respect to immoral or illegal behavior of the parents, this was a concomitant of some other kind of mistreatment in over half the court cases, but in only one-fourth of the other group. Recalling that there were only a few cases overall that involved *only* this kind of parental behavior, its importance here in determining court action is only as a contributing factor in the presence of more serious kinds of mistreatment. In a sense, "seriousness" of mistreatment for purposes of court definition is determined not so much on a criterion of absolute seriousness of a particular kind of mistreatment but rather on a criterion of cumulative seriousness of multiple kinds of mistreatment (see table 5–3B).

These data indicate that the seriousness of mistreatment is linked to the kinds of dispositions made. The most serious kinds of mistreatment—serious as judged by all the groups studied—are more likely to result in the more extreme dispositions, and even

TABLE 5-3. Discriminant Analysis and Classification: Court Removal versus Voluntary In-Home Supervision by Categories of Mistreatment and Caretaker Attitudes

A: County 1

Category of Mistreatment	PERCENTAGE OF CASES IN DISPOSITION TYPE		F-Ratio
	Court Removal	Voluntary Home	
Failure-to-provide	46%	50%	0.39
Physical injury	47	25	12.34†
Inadequate environs	43	48	0.53
Emotional neglect	51	61	2.49
Sexual abuse	26	13	6.04*
Moral/legal	36	33	0.29
Child behavior	21	25	0.18
Drugs/alcohol (parents)	07	05	0.43
Parents want emotional help	23	50	17.45†
Parents want removal	31	06	24.95†

* $p < .05$
† $p < .01$
Eigenvalue: .33
Canonical correlation: .50

Classification

Actual Group	N	PREDICTED GROUP MEMBERSHIP	
		I	II
I Court removal	(118)	66.9% (79)	33.1% (39)
II Voluntary home	(106)	24.5% (26)	75.5% (80)

Percentage of cases correctly classified: 70.98%.

B: Counties 2, 3, and 4

Category of Mistreatment	PERCENTAGE OF CASES IN DISPOSITION TYPE		F-Ratio
	Court Removal	Voluntary Home	
Failure-to-provide	50%	36%	4.62*
Physical injury	42	25	8.56†
Inadequate environs	50	37	4.42*
Emotional neglect	81	60	12.02†
Sexual abuse	17	08	5.80*
Moral/legal	53	23	27.65†
Child behavior	32	32	0.23
Drugs/alcohol (parents)	11	06	2.28
Parents want emotional help	21	47	18.70†

TABLE 5–3.   Continued

B: Counties 2, 3 and 4

Category of Mistreatment	Percentage of Cases in Disposition Type		F-Ratio
	Court Removal	Voluntary Home	
Parents want removal	38	07	64.18†

* p < .05, 1 and 440 d.f.
† p < .01
Eigenvalue: .35
Canonical correlation: .51

Actual Group	N	Predicted Group Membership	
		I	II
I Court removal	(74)	70.3%	29.7%
		(52)	(22)
II Voluntary home	(368)	17.9%	82.1%
		(66)	(302)

Percentage of cases correctly classified: 80.1%.

more likely when combined with other types of mistreatment, though these are less serious ones in themselves. However, judging from the percentage of cases that could be correctly classified on the basis of the mistreatment (65 percent and 71 percent) alone, many other factors played a part in the decisions that were made. There was a large proportion of cases with mistreatment similar to that in court removal where the children were left in their homes. Two other pieces of information about the families were investigated along with the kinds of mistreatment as possible factors influencing this discrepancy, both reflecting attitudes of the parents. There was a question on the form filled out by the workers asking what the parents thought would be helpful to them in resolving the situation. The workers asked this of the parents and recorded their anwers. There were nine categories of responses, including "parent saw no problem," "wanted practical help" (such as babysitting, housing), "wanted emotional help" (including casework services, psychotherapy, or someone to talk to), and "parents wanted removal of child." Two of these categories of responses to the parents' perception of a solution when added to the discriminant analysis increased the proportion of cases correctly classified. These reponses were "want emotional help" and "want removal of child." That these two particular attitudes would influence disposition makes sense. Since intervention without court action takes some degree of cooperation on the part of the parent, the fact that parents actually sought help for themselves, especially emotional help, is probably a good indicator that they are willing to cooperate, without resort to court coercion. The parents' wish for removal of the child, on the other hand, would seem to mitigate against leaving the children in the home. The kind of disposition made was related both to the seriousness of the mistreatment and to the interaction of the mistreatment itself and the attitudes of the parents.

In the first county the proportion of cases correctly classified increased from 65 percent to 71 percent when information about the parents' attitudes was added to the analysis. In the other three counties the increase in correctly classified cases was from 71 percent to 80 percent. For all counties the patterning of the interaction was the same. If there were multiple kinds of mistreatment and/or very serious mistreatment and the parents did *not* want emotional help, and/or wanted the child removed, the likelihood of court removal increased.

While the parents' attitudes did have an effect on the kind of disposition made, this effect was not independent of the kind of mistreatment involved. In the absence of serious mistreatment, the parents' attitudes did not increase the likelihood of court removal. Rather, the presence of more positive attitudes on the part of the parents in part seemed to explain why some cases with very serious or multiple kinds of mistreatment still were thought to be safely manageable at home, without court action. What this suggests, of course, is that criteria utilized by the courts in these counties establish the parameters of admissible cases along lines of the seriousness of different kinds of mistreatment, especially physical injury and sexual abuse. However, this does not mean that families where there is such serious mistreatment must be taken to court or the children removed. Rather, there is some discretion, and depending on other circumstances, the other options in disposition can be exercised: services to the child and family in their own home or voluntary foster home placement.

What do these data suggest about the definitional processes in the protective systems of these counties? There is some evidence that the use of multiple definers—the community, the social workers, and the courts—results in an interdependence in the kinds

of criteria utilized by each set of definers. Those kinds of mistreatment that were least likely to have been processed by the courts
were also those least likely to have been entered into the protective
network at all, unless they were a concomitant of more serious
kinds of mistreatment. If entered into the system the least serious
kinds of mistreatment were least likely to go to court, but the
reverse is not necessarily so. With respect to cases serious enough to
be court-admissible, other factors intervene, including parents' attitudes and willingness to cooperate. Those situations where the
mistreatment is of a less serious nature, and the parents are not
willing to cooperate with interventive methods, are likely to be
dropped out of the protective network altogether. In a sense this
kind of definitional process reflects an adjustment to the sometimes
conflicting interests that inhere in problems of mistreatment—the
interests of the parents, the children, and the community. The seriousness of the mistreatment becomes grounds for overriding the interests of the parents in favor of those of the children and the community. In the face of less serious mistreatment, the interest of the
parents takes priority over the others. The concept of relative
seriousness of different kinds of mistreatment, then, becomes a
crucial criterion in determining the social response. In a very practical sense the seriousness of mistreatment determines whether a
specific case will be defined as one of mistreatment or not. In less
serious cases, other criteria, such as parental attitudes and the
availability of interventive resources, may be more crucial determinants of definition. In instances of more serious mistreatment,
the kind of mistreatment itself can be the sole determinant of
definition, leading to coercive family intrusion and separation of
children from their families.

   If one of the determining factors in defining a case of mistreatment is the cooperativeness of parents, then the acceptability to
them of the interventions offered is very likely to affect their
cooperativeness, and hence how the case is labeled, if it is labeled
at all. Whether a service is in fact given or not depends partly on its
acceptability but also on its availability. Both the availability and
acceptability of services can influence whether a case becomes
labeled as one of the mistreatment at all, providing the mistreatment is not of a serious enough nature to warrant court intrusion
and/or placement. If, for example, a case involved mild failure to
provide, and counseling was thought appropriate, the case might
be kept in a protective service caseload—labeled as one of mistreat-

ment—only if the counseling was available and acceptable; otherwise it might just be dropped altogether. In the next part of this chapter we present information about the resources the workers deemed useful to these families, the acceptability of these resources to the parents, and their actual availability.

DEFINITION OF MISTREATMENT AND ALLOCATION OF RESOURCES

An item on the questionnaire contained a checklist of resources and services. The workers checked off for each case those that they would ideally recommend for these families and their situations, and then whether it was available, and if so, acceptable to the client.[8] These resources were considered applicable to a case regardless of the kinds of dispositions made—that is, whether the child remained at home or was placed, or whether the case was handled through the courts or not. A child might be placed through the courts, for example, as the disposition, but an additional resource recommended along with this action might be mental health services for the mother, before the child could be placed back at home. As with the parental attitudes described in the previous section, the availability of resources would be a secondary consideration, if one at all, to the seriousness of mistreatment in determining the more extreme situations, but it might be a more important determinant of keeping a family in protective services voluntarily in less serious mistreatment cases.

The resources recommended are categorized as: (1) those of a therapeutic or educational nature; (2) support in child caring; and (3) economic supports.

---

[8] This was a different question from the one referred to earlier, which asked what parents thought would be helpful. That question was intended to get at parents' attitudes about their situations and the locus of the problem, while this one was intended to tap the workers' opinions. In the parents' questions, responses were not limited to formal kinds of institutional services, but included a variety of things such as removal of a disturbing family member, removal of the child, and even the perception that they saw no problem at all. There was, of course, overlap, such as parents who thought the problem centered on inadequate income, who also had "increased income" checked as a recommended resource. But there was no deliberate overlap (parents could have answered any way they wished), and thus the responses on the two questions cannot justifiably be compared. The parents' opinions about the resources offered them are reflected, however, in whether or not the workers rated the resource as acceptable to the clients.

There was a negative correlation between the availability of the resources and their acceptability to the clients that strikes a sad note.[9] The resources most often available were among those least often acceptable, and conversely the least available were the most often acceptable. The most available resources were those of a therapeutic, educative nature, including mental health services, parent education, instruction in money management, and Parents Anonymous. About half of the parents for whom parent education and/or money-management instruction were recommended were accepting of these services. Only about a third of those for whom mental health and Parents Anonymous groups were recommended were willing to participate in those programs. These services were available in over 90 percent of the situations for which they were thought suitable resources.

Services to assist parents in child care were available in only about 75 percent of the situations, but compared with the educative/therapeutic services, they were much more often acceptable: in over 70 percent of the cases where they were recommended. These services included homemakers, housekeepers, day care, nursery, and babysitting services. The least available of these was homemaker services, unavailable to 40 percent of the families where recommended. Although these kinds of child care supports were much more acceptable to these clients than were the therapeutic and educative services, still there were about a fourth who were not accepting of them. Child care services were apparently viewed as welcome supports by most, but to about a fourth of the parents surrendering the child to a day care center or having a homemaker may have been viewed as an unwelcome intrusion into their lives and their relationships with their children. Here again the issue arises as to when mistreatment is serious enough to warrant coercive action in order to elicit acceptance of this kind of "help." Neither the therapeutic nor the more tangible supports can in any way be construed as punitive. Quite to the contrary, they are traditional parts of the social service armamentarium, the core of the rehabilitative approach to the handling of mistreatment.

These situations bring into focus the potential clash between the therapeutic and the legalistic approaches to mistreatment, a clash that goes far back in history. At issue is the right of parents to refuse help, no matter how well intentioned or beneficent that help might be, a right that is lost when the authority of the court is in-

[9] Tabular presentation is given in appendix B, table B–3.

voked to force parents to accept help and services that, for whatever reasons, they do not want. Apparently in these counties there were very few such situations. In only a small number of cases that had come to the attention of the courts were the children left with their parents but under the supervision of the court. If mistreatment was not sufficiently serious to warrant removal of the child, then the provision of services to alleviate the problem was very dependent on the willingness of parents to accept these services voluntarily. There is, of course, no way of knowing how many parents of children placed by the courts might "accept" a service that they did not want, only as a means of getting their children back.

The recommendations as to what would be helpful to these families, both from their own and the workers' perspective, was not limited to social services but included resources of an economic and environmental nature—namely employment, supplementary income, and housing. These resources were virtually beyond the power of the protective agencies to provide and were hence much less widely available than personal social services of any kind. Although they were not recommended in a large proportion of cases, when these resources were deemed suitable, they were for the most part unavailable. But they would have been acceptable to a much higher proportion of the clientele than any of the other services. Help with housing would have been acceptable to 78 percent of those for whom it was recommended but was available to only 58 percent. Employment would have been acceptable to three-fourths of the parents but was available slightly more than half the time. Finally, increased income was acceptable to almost all but was available to only 9 percent. These economic resources were recommended in fewer than 20 percent of the cases. Their general unavailability may have precluded many of these workers from even thinking about them as a resolution to the problems of these families. However, in the next section it will be clear that financial difficulties were very common among these families, particularly among those where the mistreatment involved failure-to-provide.

CIRCUMSTANCES OF POVERTY AND
DEFINITIONS OF MISTREATMENT

In chapter 2 it was brought out that, until very recently, children of parents dependent on public support were routinely taken away from them as a means of coping with the dependency. With the advent of federal public-assistance programs, this practice waned. In principle children are removed only if they have been mistreated.

One of the last kinds of mistreatment to be included in mistreatment statutes was the physical neglect of children, and among those who spurred its inclusion were social workers who went into the homes of the poor and deplored the conditions they saw. Critics of social workers' approaches to the problems of mistreatment, especially those in the legal profession, in the past and currently, have charged that the social workers have confused the circumstances of poverty with parental mistreatment. The imposition of middle-class values on the poor has led to the erroneous definition of a poor environment as mistreatment. The kinds of situations involved are those encompassed in our category of failure-to-provide; poor supervision, inadequate feeding, lack of cleanliness. The professionals studied in the research, the community members, and the workers from these counties all perceived these kinds of mistreatment as less serious than most others. Hence there is consensus both as to what constitutes this kind of mistreatment and as to its relative seriousness. What is the link, then, between this generally recognized form of mistreatment and the circumstances of poverty? We ask this not in an attempt to demonstrate that poverty itself causes these kinds of parental failure. Rather, our interest is to ascertain how enmeshed in poverty conditions are the families where failure to provide exists. Whether causal or not, poverty conditions are important components of the total psychosocial context of poor families' lives. Managing these cases, and extension of help to the families and children, must inevitably take place within that context.

We examined the question by dividing the cases into six groups: (1) cases where the only form of mistreatment was failure to provide,[10] (2) failure-to-provide and at least one other kind of mistreatment except a physical injury, (3) failure-to-provide along with a physical injury, (4) physical injury was the only kind of mistreatment, (5) physical injury was present and also another form of mistreatment but not failure to provide, and finally (6) cases without either failure-to-provide or a physical injury (the majority of these [65 percent] involved children's behavior problems or emotional

[10] For this computation, cases with failure-to-provide and/or inadequate physical environs were grouped together as failure-to-provide.

mistreatment). We then compared these groups on several factors indicative of financial hardship.

The results were clear. Among families where the mistreatment involved failure-to-provide with or without some other form of mistreatment but not physical injury of the child, poverty was not only typical but much more characteristic than among families with the more serious mistreatment involving physical injury. Only a third of the two failure-to-provide groups were judged able to meet basic costs of living, compared with two-thirds of the other groups. Two thirds of the failure-to-provide group were welfare recipients, while only one-third of the total families were receiving welfare. Linked to the financial circumstances was the fact that in only one-fourth of the failure-to-provide families was the father residing in the home, and in those few families, over a third of the fathers were unemployed.[11] Although these families typically had no more children than did other kinds of mistreating families, the ratio of children to adults was generally higher, owing, of course, to the absence of one parent. In over half of these families the ratio of children to adults in the household was three to one, while in the other groups such a high ratio obtained in only one-fourth of the families.

In one-fourth of these failure-to-provide cases the housing was judged to be inadequate and was, in fact, part of the reason for the complaint of mistreatment, a factor noted in less than 10 percent of the physical-injury cases. Less than half had a working telephone, and only one-third had an automobile (which in these California counties is a hardship), while three-fourths of the other families had these conveniences. The conditions of material deprivation were not uncommon among other families. Certainly relative to the general population the entire parent group was skewed toward the lower end of the financial spectrum. However, these factors were two or three times more common among families in the

[11] On almost all these variables the cases involving both failure-to-provide and a physical injury were more like the failure-to-provide than the physical-injury groups. However, with respect to father presence/absence the failure-to-provide/physical-injury group was more likely to have a father in the home (43 percent) than the other failure-to-provide families. Cases overall where a physical injury had been inflicted were more likely to have a father present. The greater involvement of fathers and other males in physical abuse is gradually being recognized. The 1978 data from the American Humane Association showed that in 13,558 cases of "abuse only," 55 percent of the perpetrators were males (1978, p. 7). Tabular presentation of these data is given in appendix B, table B–4.

failure-to-provide categories than among those where this was not a part of the problem.

Of principal concern are those families where failure to provide is the only kind of mistreatment. These families were also the least likely to have been taken to court: only about one-fourth as compared with one-third of those where there had been a physical injury and half of those where there were multiple kinds of mistreatment. It would appear that the children of these poor families were not being removed from their families very often. The major point of concern, then, would not be the issue of coercive action but the cooperativeness of the parents as crucial to protective intervention. Should parental failure of a less serious nature be defined as mistreatment when it is enmeshed in conditions of poverty? The issue is a practical one. What is the purpose of defining these families as mistreating if the social responses available have little to do with reducing the circumstances of poverty?

If we relate the information on the circumstances of these families and the kinds of services and resources that were most available to the protective workers trying to help them, then serious questions can indeed be raised as to the possibility of alleviating the circumstances at all. The provision of increased income, employment, and better housing is beyond the scope of the protective agency. Increasing the availability of such resources calls for a reallocation of total societal resources and basic structural changes in the socioeconomic system. The basic economic situation of most of these families is entwined with the single-parent status of the mother and the generally disadvantaged position of women. Hence the economic hardship of most is compounded by the increased responsibilities of single parenthood. Supportive child care services can relieve some of this strain, but it cannot change the financial and material deprivation under which they live. Instruction in money management might help some to stretch the available dollars, but given the dire straits many are in, it seems unlikely that any but the star pupils would benefit. And mental health services, while they might improve the psychosocial functioning of some of these mothers, cannot be expected to improve their economic functioning in a system that places little value on what they have to offer.

The primary purpose of defining mistreatment is, or should be, to protect children. In these situations, where the only mistreatment is inextricably entwined with the circumstances of poverty, it might be possible to protect the children by removing them from their families and from the circumstances of poverty, but in the past hundred years we as a society have come to reject this alternative. Short of this, the kinds of resources with which the society responds to the definition of mistreatment are not likely to alter their circumstances. These resources cannot protect the children or their families from the hardship of poverty. Unlike the more serious kinds of mistreatment, which can be defined independently of the circumstances under which they take place, here the primary issue in the definition of mistreatment is not the matter of family intrusion through coercive action but, rather, the allocation of resources in protective intervention.

SUMMARY

In the two previous chapters we have presented detailed research findings concerning the opinions of key professionals and the general population about the seriousness of various kinds of child mistreatment. In this chapter we have examined the definitional process involved in 949 actual cases of families that had been defined as mistreating. We found that the lay population, especially those most like the families themselves—relatives and neighbors—are much more likely to have made the initial definition of mistreatment than any single group of professionals in these communities.

In examining the specific incidents of mistreatment that precipitated protective action in these cases, we found further corroboration of the consensus in definition revealed in the opinion studies. Consensus was found among the protective agents managing these cases with respect to perceptions of different kinds of mistreatment and their relative seriousness. The categories of mistreatment distinguished by these protective workers were very similar to those identified by other professionals, as was their assessment of the relative seriousness of these kinds of mistreatment. The dispositions made in these cases were demonstrated to be related to the relative seriousness of the mistreatment. There were very few cases in which the only kind of mistreatment was one generally considered less serious, or one that was controversial, including the moral behavior of the parents and emotional mistreatment. Such situations seemed likely to have been screened out of the protective network early in the process. Cases in which the disposition was the most extreme intervention, removal of the children through court action, were distinguished from others by the presence of more serious kinds of mistreatment—physical injury and sexual abuse—and by the presence of multiple kinds of mistreatment of varying degrees of seriousness. This suggests that the professionals making these decisions, primarily social workers, were influenced not only by their own opinions about mistreatment but by those in the court system. Their discretion regarding which cases to take to court is limited.

Parental attitudes also added to the distinctions that could be made among types of dispositions. Even in cases of very serious mistreatment, parental cooperativeness and motivation could mitigate against court action. However, in the absence of serious mistreatment, uncooperativeness was not likely to have resulted in court action. The latitude of discretion parental attitudes permit is in choosing cases *not* to take to court, rather than influencing court action independent of mistreatment criteria. We conclude that the presence of multiple definers in the entire protective system, from the lay person to the courts, tends toward more stringent criteria in defining mistreatment.

Finally we examined the characteristics associated with one particular kind of mistreatment, failure-to-provide, and demonstrated that when this kind of parental failure was not accompanied by more serious kinds of mistreatment, it most likely had occurred in families living under circumstances of extreme financial hardship. However, the resources available to protective agencies are not likely to alleviate such hardship.

In the final chapter we discuss the policy implications of these data and those of the opinion surveys with respect to the potential for pinpointing issues in the definition of mistreatment and finding potential resolutions.

CHAPTER 6

Social Policy Issues
in the Definition
of Child Mistreatment

IN THE PREVIOUS CHAPTERS we presented the results of our research on the social definition of child mistreatment. In this final chapter we focus on the social policy implications of the results of that research. We begin with a summary of the major findings of the research and then discuss the policy implications of those findings with respect to research and program evaluation, statutory changes, and resource allocation.

Can child mistreatment be defined more precisely? We began with the assumption that it is not an absolute entity but, rather, is socially defined and cannot be divorced from the social contexts in which it occurs. We further posited that mistreatment is not a unitary phenomenon but encompasses a broad range of acts, acts that can be distinguished from one another both conceptually and operationally. The history of child protection, reviewed in chapter 2, and the results of the research bear out these assumptions. Historically we saw that at different times, in different social contexts, different facets of parental role failure have been considered as socially deviant. Early in the country's history, social conformity and industriousness in children were highly valued and hence of paramount concern in judging the fitness of their parents. Today the very industriousness of children, so valued in colonial times, is itself a violation of the child labor laws and a form of mistreatment. When laws specific to the protection of children were first passed, the kinds of mistreatment they proscribed focused on the physical injury of children and sexual assault and very much on the moral behavior of both children and parents. It was not until the present century that the physical care of children became a matter that could bring them under the protective aegis of the state. And only very recently has the emotional aspect of child rearing come into focus as a matter possibly warranting state intervention. The social definitions have changed over time, and the changes have not been without controversy.

In pursuit of knowledge about the present status of definitions, we systematically sought the opinions of those involved in the definitional processes in one community—the professional and the lay populations. From their responses it was clear that neither professionals nor lay people perceive of child abuse and neglect as single entities. Both groups distinguished among different types of mistreatment and, more important, placed different valuations on these different types. The research technique used is relevant here, since the opinions we sought were about specific incidents. The results demonstrated that the professionals and lay people alike shared perceptions of the underlying commonalities among the specific incidents and made similar demarcation of the boundaries between broader classifications of incidents. Since all definitions are in essence classification schemes, these results argue not only for the necessity but also for the feasibility of more precise definitions of different kinds of mistreatment. Indeed, there could be no definition without socially shared perceptions of the actual ingredients of the definitions. The data confirmed that such socially shared perceptions exist. The potential for more precise definitions was validated by the data.

Although the respondents concurred on the boundaries of different kinds of mistreatment, there was not always agreement about the valuations placed on each. Community members saw most kinds of mistreatment as more serious than did professionals, and among professionals, lawyers especially dissented from the other groups, generally regarding mistreatment as less serious than the others did. However, there was amazing similarity in the judgments of the relative seriousness of different *kinds* of mistreatment both among the professionals and among the lay respondents.

There were some notable exceptions to this general pattern. Among the professionals, police and social workers saw most kinds of mistreatment as more serious than did lawyers or pediatricians. This difference in opinion was most clearly related to the roles they play in the protective network as gatekeepers who make the initial decision as to whether a situation will be defined as one of mistreatment at all. This role provided them with particular kinds of responsibilities and experiences. Among the community respondents, differences in opinions related to ethnicity and social class. Contrary to common speculation, Black and Hispanic respondents and those of lower socioeconomic statuses exhibited greater concern about all kinds of mistreatment. Further, socioeconomic status of the respondents, while shown to be related to their perceptions of mistreatment, was not a factor that operated independently of their ethnicity. Rather, the ways in which social class and cultural values affected opinions about mistreatment were demonstrated to be very complex and not uniform across all ethnic groups.

Finally, data were presented from a study of 949 actual cases of mistreatment from four counties in California. In over half these cases the initial reports of mistreatment had been generated by community members, not by professionals, again indicating that deviant parenting is recognized among all social classes and ethnic groups. The seriousness of the different kinds of mistreatment involved in these cases was related to the kinds of dispositions made. The more serious the mistreatment, the more likely it was that the courts had intervened and removed the children from their homes. Less serious kinds of mistreatment were less likely to receive such extreme intervention and, in fact, unless accompanied by more serious mistreatment, were not likely to have been processed into the protective networks of these counties at all. One particular kind of mistreatment involving improper physical care of children—commonly thought of as neglect—was found to be particularly common among families living under extreme financial hardships.

POLICY ISSUES IN
SPECIFIC KINDS OF MISTREATMENT

Throughout the preceding chapters we have stressed the complexity of the issues involved in societal intervention into situations of child abuse and neglect, a complexity based on reconciling the interests of the child, the parents, and the state. There are two dimensions to social intervention. One is the legal dimension, which comes into play when the courts are used to intrude into family privacy. The other dimension involves the allocation of social resources used in the management of the problems. The policy issues involved in specific kinds of mistreatment revolve around both dimensions. Thus as we detail the issues involved in each kind of mistreatment, both dimensions are kept in mind. With respect to definitional criteria for coercive intervention, we have oriented the discussion in part around the criteria suggested by the Juvenile Justice Standards Project discussed in chapter 3. We have done so because this is the most explicit policy statement available on the issues involved in coercive intervention.

Physical Mistreatment

Sexual abuse: Among all the groups studied, there was greater consensus about the extreme seriousness of this kind of child mistreatment than about any other. Historically, sexual abuse of children has always been considered a very serious kind of mistreatment. The JJSP established a separate standard for sexual abuse: "Coercive intervention should be authorized when a child has been sexually abused by his/her parents or a member of his/her household." The unanimity of opinion may reflect, however, not a primary concern with the welfare of children but the fact that sexual abuse of children is first of all a violation of societal taboo. Very little is known about the actual harm done to children who are sexually molested. Physical harm is not always a concomitant, especially among older children. The concern about sexual abuse usually rests on the presumed effects on their subsequent psychological adjustment and their moral character, but even after several years of research in the field of child abuse and neglect, the National Center on Child Abuse and Neglect has stated: "Sexual abuse of children, especially in cases of incest, is perhaps one of the least understood and, consequently most mishandled forms of child mistreatment. . . . There is often as much harm done to the child by the systems' handling of the case as the trauma associated with the abuse" (*Federal Register*, Jan. 23, 1978, part 2, p. 3244).

If indeed the major concern for the children centers on their psychological and moral development, then clearly the most important issues concern the ways in which they are treated in the protective intervention. Perhaps nothing is more clearly socially determined than the bounds of acceptable sexual behavior, and clearly in this society sexual activity between adults and children, especially when they are related by blood, is considered as highly deviant. However, enlightened self-interest dictates that while the society upholds its standards of sexual behavior, care must be exercised lest the very social interventions employed produce in children the very outcomes that are feared.

Physical injury: Physically injuring a child, the most specific meaning of child abuse, might well have been expected to be the least controversial kind of mistreatment. In one sense this was so, but only with respect to extreme kinds of injuries. Less extreme forms of physical punishment—spanking a child and even hitting him with a wooden stick—generated considerable disagreement among all respondents. Very serious injuries were considered among the most serious of all specific incidents, but the minor ones were considered among the least serious. Further, the relative seriousness of all kinds of physical injuries simply were not perceived as gravely by the community as by professionals. Clearly, what is reflected in the data is a general acceptance of corporal punishment in this country. Since hitting children is acceptable, the demarcation of "normal punishment" and "child abuse" becomes a matter of the degree of physical injury inflicted. Indeed, although the rights of parents, in fact the duty of parents, to chastise their children has been modified since colonial times, they have been only modified, not eliminated.

There are at least two policy implications to be drawn from this finding. The first concerns the general education of the public about child abuse, abusive behavior by parents themselves, and judgments about others' abusive behavior. The public view seems to be: "It's all right to hit your child, but not too hard; in fact it's all right to hurt your child—but not too badly." This issue needs to be faced more squarely than it is at present. As long as we as a society condone corporal punishment of children, we must admit that we are also willing to place some children in danger of being hurt badly. Child abuse education programs would do well to emphasize not so much the bizarre, extreme situations but the borderline types of mistreatment, the bruises and welts that come from "normal" hitting, the threshold of child abuse. The ambiguity that surrounds the demarcation of that threshold increases the risk generated by the social acceptance of physical punishment. In a very real sense, all parents are at risk of at some time crossing the threshold into "child abuse."

With respect to public policy regarding physical injury of children and the right of the state to intervene coercively, a similar ambiguity prevails. The JJSP standards with respect to physical abuse bear this contention out. The standard for permitting coercive intervention is "a child has suffered a physical harm, inflicted non-accidentally . . . which causes, or creates a *substantial risk* of causing disfigurement, impairment of bodily functioning, or other serious physical injury" (emphasis added). In the narrative explaining the standard, bruises are specifically singled out as questionable instances of "serious physical injury." According to all available data, bruises alone are the commonest form of reported physical injury subsequently classified as child abuse. Adherence to this standard implies that those who engage in the process of defining specific cases of "abuse" must make two kinds of judgments. One is the normative judgment implied in all kinds of mistreatment—that is, whether this parental practice or failure is sufficiently deviant from social norms to warrant social intervention. This in itself is a difficult judgment to make. However, the notion of "creating a substantial risk" calls for a predictive judgment as well. The definers must judge from among all the cases of bruised children which ones are likely to suffer broken bones or skull fractures the next time. This is by no means an easy task, but the penalty for misjudgment can be a severe one for children. We can only conclude that the lower definitional boundary of physical injury is shrouded in ambiguity. In the midst of the ambiguity is the delicate balance between children's rights to protection and parents' rights to autonomy. And at the heart of the ambiguity is our own societal ambivalence about the rights of children.

The next two kinds of mistreatment to be considered are related to failures in performing the usual duties of parents, particularly with respect to the physical care of children. On the basis of our data we think the distinction between supervision and failure to provide as separate domains of child care is a proper one to maintain, since both the professional and the community respondents made such distinction between these aspects of parental care and others.

Supervision: The kinds of parental failure encompassed by this kind of mistreatment all involve leaving a child alone, at various times of the day, for varying periods of time, in or out of their home. Neither the professionals nor the community members saw this kind of neglect of children as having a commonality with leaving a child *not alone*, but in the care of another, potentially unreliable person. This category of child neglect was a major source of disagreement between lawyers and other professionals (pediatricians, police, and social workers) but not between these other professionals and the community. Hence there is reason to suspect that the lawyers' opinions are not representative of most persons' opinions. The perceptions of lawyers with respect to leaving children alone revealed in this study are similar to those expressed in the JJSP standards; they center on the distinction between *potential* and *actual* physical harm to children. The standards proposed do not single out supervision as a separate entity but rather subsume it under the more general category of "inadequate parenting." Part of the commentary on that category deals with leaving a child unsupervised: "Intervention would not be justified solely because a home is dirty, because a parent leaves a child unattended for a brief period of time, or because of inadequate care or attention to the child." The standard applied is very similar to that recommended for physical abuse, the only difference being that the harm to the child is caused by parental failure to act (neglect) rather than deliberately inflicted: "a child has suffered . . . or there is substantial danger of physical harm causing disfigurement, impairment of bodily functioning, or other serious physical injury as a result of conditions created by his/her parents or by the failure of the parents to *adequately supervise* or protect him/her" (emphasis added).

Clearly the issue at hand is whether some physical harm must befall a child as a result of having been left alone before coercive intervention is justified. We believe, on the basis of our data, that most lay people do not think so. Rather, they see lack of supervision as a distinct kind of failure in parental role performance and a relatively serious one, whether or not the child suffers serious physical harm. The criterion of potential harm seemed to have much salience among all our respondents except the lawyers.

Two points should be clearly distinguished here. The first is that the indicents referred to in this research all concerned a child left *alone*, without any supervision.[1] Hence, the appropriateness of

---

[1] Although items had been included referring to leaving a child with an uncertain babysitter, the ratings of these were not correlated with those items where the child was left all alone, indicating an underlying commonality was not perceived between these two types of situations.

any given parental surrogate is not at issue, be it another child, a relative, or a neighbor. Leaving a child all alone is considered deviant and dangerous by most, and we suggest that this is a form of mistreatment worthy of consideration when coercive intervention is at issue.

To suggest that lack of supervision may be serious enough to warrant coercive intervention does not mean that this is necessarily the optimal solution. Clearly one way to relieve the danger to children from being left alone is to provide substitute caretakers. Hence, the reason children are left alone is a crucial policy consideration when developing more general approaches to the problem.[2] Parents, especially single parents overburdened by a variety of circumstances, may leave a child alone not altogether willingly. Certainly, the phenomenon of the "latch-key child" of the working parent is not only long recognized but quite acceptable to the American public. To this day we are unwilling to allocate much in the way of public resources to protect such a child. Hence, the problem of children left alone, perhaps in a majority of cases, might best be alleviated not through coercive intervention but rather through the provision of child care supports to parents, especially single parents. If the parents are willing to accept such help but it is not available, then the dilemma becomes one of a choice between two societal injustices, removal of the child from an otherwise adequate parent, and failure to protect the child. But if the help is available and the parents are unwilling to ensure the child protection through proper supervision, we do not believe, nor did most of our respondents, that societal intervention has to be suspended until the child is severely damaged.

Failure-to-provide: This kind of mistreatment, commonly thought of as physical neglect, might have been expected to be among the most controversial, but among our respondents it actually was not. While police and social workers thought this type of neglect more serious than did other professionals, all the professionals saw it as relatively less serious than most other kinds of mistreatment. As a category of mistreatment it would appear to be

[2] With respect to a given case obviously the age of the child and where and how left alone condition the seriousness. Here we found unanimity in terms of relative seriousness by designing the vignettes according to the criteria used by the Child Welfare League of America: worse a preschool child, worse left alone at night than during the day, and worse outside the home than inside.

at best at the threshold of those matters warranting coercive intervention. The standard applied to this form of mistreatment by the JJSP has been cited, and is essentially the same as that for physical injury: the result of the physical lack of care must be manifested in serious physical impairment before coercive action can be taken. We would tend to agree, for two reasons. First of all, historically, poor families have been in unique jeopardy with respect to their rights to autonomy, freedom from intrusion, and, in fact, their children. It is not so long ago that children could be taken from the poor simply because of their poverty. Given the data detailed in chapter 5, data corroborated by others, failure-to-provide is deeply enmeshed in circumstances of poverty. Clearly there is a qualitative difference between parents who live in the same squalor as their children and those whose children live in squalor while they live in luxury. The former is an all too common situation; the latter a rare and even bizarre occurrence. How are we to draw the line between removing children because of poverty and removing them because of circumstances engendered by poverty? It seems justifiable to exert extreme caution in the use of such interventions when the *only* form of mistreatment present is the failure to provide adequate physical care. We therefore concur with the JJSP regarding the stringency of criteria for exercising coercive intervention when this is the only form of mistreatment present. Noncoercive intervention is another matter, and here the issues very centrally concern the allocation of resources. If parents are willing to accept whatever help might be forthcoming, there seems no logical reason to deny that help. But the expectations of what kinds of help can reasonably be achieved must be tempered by the realities of the situations. Material lack is material lack, and if this lack cannot be made up for, especially by an affluent society such as our own, the children will continue to suffer the consequences. Indeed, more than any other kind of mistreatment, it might be said the real failure to provide is that of the society, not of the parents.

But what of those cases that do meet the more stringent criteria of physical harm, cases where court intrusion does seem indicated? Who is to make the judgment as to whether there is serious physical impairment stemming from the neglect? Here we believe there should be more medical resources allocated to protective systems and that physicians should be utilized routinely in examining children who have not been properly cared for in this way. We particularly note here the discrepancy between the other professionals' and the pediatricians' valuations of the medical consequences described for these kinds of incidents, indicating that the other professions may lack the expertise to make the judgments. Medical examination is far from routine in cases of neglect, and the lack of it may itself constitute a form of negligence. From the standpoint of making a judgment as to whether a child has been harmed by improper feeding, for example, or, equally important, of correcting the effects of malnutrition, it would seem appropriate that medical opinion be invoked in such cases. Among the children in the study reported on in chapter 5, very few who had not been physically injured had received any medical examination at all. While we agree with the standard of serious physical impairment, we suggest that the evaluation be made by a physician in cases where this is at issue, and that medical examination and treatment, if necessary, be provided even if coercive intervention is not being sought.

Nonphysical Mistreatment

The next five kinds of mistreatment, while not exactly overlapping, are discussed as a group because some of the underlying policy issues with respect to disposition are deeply entwined. These matters transcend the physical care of children and involve their emotional and behavioral adjustments. The linkage among all the categories of fostering delinquency, emotional neglect, child behavior problem, drugs/alcohol use by children, and educational neglect is the actual or potential undesirable behavior of the children. Some of the undesirable consequences of emotional neglect involve the kind of antisocial behavior thought of as delinquent. Policy issues as to when and how such problems should be handled and by whom are thus interwoven and, as demonstrated in the historical review, have been interwoven for over 150 years.

Fostering delinquency: Actually engaging or encouraging a child in the commission of a crime was thought to be one of the three most serious kinds of mistreatment by all respondents and was one of the first kinds of mistreatment enunciated in child neglect laws. The JJSP standards provide for it as a separate category of mistreatment worthy of coercive intervention: "A child is committing delinquent acts as a result of parental encouragement, guidance or approval." In the discussion of the standards the point is made that the parents must actively be engaged in the child's delinquency in some way, not simply committing crimes themselves without involving the child. (This was also the way in which the respondents in this study seemed to interpret the category; criminality in the household was not perceived as having an underlying commonality with actually engaging a child in stealing.) It would appear that this kind of parental action is not controversial with respect to its seriousness or its implications for coercive action. However, the matter may not be so clear cut as it might seem. The clarity of definition rests not only on the parents' involvement but also on the definition of "delinquent acts." As the social definitions of "delinquency" change, this aspect of mistreatment also is subject to definitional change.

What of children who are committing delinquent acts, not only without parental encouragement but to parental dismay? Although we did not include situations among the ones submitted to respondents in the opinion survey, they did emerge as a distinct category in the study of actual cases. A major policy issue, one with serious implications, relates to the uses that should be made of resources allocated to protective intervention programs. Many states, at the prompting of groups concerned with the rights of children, are removing from their statutes acts that are considered as delinquent only because of the age of the perpetrator, acts that are not criminal for adults, including running away, incorrigibility, and generally being beyond the control of the parents. The resources of the courts are gradually being closed to situations involving such children, known as PINS (persons in need of supervision) or status offenders. There is evidence, however, that court sanction is being successfully sought by the parents of such children, not through their prosecution as delinquents but actually as neglected children. Given the broadness of most neglect statutes, it is quite possible to do this. Further, this development is encouraged by the fact that though many such parents would voluntarily, even gladly, surrender their children for placement, federal funding policies preclude reimbursement to states and counties for expenses of such voluntary placement. Hence court action is sought as much for funding purposes as for reasons of necessity.

The situation is not at all unlike that which existed in the early days of the reformatory, when that institution, presumably intended for the rehabilitation of delinquents, was used quite indiscriminately to resolve a variety of problems involving children.

The issues are complex. Clearly the intent of protecting children's rights by eliminating status offenses is in part defeated through a shunting of children, with the same effects for them, into the system for neglected children. Linked to this is the problem of resource allocation. Are protective systems, already overburdened, going to be able to absorb this additional burden, both from the standpoint of expertise in dealing with these children and from that of their limited resources? And what of the parents? Where are they to turn if both the protective and delinquency systems are closed to them? In a very real sense one of the most crucial definitional problems that may be emerging with respect to mistreatment is whether or not, for practical purposes of social intervention, such situations should be considered as mistreatment. The unresolved dilemmas of 1830 regarding the use of the *parens patriae* argument are still very much with us. And the dilemmas of the proper use of the reformatory or orphanage are reincarnated in issues regarding the proper use of the foster home, the group treatment home, and the protective services.

Emotional mistreatment: The controversial nature of emotional mistreatment could easily be anticipated from the public writings and debates among professionals. However, neither the professionals nor the community considered emotional mistreatment to be as serious as physical or sexual assaults on children or contributing to their delinquency. The issue seems to be not recognition of emotional mistreatment as an entity but rather the rightness or wrongness of invoking coercive intervention. Reflecting in part the criterion of actual versus potential harm, the JJSP standards recommend that coercive intervention be invoked for a child "suffering serious emotional damage, evidenced by severe anxiety, depression or withdrawal, or untoward aggressive behavior toward self or others and the child's parents are not willing to provide treatment for him/her." Parental behavior thought likely to produce such symptoms in children at some future time would not be grounds for coercive intervention.

Given the controversial nature of the matter and the fact that no evidence has yet emerged to resolve the controversy, we would concur that the standard proposed is at present the most viable approach. Perhaps emotional mistreatment is best viewed through analogy with serious physical illness. If the courts can be invoked in situations where parents refuse medical treatment of the child for physical illnesses, then the invocation of court authority is justified to obtain treatment for serious emotional maladies. As suggested previously with respect to physical impairment due to parental failure, the judgment as to the severity of the condition should be made by an independent mental health professional. This is in no way to impugn the capacities of social workers in making such judgments; indeed, the mental health professional may well be a social worker by training. But given the controversial nature of judging emotional well-being, an independent evaluation would seem to be imperative. This does mean the addition of resources to the courts and protective systems, resources that could be supplied by other community or state mental health agencies.

What are the implications of hinging the matter on parental willingness? If parents themselves are to be involved in treatment, as most models of child treatment, at least with younger children, would prescribe, can their participation be mandated by a court? In part this question can be answered only by representatives of the mental health system itself. Are they willing and able to work with situations involving unwilling parents? Until this issue of the necessity for parental willingness to participate in treatment is resolved, hinging the definition of emotional mistreatment on parents' being *unwilling* to get treatment for an emotionally disturbed child is an empty solution in getting help for the child. And what if the child himself does not want treatment, especially the older child? Does this not raise the very issues involved in the elimination of status offenders from court intervention? In our opinion, no amount of dialogue is going to resolve the issues surrounding emotional mistreatment while the actors are limited to those within the child protective system. If another system, mental health, is the ultimate recourse, then the key actors really are the members of that system. Their resources, their capabilities, and their views are ultimately going to decide the actual outcome of these cases. This also includes those cases where the parents are willing to obtain treatment.

Mental health services for children have existed side by side with protective services for over fifty years. Why should the emotional disturbances of one group of children be dealt with in one system, the protective one, while others are treated in child guidance clinics by specialized child therapists? The reason is, in part, social class. Child guidance clinics started out as an arm of the juvenile courts but for a variety of reasons quickly moved away to become independent entities, with increasingly middle-class clientele (Levine and Levine 1971). Placing the emotional problems of some children, or those of their parents, under the aegis of protective services would seem to be a validation of the practice of bifurcating mental health services along social class lines. From this perspective, both services and statutes dealing with the emotional well-being of children, their mental health, might well be eliminated entirely from the purview of mistreatment and protective legislation. Both the laws and the services relating to emotionally mistreated children should be reserved as the province of the mental health system of each state and each community, regardless of the social class of the children or families involved. If it does not make sense to separate children's problems in this way, their physical and emotional ones, their delinquency and neglect, then that is another matter, one calling for a different kind of solution: comprehensive programs for *children*, not for categories of problems. But as long as we as a society persist in treating children not as a single entity but categorically, then we must exert persistent vigilance to ensure that the ways in which we categorize their problems and attempt to handle them are not simply a reflection of how much we value the social class, skin color, or language of their parents.

Educational neglect: The parents' failure—willingly or unwillingly—to see to it that their children go to school was considered as one of the two least serious kinds of mistreatment—in fact, at the borderline of being considered as mistreatment at all. It was once a very highly valued aspect of parental performance but seems not to be any longer. The JJSP standards do not deal with the matter at all. In reality there are probably very few parents who deliberately keep their children from obtaining an education, and very few of these who would not be mistreating them in some other way as well. A more common problem is linked to the kinds just discussed, a problem enmeshed in a more general pattern, where children are beyond the control of their parents. Truancy in and of itself is one of the status offenses now being questioned as a form of delinquency.

Utilizing the courts' authority to oblige parents to make their children go to school may be a futile gesture, for the parents may be powerless. Very often, especially with troublesome youngsters, the reason they are not in school is not that their parents do not want them to be there but rather that the schools do not want them. Because of the many problems and inequities in our present educational system, educational neglect by parents is a very minor problem compared with institutional neglect of the educational needs of a vast proportion of children. As is mental health, education is integrally involved with a major system apart from the protective one. Hence, it would seem to be a matter best handled within that system, including the legal aspects, and not a matter to be dealt with by the protective mechanisms established for other kinds of mistreatment.

Parental sexual mores: A major preoccupation of the early neglect laws, the sexual behavior of parents, was clearly seen as the least serious of any kind of mistreatment by all the respondents in this study. The JJSP did not establish any standard for dealing with these matters; in fact it explicitly rejected them as grounds for coercive intervention. Attitudes about sexual expression do appear to be changing, and rather rapidly. As part of the change, parents' sexual behavior unrelated to their children is not usually socially defined as deviant, much less as mistreatment warranting protective intervention. But the old laws, some more than a hundred years old, remain on the books. Our data on actual cases indicate that in practice very few, if any, parents are being intruded upon solely because of their sexual habits. The major policy issue, as is so often the case, may be revision of the law to catch up with the changing sexual mores. We are, of course, cognizant that such changes in mores and attitudes are not occurring at the same pace throughout all strata of the society or all sections or regions of the country. Changes in the protective laws will no doubt arouse controversy in many areas. It would seem that the time has come for full emergence of the controversy, and that the older resolutions are no longer valid ones.

Drug/alcohol abuse on the part of parents: Closely linked in the minds of many with sexual morality, rightly or wrongly, is parental abuse of drugs and alcohol. Some underlying commonalities were perceived between the two by community members, while professionals saw them as separate and distinct. However, even community people saw the drug and alcohol issues as more serious than the sexual ones. The JJSP does not deal with the matter, and this is in keeping with its general stance that mistreatment should be defined only with reference to its effects on the child. The nub of the issue is whether addiction of parents that has not had a demonstrably negative effect on the children should be considered as parental failure in and of itself. That it should be is the position taken in early protective legislation, which is still in effect.

In most instances the issue may be academic. It is very difficult to see how chronic alcoholism or drug addiction, which so impair psychological functioning, would not also impair parental performance. How can an otherwise malfunctioning individual exercise competent child care? Our own data indicated that in fully 40 percent of the cases we studied, drug and alcohol abuse were a concomitant of other kinds of mistreatment, often very serious mistreatment. There is one kind of situation in which drug abuse of parents does not affect the care of their children: where someone else is actually caring for the children, especially grandparents and nonaddicted spouses. It is very often these substitute caretakers who seek protective intervention on behalf of the children. There is a high potential for children to be torn between the parties in these situations.

We believe that matters concerning drug and alcohol abuse should be resolved with the children's interests as the primary and only concern. If indeed an addicted individual is capable of caring *independently* and *consistently* for children, then the addiction in and of itself should not be considered grounds for intervention. But when he or she is not, the addiction should be considered as a form of mistreatment in and of itself, and grounds, if necessary, for a court's intrusion. The concept of parental rights does not or should not include the right of parents to destroy themselves and their children.

Having looked at policy implications with respect to specific kinds of mistreatment, we turn now to discussion of more general issues. We begin first with definitional issues involved in statistical and accountability reporting, research, and evaluation. Next, we consider the policy issues in statutory development, and finally those with respect to resource allocation.

ACCOUNTABILITY, RESEARCH, AND EVALUATION

Statistical Reporting

Whether a totally rational social policy is an attainable goal is a moot question, but no policy formulation can be even quasi-rational unless it is informed by accurate factual data. The definitional chaos that has surrounded the problems of child abuse and neglect has precluded such rationality. Such confusion is unnecessary. First of all, with respect to any kind of statistical reporting, be it for purposes of accountability or for the maintenance of central registries, the terms "abuse" and "neglect" should be abandoned. It makes no sense to spend time and energy counting meaningless units. At the very least, the units of analysis should be as precise as the subclassifications developed in this study.

But we see no reason why the precision should stop there. The specific incidents subsumed under each category should also be spelled out. In the research described in chapter 5, a checklist of 104 such incidents sufficed to describe the specific kinds of mistreatment involved in 949 actual cases. Hence, there is no reason to believe that the potential pool of specific incidents is infinite. The accounting of specific aspects of mistreatment is important, since there are differences not only in the relative seriousness of different kinds of mistreatment but within types. Many reporting forms, such as that developed by the National Clearinghouse on Child Abuse and Neglect of the American Humane Association, already provide such detailed listings for the recording of different kinds of physical injuries (broken bones, bruises, and so on). That form also provides information on more precise subclassifications, such as supervision and medical neglect. In its most recent compilation of data from states using the form, the American Humane Association reported that the most common form of mistreatment involved supervision, present in 47 percent of the cases (American Humane Association 1978). It would be well to know how serious was the lack of supervision in this very large proportion of cases. How many of the children were actually left alone? In or out of their homes? During the day or at night or both? Surely the potential consequences of lack of supervision were not the same for all 47 percent, but there is no way of knowing from such grossly aggregated data.

We are not suggesting more paperwork for already overburdened protective workers. On the contrary, we suggest that priorities be set for the kinds of information that should be gathered routinely if we are to come to any better understanding of just what kinds of situations are being processed through our protective networks. If the primary function of child protective work is to protect children, then the highest priority should be accorded to obtaining the very best information about what has happened to the children, what they are being protected from. Any additional information, including the age, sex, and race of the children, is meaningless, unless it can be placed in the context of the nature of the mistreatment. We would suggest that all kinds of statistical reporting forms be designed with this priority in mind, whether the reporting purpose is for funding and resource allocation or for computing estimates of incidence. Additional pieces of information should be added only after this primary purpose is fulfilled.

Politically, more precise information can be a double-edged sword. If the public and its representatives are told, for example, that the problem of child mistreatment involves 6 million children a year, and their referent for the concept of "abused" is a severely battered child, the response might be more sympathetic and generous than if the referent included the less severely mistreated child. As in all politically sensitive matters, greater specificity and factual information are less likely to produce the desired emotional response. However, public policy based on misrepresentation always treads a precarious path. Those accountable to the public, should they be challenged, can find themselves losing battles that might not be lost had they available documentation to justify their positions and use of public funds. The present state of information about child abuse and neglect suggests that those who manage public programs may well be in just that situation.

Research and Program Evaluation

A more rational policy formation requires greater specificity in policy-related research endeavors, including epidemiological, etiological, and evaluative research. Until there is further delineation of that which is to be counted and estimates of its dispersion, epidemiologic and incidence estimation would seem futile. Similarly, etiological research may be premature until there is a more detailed specification of the phenomena for which the causes are being sought. Specification of the manifestations of abusive and neglectful behavior and the development of more refined manifestational taxonomies, such as the classifications developed in this study, would seem necessary before any etiological investigation could take place. Before events can be expected to have a common etiology, the events themselves must share some commonality. Such commonality is yet to be demonstrated in the diverse phenomena that are considered to be manifestations of abuse and neglect.

Finally, more specific data are necessary for evaluative research. The efficacy of any interventive modality can be judged only with reference to the difficulty of achieving the treatment goals. Insofar as both the type and the severity of abuse and neglect might contribute to the overall difficulty of treatment prognostication, comparisons of evaluation outcomes of differing treatment modalities simply are not logical. Hence, a requirement of all evaluative endeavors should be specific measures to assess the types and severity of the mistreatment that have formed the basis for the treatment provision.

Statutory Implications

Throughout we have maintained and demonstrated that the components of child mistreatment are socially defined, and that such definitions, tied as they are to social contexts, are subject to change over time. Insofar as our laws, especially those regulating intimate and personal relationships, should reflect the values of the society, one of the most important issues arising out of this study is the necessity to update our present laws regulating child mistreatment. How they are updated, what should be added and what deleted, may indeed be controversial. But explicit controversy is more apt to result in socially responsive laws than is complacency with the continuance of outmoded ones. Such complacency is often tolerated only because the laws themselves are skirted or ignored, a situation that breeds contempt for the law and those who enforce it, a demoralizing situation for any society. Further, the existence of an archaic statute does not preclude it from being invoked from time to time. Some readers may have smiled at the language and concepts in some of the nineteenth-century mistreatment laws we have quoted. Yet at the very time this book was being written, the New York Society for the Prevention of Cruelty to Children was bringing charges against the Barnum and Bailey Ringling Brothers Circus under an 1840 statute prohibiting the employment of children in carnivals.

Nineteenth-century statutes cannot capture twentieth-century social values or twentieth-century conditions. In part, definitions of child mistreatment are social barometers, barometers that should be measuring minimum standards of care, below which no child should have to suffer. When those minimum standards change, so also should the laws intended to enforce them. Hence, constant review and updating of our laws would seem to be imperative if children are to be adequately protected, and if the rights of their parents are also to be protected. Change thus might encompass both the elimination of some kinds of parental behaviors as socially unacceptable, and the addition of others because of changes in achievable minimum standards. At a time of heightened interest in child mistreatment, it would seem only appropriate that states review their child protective legislation. The elimination of archaic laws is just as necessary as is the addition of new laws to accommodate changing social values and standards.

How should the laws be changed? The research in this book has direct relevance to the issue of greater specificity of the laws that regulate child mistreatment. At the present time these laws are of three types: those that spell out the conditions under which parental authority can be overriden by the state, those mandating the reporting of specific kinds of mistreatment, and those specifying criminal acts and procedures. We deal only with the first two.

The major argument against changing the currently vague and general statutes regulating the management of mistreatment is that the vagueness itself is more adaptable to different community standards and thus serves as a kind of protection against the imposition of one community's or state's values on another. Courts are thus empowered by such vague laws to make more sensitive judgments in individual cases. To be sure, more specific legislation would curtail the power of the courts. However, this argument does not take into account the fact that pluralistic values prevail within a given community just as they do from state to state and from region to region. The interests of a given group in a community may need protection most from other groups in that same community. Providing equal protection of diverse values in child rearing under the law would seem to call for *less* subjectivity on the part of local judiciary, not more. Such subjectivity can be mediated only through more specific laws. Catchall phrases like "the general welfare of children" should be eliminated. Rather, specific kinds of mistreatment should be spelled out in the law, as should criteria for deciding which cases do and do not belong under each category. This is the approach taken by the JJSP, and although we have already expressed dissension from the specifics of some of those criteria, we certainly concur with the general preference for specificity. Culturally diverse values would be better protected by more specific, rather than less specific, definitions and criteria, especially in judging the relative seriousness of given types of mistreatment.

Wald's reasoning is applicable here. He argued that greater specificity of statutes and of legal standards for interpreting would reduce judicial discretion, thus facilitating proper legal representation of all parties in that "lawyers could perform their traditional role of seeing that the judicial standard meet the legal standards" (Wald 1975, p. 1035). This is a very important point. If one solution to the complex problem of protecting the interests of all parties concerned in cases of child mistreatment is the provision of counsel for each, it is no solution at all if the laws preclude their adequate functioning as legal representatives. The data from our empirical study demonstrate both the necessity and the feasibility of more precise legal definitions of mistreatment.

Implications for Resource Allocation

Professionals in this study evidenced both agreement and disagreement about various kinds of mistreatment. The disagreement was most clearly related to the professional roles they play in the protective network. The strongest and most systematic differences found were between those who have primary responsibility for screening cases into or out of protective intervention (police and social workers) and those who have only secondary responsibility in this regard (lawyers and physicians). Is this disagreement undesirable? We believe not. The complexity of interests to be protected in child abuse and neglect demands that management be an interdisciplinary endeavor. The nature of the problems not only provokes multiple perspectives but requires them for optimal resolution.

The identification of child abuse and neglect, as of other forms of deviance, has the potential for two types of error that can occur in any classification process: failure to identify cases that properly belong within the classification, and misidentification of cases as belonging to a category when in fact they do not. Both kinds of error in protective services work can cause harm to children and their families. Hence, it may be that the well-functioning protective services system is one that facilitates the performance of personnel in such a fashion as to guard against both types of error.

Nagi discussed the differences in professional orientations when he applied Scheff's distinctions between the orientations of lawyers and those of physicians to case identification of abuse. For physicians it is far more culpable to dismiss a sick person than to retain a well one, but the legal dictum is that "a man is innocent until proven guilty." The protection of children may be enhanced by the former kind of orientation; the protection of familial integrity may be balanced by the latter. In this study, the role that police and social workers play as primary screeners of cases into protective systems may reflect an orientation similar to Scheff's description of physicians; their primary-type role may give rise to their generally higher ratings of seriousness for various acts. The uniformly low ratings of lawyers similarly may reflect Scheff's concept of the legal perspective. Both perspectives are necessary (Nagi 1977, p. 111; Scheff 1965, p. 69).

It should be stressed here that there is a difference between disagreement and confusion. The currently vague definitions of child abuse and neglect and the lack of specific criteria for making judgments invite confusion. Without some more explicit set of standards, valid disagreement as to whether a particular case meets a standard or not cannot find coherent expression or result in objective resolution. Such confusion is unwarranted. The professionals in this research gave clear evidence of the capacity to make fine distinctions among different incidents and classes of mistreatment; they can agree on what they see. But this professional capacity is neither enhanced nor fully utilized if the laws under which they operate do not make such distinctions. More precise definitions and criteria will not éliminate disagreement that stems from different values and perspectives. There will always be borderline cases, and it is most important with respect to such cases that there be full representation of the different perspectives and interests of the parties involved.

Nagi observed this in discussing his findings regarding professional dissatisfaction with the vague criteria under which they now must operate:

> The problem of "where to draw the line" arises not only in identifying the categories of children to whom the terms *abuse* or *neglect* apply, for example, but also in distinguishing subclasses of children on the basis of the types and degrees of abuse and neglect inflicted. There is always the possibility of borderline cases, wherever the lines may be drawn. To be aware of open meanings for crucial concepts and terms and to recognize vagueness around the lines of differentiation, is not, however, to sanction apathy and the carelessness. Rather, the purpose is to emphasize one of the major problems underlying difficulties in the delivery of services and the administration of justice in this field [Nagi 1976, p. 108].

The results of this study would indicate that both apathy and intellectual despair at resolving the problems of definition and criteria are unwarranted.

Confusion and misrepresentation can arise not just from inadequate concept definitions but also from poorly defined roles. No one profession can represent the perspective of another as well as its own. Social workers should not be called upon to act as lawyers, and lawyers should not act as social workers. If protective systems are to operate optimally, resources must be allocated to them so that the necessary roles and functions can be carried out by personnel qualified to fulfill them, including adequate legal representation and medical advice.

Increased resources alone will not solve the problem of protecting divergent interests. Pluralistic interests can be protected only by pluralistic representation. The data in this study with respect to ethnic variation in perceptions of child mistreatment underscore this point. Not only has the diversity itself been overlooked, but the values of these ethnic groups have been grossly misrepresented in the published writings of leaders in the field. There is no substitute for equality of participation in ensuring equal protection of diverse values. The social definition of child mistreatment brings with it serious social consequences for all involved. Until members of these ethnic groups have full representation at all steps in the definitional process—among the legislators who make the laws and among the professionals who interpret and research the issues—that definitional process cannot be a just one, and the definitions will remain inadequate.

Categories of Mistreatment and Professionals' Ratings

TABLE A-1.   Categories and Ratings by Professionals

OLD AND NEW CHILD ABUSE AND NEGLECT CATEGORIES

			PROFESSIONALS' RATINGS			
Hypothesized Categories	Categories Generated by Factor Analysis	Overall Rating	Lawyers	Pediatricians	Social Workers	Police
Physical Abuse (6.89)						
1. Physical abuse	The parent burned the child on the buttocks and chest with a cigarette.	8.45 (1.19)	8.04 (1.45)	8.44 (1.04)	8.60 (1.20)	8.70 (0.70)
2. Physical abuse	The parent immersed the child in a tub of hot water.	7.88 (2.06)	6.98 (2.67)	8.05 (1.53)	7.92 (2.20)	8.72 (0.66)
3. Physical abuse	The parent hit the child in the face.	6.98 (2.12)	6.23 (2.12)	7.20 (2.05)	7.09 (2.18)	7.38 (1.95)
4. Physical abuse	The parent banged the child against the wall while shaking him by the shoulders.	6.95 (2.24)	5.67 (2.44)	7.04 (1.98)	7.77 (1.78)	6.83 (2.46)
5. Physical abuse	The parent struck the child with a wooden stick.	6.23 (2.68)	5.39 (2.57)	6.43 (2.51)	6.31 (2.79)	7.03 (2.58)
6. Physical abuse	The parents usually punish their child by spanking him with a leather strap.	4.76 (2.54)	3.83 (2.62)	4.55 (2.27)	5.58 (2.47)	4.64 (2.58)
Sexual Abuse (6.67)						
1. Sexual abuse	On one occasion, the parent and the child engaged in sexual intercourse.	8.24 (1.39)	8.02 (1.45)	7.98 (1.61)	8.31 (1.37)	8.73 (0.81)
2. Sexual abuse	On one occasion, the parent and the child engaged in mutual masturbation.	7.27 (1.96)	6.77 (2.32)	6.79 (2.16)	7.52 (1.69)	8.17 (1.12)
3. Sexual abuse	The parent repeatedly suggested to the child that they have sexual relations.	7.05 (2.16)	6.15 (2.32)	6.87 (2.16)	7.49 (1.69)	7.89 (1.12)

4. Sexual abuse	The parent repeatedly showed the child pornographic pictures.	6.13 (2.23)	5.11 (2.58)	5.87 (2.30)	6.47 (2.00)	7.13 (1.85)
5. Sexual abuse	On one occasion, the parent fondled the child's genital area.	6.02 (2.56)	5.69 (2.44)	4.90 (2.61)	6.20 (2.44)	7.82 (1.85)
6. Parental sexual mores	The parents have intercourse where the child can see them.	5.04 (2.48)	3.12 (1.90)	4.37 (2.54)	5.95 (2.15)	6.39 (1.91)
Fostering Delinquency (6.55)						
1. Fostering delinquency	The parents make their child steal small articles from the supermarket.	6.66 (1.86)	6.42 (1.93)	6.88 (2.02)	6.67 (1.77)	6.63 (1.76)
2. Fostering delinquency	The parents make their child take stolen merchandise to a store that sells it illegally.	6.42 (2.06)	5.41 (2.29)	6.40 (1.99)	6.68 (1.90)	7.18 (1.74)
Supervision (5.19)						
1. Supervision	The parents regularly left their child alone outside the house after dark, often as late as midnight.	6.20 (2.17)	4.65 (1.79)	5.84 (2.25)	7.09 (1.88)	6.85 (1.89)
2. Supervision	The parents regularly left their child alone inside the house after dark. Often they did not return until midnight.	6.13 (2.25)	4.53 (1.77)	6.02 (2.44)	6.89 (1.94)	6.54 (2.23)
3. Supervision	The parents regularly left their child alone inside the house during the day. Often they did not return until almost dark.	5.59 (2.21)	4.37 (1.87)	5.65 (2.36)	6.09 (2.00)	6.21 (2.26)
4. Supervision	On one occasion, the parents left their child alone all night.	5.55 (2.52)	4.17 (2.37)	5.09 (2.49)	6.52 (2.32)	6.26 (2.18)
5. Supervision	The parents regularly left their child alone outside the house during the day until almost dark.	4.57 (2.21)	3.67 (2.23)	4.63 (2.20)	4.92 (2.17)	4.90 (1.95)

TABLE A-1. Continued

OLD AND NEW CHILD ABUSE AND NEGLECT CATEGORIES			PROFESSIONALS' RATINGS			
Hypothesized Categories	Categories Generated by Factor Analysis	Overall Rating	Lawyers	Pediatricians	Social Workers	Police
6. Supervision	The parents regularly left their child with their neighbors, without knowing who would assume responsibility and be in charge.	4.45 (2.13)	3.46 (1.70)	4.52 (2.19)	4.93 (2.25)	4.88 (1.85)
7. Housing	The parents live with their child in an old house. Two windows in the living room where the child plays have been broken for some time and the glass has very jagged edges.	4.12 (2.13)	3.22 (1.70)	3.59 (2.19)	4.59 (2.25)	4.98 (1.85)
	Emotional Mistreatment (5.05)					
1. Emotional mistreatment	The parents dress their son in girl's clothing, sometimes putting makeup on him. They keep long curls on him.	5.93 (2.16)	4.93 (2.16)	5.57 (2.54)	6.69 (2.10)	6.20 (1.97)
2. Emotional mistreatment	A child is severely emotionally disturbed. The parents refuse to accept treatment for themselves or for their child.	5.55 (2.40)	4.62 (2.45)	5.37 (2.29)	6.31 (2.32)	5.46 (2.19)
3. Emotional mistreatment	A child has severe behavior problems. The parents refuse to accept treatment for themselves or for their child.	5.03 (2.22)	4.18 (2.10)	4.55 (2.33)	5.86 (2.11)	5.11 (1.83)
4. Emotional mistreatment	The parents are constantly screaming at their child, calling him foul names.	4.95 (2.24)	3.92 (1.86)	5.17 (2.36)	5.43 (2.22)	4.95 (2.19)
5. Emotional mistreatment	The parents ignore their child most of the time, seldom talking with him or listening to him.	4.64 (2.30)	3.60 (2.18)	4.81 (2.28)	5.49 (2.21)	3.93 (1.93)

6. Emotional mistreatment	The parents dress their daughter in boy's clothing and keep her hair cropped short like a boy's.	4.96 (2.37)	5.20 (2.56)	4.56 (2.52)	3.59 (2.03)	4.63 (2.47)
7. Emotional mistreatment	The parents constantly compare their child with his younger sibling, sometimes implying that the child is not really their own.	3.88 (2.30)	5.32 (2.19)	4.82 (2.37)	3.47 (2.10)	4.56 (2.35)
Drug/Alcohol (4.62)						
1. Drug/alcohol	The parents always allow their child to stay around when they have friends over to experiment with cocaine.	7.74 (1.35)	6.41 (2.08)	5.82 (2.46)	5.08 (2.38)	6.14 (2.32)
2. Drug/alcohol	The parent experimented with cocaine while alone taking care of the child.	6.76 (1.70)	5.78 (2.45)	5.26 (2.41)	4.29 (2.10)	5.44 (2.38)
3. Drug/alcohol	The parents use marijuana occasionally, but the father's brother, who is an addict, visits their home often and has used cocaine in front of their child.	6.69 (2.01)	5.22 (2.26)	4.76 (2.23)	4.12 (2.24)	5.09 (2.34)
4. Drug/alcohol	A parent became very drunk while alone taking care of the child.	5.55 (1.97)	5.13 (2.32)	5.30 (2.17)	3.31 (1.83)	4.80 (2.27)
5. Drug/alcohol	A parent got very high smoking marijuana while alone taking care of the child.	6.71 (1.86)	4.75 (2.62)	4.33 (2.56)	3.13 (1.89)	4.61 (2.58)
6. Drug/alcohol	The parents always allow their child to stay around when they have friends over to smoke marijuana.	6.74 (2.00)	4.56 (2.47)	3.86 (2.39)	3.33 (2.37)	4.47 (2.59)
7. Drug/alcohol	The parents always allow their child to stay around when they have drinking parties.	5.00 (1.85)	4.00 (2.37)	4.39 (2.55)	3.27 (1.79)	4.11 (2.28)

TABLE A-1. Continued

OLD AND NEW CHILD ABUSE AND NEGLECT CATEGORIES			PROFESSIONALS' RATINGS			
Hypothesized Categories	Categories Generated by Factor Analysis	Overall Rating	Lawyers	Pedia-tricians	Social Workers	Police
8. Drug/alcohol	The parents leave bottles of whiskey around the house in place where the child can get to them.	4.07 (2.26)	2.74 (1.52)	4.54 (2.40)	4.48 (2.39)	4.33 (2.00)
9. Drug/alcohol	The parents let their child sip out of their glasses when they are drinking whiskey.	3.86 (2.27)	2.79 (1.85)	3.94 (2.48)	4.10 (2.29)	4.66 (1.93)
10. Drug/alcohol	The parents are moderate drinkers, but the father's brother, who is an alcoholic, visits their home often, drinking constantly in front of their child.	3.52 (2.21)	2.87 (1.91)	4.03 (2.42)	3.31 (2.20)	4.02 (2.02)
	Failure-to-Provide (4.23)					
1. Medical neglect	The parents ignored the fact that their child was obviously ill, crying constantly and not eating.	6.81 (2.13)	5.64 (1.97)	6.42 (2.51)	7.79 (1.42)	6.89 (2.08)
2. Medical neglect	The parents ignored their child's complaint of an earache and chronic ear drainage.	6.08 (2.05)	5.15 (1.95)	5.59 (1.98)	6.87 (1.83)	6.41 (2.11)
3. Cleanliness	The parents usually leave their child on a filthy, sodden mattress.	5.77 (2.24)	4.59 (2.17)	5.37 (2.00)	6.23 (2.17)	6.90 (1.99)
4. Medical neglect	The parents have repeatedly failed to keep medical appointments for their child.	5.67 (2.42)	5.07 (2.16)	4.58 (2.21)	6.72 (2.15)	6.15 (2.62)
5. Cleanliness	The parents do not wash their child at all.	5.50 (2.50)	4.91 (2.39)	4.89 (2.33)	6.01 (2.60)	6.08 (2.36)

6.	Medical neglect	The parents do not provide any health care for their child.	5.35 (2.28)	4.65 (2.04)	4.95 (2.41)	5.79 (2.17)	6.03 (2.32)
7.	Cleanliness	The parents do not wash their child's hair or bathe him for weeks at a time.	5.00 (2.29)	4.44 (1.90)	4.31 (2.30)	5.54 (2.29)	5.84 (2.31)
8.	Medical neglect	The parents have not given their child medication prescribed by a physician.	4.58 (2.25)	4.16 (1.98)	3.88 (2.04)	5.05 (2.38)	5.08 (2.32)
9.	Cleanliness	The parents make no effort to keep their child clean.	4.55 (2.33)	3.79 (1.98)	3.91 (2.04)	5.03 (2.53)	5.40 (2.15)
10.	Nutritional neglect	The parents fail to prepare regular meals for their child. The child has often had to fix his own supper.	4.15 (2.14)	3.07 (1.88)	4.05 (2.23)	4.56 (2.12)	4.88 (1.93)
11.	Medical neglect	The parents have not taken their child to a dentist.	3.90 (2.34)	3.08 (1.97)	3.64 (1.98)	4.36 (2.53)	4.56 (2.54)
12.	Housing	The parents live with their child in a hotel apartment. There are no adequate cooking facilities.	3.62 (2.44)	2.95 (2.18)	3.42 (2.30)	3.99 (2.51)	4.02 (2.65)
13.	Housing	The parents live with their child in a small rented house. No one ever straightens up.	3.61 (2.60)	2.68 (1.94)	3.29 (2.33)	4.24 (2.93)	4.18 (2.66)
14.	Medical neglect	The parents have failed to obtain an eye examination for their child.	3.44 (2.19)	2.54 (1.55)	3.23 (2.02)	3.95 (2.46)	3.71 (2.16)
15.	Clothing	The parents do not see to it that their child has clean clothing.	3.31 (1.94)	2.53 (1.36)	3.67 (2.25)	3.54 (2.04)	3.38 (1.71)
16.	Nutritional neglect	The parents always insist that their child clean his plate, which they heap full of food.	3.31 (2.15)	2.73 (1.67)	3.28 (2.10)	3.95 (2.44)	2.75 (1.81)
17.	Cleanliness	The parents do not see to it that their child brushes his teeth.	2.79 (1.99)	2.53 (1.70)	2.72 (1.92)	2.86 (2.15)	3.14 (2.16)

TABLE A-1. Continued

OLD AND NEW CHILD ABUSE AND NEGLECT CATEGORIES

Hypothesized Categories	Categories Generated by Factor Analysis	Overall Rating	PROFESSIONALS' RATINGS			
			Lawyers	Pedia-tricians	Social Workers	Police
	Educational Neglect (4.06)					
1. Educational neglect	The parents frequently keep their child out of school.	4.56 (1.90)	4.47 (1.84)	4.68 (1.94)	4.66 (1.96)	4.27 (1.82)
2. Educational neglect	The parents know their child is often truant, but they don't do anything about it.	4.44 (1.83)	4.00 (1.73)	4.49 (2.00)	4.80 (1.67)	4.31 (1.94)
3. Educational neglect	The parents frequently let their school-age child stay home from school for no reason.	4.22 (2.07)	3.80 (1.84)	4.58 (2.04)	4.31 (2.21)	4.05 (2.01)
4. Educational neglect	The parents never see to it that their children do any homework. They let them watch TV all evening.	3.09 (1.87)	2.58 (1.66)	3.20 (1.83)	3.34 (2.11)	3.02 (1.51)
	Parental Sexual Mores (3.21)					
1. Parental sexual mores	The parents permit a relative who is a prostitute to bring customers to their house.	5.10 (2.31)	4.74 (2.28)	4.58 (2.31)	5.39 (2.26)	5.85 (2.31)
2. Parental sexual mores	A divorced mother, who has custody of her child, is a prostitute.	3.40 (2.23)	2.64 (1.80)	3.43 (2.13)	3.21 (2.10)	4.84 (2.58)
3. Parental sexual mores	A divorced mother, who has custody of her child, brings home different men often.	3.37 (2.12)	2.63 (1.78)	3.46 (2.13)	3.49 (2.18)	3.94 (2.17)
4. Parental sexual mores	A divorced mother, who has custody of her child, is a lesbian.	2.62 (2.29)	1.82 (1.50)	2.32 (2.22)	2.41 (2.09)	4.56 (2.64)

5. Parental sexual mores	A divorced father, who has custody of his child, is a homosexual.	4.72 (3.02)	2.32 (1.91)	2.67 (2.19)	1.69 (1.23)	2.62 (2.24)
6. Parental sexual mores	A divorced mother, who has custody of her child, has a steady boyfriend with whom she has intercourse often.	2.80 (2.04)	1.83 (1.68)	2.52 (2.26)	1.79 (1.34)	2.14 (1.87)
Deleted Vignettes						
1. Emotional neglect	The parents have kept their child locked in since birth. They feed and bathe the child and provide basic physical care.	8.51 (0.84)	8.52 (1.36)	8.41 (1.35)	7.82 (1.97)	8.33 (1.47)
2. Nutritional neglect	The parents regularly fail to feed the child for periods of at least twenty-four hours.	7.74 (1.63)	7.52 (1.60)	7.45 (1.85)	6.24 (2.21)	7.26 (1.89)
3. Drug/alcohol	Both parents are drug addicts.	7.23 (2.16)	6.60 (2.35)	5.78 (2.62)	4.59 (2.71)	6.05 (2.62)
4. Nutritional neglect	The parents feed only milk to their child.	6.00 (2.43)	6.85 (1.95)	5.23 (2.52)	4.68 (2.29)	5.81 (2.41)
5. Nutritional neglect	The parents brought their child to the hospital three times for being underweight. Each time the child gained weight during his hospital stay.	5.59 (2.61)	6.18 (2.34)	5.91 (2.31)	3.96 (2.47)	5.55 (2.53)
6. Fostering delinquency	The parents allow an uncle to store stolen merchandise in their house.	4.40 (2.40)	3.45 (2.30)	3.90 (2.12)	3.38 (2.07)	3.70 (2.24)
7. Housing	The parents live with their child in a skid row neighborhood. Derelicts sleep in the doorway of the building in which they live.	3.32 (2.20)	4.04 (2.54)	2.97 (2.16)	2.76 (2.09)	3.35 (2.34)
8. Clothing	The parents always let their child run around the house and yard without any clothes on.	4.90 (2.10)	3.70 (2.09)	2.50 (1.82)	2.63 (1.67)	3.30 (2.09)

TABLE A-1. Continued

OLD AND NEW CHILD ABUSE AND NEGLECT CATEGORIES

Hypothesized Categories	Categories Generated by Factor Analysis	PROFESSIONALS' RATINGS				
		Overall Rating	Lawyers	Pedia-tricians	Social Workers	Police
9. Supervision	On several different occasions the parents left their child with a grandmother for periods of time up to ten days without providing any means of contacting them.	3.26 (1.98)	2.49 (1.73)	3.67 (2.03)	3.40 (1.97)	3.24 (2.02)
10. Clothing	The parents seldom notice how their child is dressed.	2.72 (1.78)	2.26 (1.53)	2.91 (1.79)	2.84 (1.92)	2.73 (1.62)
11. Physical abuse	The parents usually punish their child by spanking him with the hand.	2.40 (2.07)	2.08 (1.90)	3.00 (2.43)	2.39 (1.95)	1.92 (1.77)
12. Housing	The parents live in an apartment with their two childen. They have few furnishings, a bed where the parents sleep, and two mattresses where each of the children sleeps.	2.06 (1.57)	1.59 (1.14)	1.69 (1.04)	2.54 (1.96)	2.21 (1.49)
13. Housing	The parents live with their child in a small two-room apartment. The three of them have lived there for several months.	1.58 (1.31)	1.18 (0.43)	1.79 (1.59)	1.74 (1.55)	1.44 (0.88)

Research Methods Used in Chapter 5, and Additional Tables

Research Method Used in Chapter 5

Measures of Mistreatment

The measures of mistreatment were based on the ratings obtained from the probation officers and social workers, and numerical values were attached to each of the acts of mistreatment that had been noted in each case in the study. These numerical values represent the mean rating obtained for that act from these protective workers. From these numerical ratings of each act, scoring procedures were developed that would capture different kinds of information.

Three different types of scores were developed. The first was intended to capture the seriousness of the incidents without reference to the numbers of items checked across categories or within categories. For each of the eight categories of mistreatment in each case, a score was given based on the mean of the scores in the category (the sum of the scores divided by the number of items checked). The second type of score captured the information on seriousness as well as the number of different incidents involved, for each case in each category (the sum of the seriousness scores on the incidents checked in each category). Finally, a third type of score was based only on the number of items checked in each category. In addition, overall case summary scores were developed: (1) a mean score based on the sum of scores on all items across categories divided by the number of items checked; (2) a sum of all the seriousness scores—that is, all scores added together; and (3) the sum of the number of all items checked. Through these three different types of scoring it was possible to capture multiple dimensions of mistreatment. Parents may fail in many different ways. Some may fail in a variety of ways, none of them very harmful to their children. Others may fail in only one way, but in a way exceedingly harmful to their children. Still others may fail in many ways, all relatively harmful. The different scoring procedures were intended to delineate these different dimensions of mistreatment.

Degree of seriousness and disposition: The effects of the seriousness of mistreatment might occur in two ways, first the seriousness of the kind of mistreatment itself—for example, physical abuse versus failure-to-provide. The second is the degree of seriousness within a given category—for example, a skull fracture versus a bruise. We first examined the relationship between the degree of seriousness within types of mistreatment in relation to whether the case had been court-adjudicated or not. We did this by testing the significance of the difference of the mean ratings of seriousness in each type of disposition for each kind of mistreatment. In this analysis, for each type of mistreatment tested, only those cases were used where that kind of mistreatment existed. For example, in investigating failure to provide, the mean seriousness scores of all court cases that involved failure to provide were compared with the mean seriousness scores of all failure-to-provide cases in the voluntary sector. Thus the presence or absence of a particular kind of mistreatment was not at issue, only the degree of seriousness of the incidents in the particular kind of mistreatment. Additionally we compared all court and noncourt cases on the two case summary scores, the mean seriousness, which is not influenced by the number of separate specific acts of mistreatment, and the sum seriousness, which is.

As discussed in the chapter, there were no significant differences in these two kinds of dispositions, court and noncourt, in the degree of seriousness of any particular kind of mistreatment except one, physical injury. There was a significant difference on the total case mean seriousness scores, and an even greater difference in the sum seriousness scores. From this we concluded (1) that disposition is more influenced by the relative seriousness of the type of mistreatment, rather than the degree of seriousness within type, and (2) the greater the number of different incidents involved and the greater number of different kinds of mistreatment, the more likely that court intervention had been sought.

For these reasons it became apparent that combinations of mistreatment were more important determinants of disposition than was the degree of seriousness. Hence the next step in the analyses was one that could capture this information about combinations. This is the analysis presented in the text based on discriminant function analysis.

TABLE B-1.   **Mean Seriousness of Categories of Mistreatment by Type of Disposition**

| | TYPE OF DISPOSITION | | | |
| | Court | | Voluntary | |
Category of Mistreatment	N	$\bar{X}$	N	$\bar{X}$
Failure-to-provide	(131)	5.23	(266)	5.07
Inadequate physical environs	(127)	3.35	(269)	3.19
Emotional mistreatment	(161)	5.81	(433)	5.79
Child behavior problem	(72)	4.27	(236)	4.40

TABLE B–1.   Continued

Category of Mistreatment	TYPE OF DISPOSITION			
	Court		Voluntary	
	N	$\bar{X}$	N	$\bar{X}$
Drug/alcohol (child)	(24)	6.91	(51)	6.75
	(115)	5.13	(209)	5.22
Sexual abuse	(65)	7.48	(77)	7.22
Physical injury	(114)	7.66*	(167)	7.51
$\bar{X}$ seriousness	(278)	5.66*	(671)	5.28
Sum seriousness	(278)	30.60†	(671)	23.15

* $p < .05$.
† $p < .001$.

Discriminant function analyses: The mathematical objective of discriminant analysis is to combine the discriminating variables in such a way that groups are forced to be as statistically distinct as possible. If, in fact, the variables under scrutiny do not distinguish groups, the results of the analysis will not be statistically signifi-cant. The maximum number of functions that can be derived from a given set of data is dependent on the number of variables and the number of actual groups. The maximum number of functions is one less than the number of variables, or the number of groups, whichever is less. Our first set of analyses, presented in chapter 5, had two groups, the extreme outcome categories of court removal and voluntary supervision. The second set of analyses, below, had three groups: court removal, voluntary removal, and voluntary in-home supervision. When comparing two outcome types, we sought to derive one function from the mistreatment variables, and when comparing three outcomes, two functions. Then through classifica-tion procedures the predictive capacity of the variables in the derived functions were tested in relation to the disposition cate-gories. In each of the tables the first data presented are the discrim-inant function coefficients. This coefficient represents the relative contribution of its associated variable to the function. The F-ratio given for each variable is a test of the statistical significance of the variables' addition to the separation of the groups above and beyond the separation produced by the other variables. The addi-tional statistics given in the table are interpreted as follows: the eigenvalue is a measure of the relative importance of the function. In a two-group problem with only one derived function, the relative importance of two or more functions is not at issue as it is when the three-group problem is investigated. The canonical correlation when squared can be interpreted as the proportion of total variance in the discriminant function explained by the groupings. In the last two columns of the tables the proportion of cases in each disposition involving each kind of mistreatment is given.

Each table is divided into two parts. The first part gives the data on the discriminant functions and the means for each dispositional group on each kind of mistreatment; the second, the results of the classification procedure. The means may be interpreted as the percentage of cases in the outcome type that involved each of the kinds of mistreatment.

In the classification procedure, each case is classified according to its probability of belonging to a group based on its score on the derived function. This rule of highest probability defines a strict dividing line. If there is a high proportion of "marginal" cases—that is, cases with relatively close probabilities of being assigned to one group or another—the predictive accuracy of the classification can be expected to decline.

Three-group discriminant function analyses (court removal versus voluntary removal versus in-home supervision): The three types of case dispositions examined here are not conceptually distinct, overlapping as they do on the dimensions or removal and court adjudication. Hence it could be anticipated that it would be more difficult to distinguish among the three groups of cases, since in fact they do have these overlapping characteristics. These facts are borne out in the results. The proportions of cases correctly classified is not as high as in the two-group comparisons (court removal versus voluntary in-home supervision) presented in chapter 5. Equally important in the data from three counties, it was not possible to derive a statistically significant function—a set of characteristics that would distinguish the three groups from one another. In distinguishing between two groups, only one function is sought, but with three groups, two are sought.

In distinguishing among the three types of removal in these three counties, it is possible to classify correctly 70 percent of the cases. However, this degree of accuracy of classification is not at all uniform across the types of disposition. Seventy-nine percent of the voluntary in-home supervision cases are correctly classified, but only 39 percent of the court-removal cases are. In other words, the information about the kind of mistreatment and the caretaker's attitudes is less useful in distinguishing between the two types of cases where the children are removed: through the courts or voluntarily. For these counties the best summary statement might be that the *absence* of the more serious kinds of mistreatment—physical injury, sexual abuse, moral/legal transgressions, child's drugs/alcohol use, and behavior disorder in the child combined with the caretaker wanting emotional help, and *not* wanting removal of the child—increases the likelihood that a case will be managed voluntarily and at home. The *presence* of each of these factors increases the likelihood that the children will be removed, but does not influence as greatly whether that removal will be by the courts or voluntarily.

For the other county, knowledge that a case involves physical injury or sexual abuse and/or that the caretaker wanted removal and did not want emotional help results in the correct classification of 71 percent of the cases. The presence of each of these factors increases the likelihood of court removal. In distinguishing among the three types of disposition, the following information leads to the correct classification of 70 percent of the cases: presence of physical injury, caretaker *not* wanting emotional help, and the caretaker wanting removal of the child. Physical injury and caretaker not wanting emotional help increase the probability of court removal. The caretaker wanting removal of the child increases the likelihood of voluntary removal. The *absence* of any of these three factors increases the likelihood of the case being managed at home in the voluntary sector.

TABLE B-2. Discriminant Analysis and Classification: Three Disposition Types by Categories of Mistreatment and Caretaker Attitudes

A: County 1

| Category of Mistreatment | PERCENTAGE OF CASES IN DISPOSITION TYPE | | | F-Ratio |
	Court Removal	Voluntary Removal	Voluntary Home	
Failure-to-provide	45%	36%	50%	1.86
Physical injury	46	22	24	9.05†
Gross neglect	43	38	48	0.87
Emotional neglect	50	74	61	5.99*
Sexual abuse	26	16	13	3.31
Moral/legal	36	46	33	2.04
Child behavior	21	53	23	14.66†

TABLE B–2. Continued

A: County 1

Category of Mistreatment	PERCENTAGE OF CASES IN DISPOSITION TYPE			F-Ratio
	Court Removal	Voluntary Removal	Voluntary Home	
Drug/alcohol (parents)	06	14	04	3.23
Parents want emotional help	22	38	49	8.83†
Parents want removal	30	68	05	58.07†

* p < .05, 2 and 304 d.f.
† p < .01.
Eigenvalue: .44   .18
Canonical correlations: .56   .39

Classification

Actual group	N	PREDICTED GROUP MEMBERSHIP		
		I	II	III
I Court removal	(118)	45.8% (54)	22.0% (26)	32.2% (38)
II Voluntary removal	(83)	10.8% (9)	66.3% (55)	22.9% (19)
III Voluntary home	(106)	22.6% (24)	5.7% (6)	71.6% (76)

Percent of cases correctly classified: 60.26%.

B: Counties 2, 3, and 4

Category of Mistreatment	PERCENTAGE OF CASES IN DISPOSITION TYPE			F-Ratio
	Court Removal	Voluntary Removal	Voluntary Home	
Failure-to-provide	50%	42%	36%	2.51
Physical injury	41	24	25	4.50*
Gross neglect	50	49	36	3.62
Emotional neglect	81	80	60	10.64†
Sexual abuse	17	18	08	4.89*
Moral/legal	52	41	23	16.17†
Child behavior	32	50	31	5.31*
Drug/Alcohol (child) (parents)	10	12	05	2.80
Parents want emotional help	20	37	47	9.67†

TABLE B-2. Continued

B: Counties 2, 3, and 4

Category of Mistreatment	Court Removal	Voluntary Removal	Voluntary Home	F-Ratio
	PERCENTAGE OF CASES IN DISPOSITION TYPE			
Parents want removal	37	53	06	73.68†

* p < .05, 2 and 516 d.f.
† p < .01.
Eigenvalue: .47   .18
Canonical correlation: .56   .38

Classification

Actual Group	N	PREDICTED GROUP MEMBERSHIP		
		I	II	III
I Court removal	(74)	39.2% (29)	31.1% (23)	29.7% (22)
II Voluntary removal	(77)	18.2% (14)	54.5% (42)	27.3% (21)
III Voluntary home	(368)	12.8% (47)	7.9% (29)	79.3% (292)

Percent of cases correctly classified: 69.94%.

TABLE B-3. Resources Recommended by Availability and Acceptance of Recommendation

RESOURCE	CASES FOR WHICH RECOMMENDED*	CASES FOR WHICH RECOMMENDED ACCEPTING	CASES FOR WHICH RECOMMENDED AVAILABLE
Casework/counseling with protective agent	73%	84%	80%
Mental health	58	43	99
Parent education	52	52	94
Instruction in money management	21	51	92
Parents Anonymous	27	33	95
Homemaker/housekeeper	15	72	59
Day care/nursery	22	70	78
Respite care/babysitting	29	77	74
Increased income	20	94	9
Employment	13	76	55
Housing	27	78	58

* N = 910 due to missing information.

TABLE B-4. Type of Mistreatment by Selected Family Characteristics

	FTP	FTP + OTHER	FTP + PA	PA	PA + OTHER	OTHER/NOT	FTP OR PA (TOTALS*)
Welfare Recipient							
YES	68%	68%	60%	35%	42%	51%	324
	(97)	(177)	(78)	(33)	(23)	(129)	537
NO	32%	32%	40%	65%	58%	49%	276
	(47)	(82)	(52)	(62)	(32)	(123)	398
TOTALS	144	259	130	95	55	252	935
Able to Meet Basic Costs							
YES	31%	29%	30%	53%	45%	50%	238
	(43)	(74)	(39)	(50)	(24)	(124)	354
NO	69%	71%	70%	47%	55%	50%	362
	(97)	(181)	(90)	(44)	(29)	(123)	564
TOTALS	140	181	129	94	53	147	744
Have Working Telephone							
YES	53%	63%	52%	72%	89%	83%	412
	(76)	(159)	(67)	(68)	(49)	(206)	625
NO	47%	37%	48%	28%	11%	17%	188
	(66)	(94)	(61)	(27)	(6)	(41)	295
TOTALS	142	253	128	95	55	247	920
Have Automobile							
YES	50%	59%	55%	78%	78%	76%	396
	(70)	(145)	(69)	(73)	(42)	(185)	584
NO	50%	41%	45%	22%	22%	24%	204
	(70)	(99)	(56)	(21)	(12)	(58)	316
TOTALS	140	244	125	94	54	243	900

See end of table (p. 283) for footnote.

TABLE B-4. Continued

	FTP	FTP + OTHER	FTP + PA	PA	PA + OTHER	OTHER/NOT	FTP OR PA
Housing Part of Complaint							
YES	26%	34%	26%	7%	13%	10%	116
	(34)	(86)	(33)	(7)	(7)	(26)	193
NO	74%	66%	74%	93%	87%	90%	489
	(99)	(165)	(94)	(86)	(48)	(225)	717
TOTALS	133	251	127	93	55	251	910
Father in home							TOTALS*
YES	21%	25%	40%	53%	43%	27%	209
	(31)	(65)	(49)	(49)	(23)	(68)	285
NO	79%	75%	60%	47%	57%	73%	637
	(113)	(194)	(75)	(43)	(30)	(182)	922
TOTALS	144	259	124	92	53	250	922
*Father employed**							
YES	68%	58%	66%	83%	65%	113	453
	(45)	(76)	(61)	(68)	(31)	(71)	352
NO	32%	42%	34%	17%	35%	29%	189
	(21)	(55)	(31)	(14)	(17)	(46)	184
TOTALS	66	131	92	82	48	159	578
Number of Children in Family							
1	56	27	75	12	39	63	272
	(38.4%)	(28.1%)	(28.4%)	(22.2%)	(30.0%)	(24.4%)	(28.7%)
2	38	39	75	20	44	82	298
	(26.0%)	(40.6%)	(28.4%)	(37.0%)	(33.8%)	(31.8%)	(31.4%)
3	28	16	57	18	22	54	195
	(19.2%)	(16.7%)	(21.6%)	(33.3%)	(16.9%)	(20.9%)	(20.6%)

	4 or more	14	57	4	25	59	183
	24 (16.4%)	14 (14.6%)	57 (21.6%)	4 (7.4%)	25 (19.2%)	59 (22.9%)	183 (19.3%)
TOTALS	146	96	264	54	130	258	948
Child/Adult Ratio							
.5–1.9	22 (15.1%)	23 (24.0%)	41 (15.5%)	10 (18.2%)	23 (17.7%)	39 (15.2%)	158 (16.7%)
2–2.9	57 (39.0%)	46 (47.9%)	87 (33.0%)	30 (54.5%)	55 (42.3%)	87 (33.9%)	362 (38.2%)
3–3.9	27 (18.5%)	15 (15.6%)	62 (23.5%)	10 (18.2%)	29 (22.3%)	81 (31.5%)	224 (23.6%)
4 +	40 (27.4%)	12 (12.5%)	74 (28.0%)	5 (9.1%)	23 (17.7%)	50 (19.5%)	204 (21.5%)
TOTALS	146	96	264	55	130	257	948 (100%)

* Totals of less than 949 indicate information missing.

TABLE B–5. Referral Pathways

	N	%
Private Individual		
Private individual	212	22.3
Law enforcement	142	14.9
DSW–DPSS	7	0.7
School	20	2.1
Medical	34	3.6
Social agency	15	1.6
Caretaker	2	0.2
Law Enforcement		
Private individual	2	0.2
Law enforcement	55	5.8
DSW–DPSS	1	0.1
Medical	4	0.4
Social agency	4	0.4
Caretaker	1	0.1
DSW–DPSS		
Private individual	2	0.2
Law enforcement	19	2.0
DSW–DPSS	67	7.1
Medical	5	0.5
Social agency	3	0.3
School		
Private individual	2	0.2
Law enforcement	23	2.4
DSW–DPSS	2	0.2
School	43	4.5
Medical	3	0.3
Social agency	4	0.4
Medical		
Private individual	7	0.7
Law enforcement	9	0.9
Medical	89	9.4
Social agency	1	0.1
Caretaker	4	0.4
Social Agency		
Private individual	1	0.1
Law enforcement	8	0.8
DSW–DPSS	2	0.2
School	2	0.2
Medical	6	0.6
Social agency	22	2.4
Caretaker	1	0.1
Caretaker		
Private individual	9	0.9
Law enforcement	26	2.7
DSW–DPSS	15	1.6
School	1	0.1
Medical	11	1.2
Social agency	3	0.3
Caretaker	60	6.3
TOTAL	919	100.0

TABLE B-6. Category of Mistreatment by Mean Seriousness, Overall Frequency, and Frequency of Single Occurrence

CATEGORY OF MISTREATMENT	MEAN SERIOUSNESS OF CASES	NUMBER OF CASES INVOLVING EACH KIND OF MISTREATMENT	NUMBER OF CASES INVOLVING ONLY PARTICULAR CATEGORY OF MISTREATMENT (EXCLUSIVE OF EMOTIONAL)
Physical Injury	8.03	281	96
Sexual Abuse	7.79	142	50
Drug/Alcohol (child)	7.06	75	10
Emotional	5.81	594	52
Moral/Legal	5.41	324	41
Failure-to-provide	4.89	397	146
Child Behavior Disorder	4.32	308	115
Inadequate Physical Environs	3.62	396	**
TOTAL			510

** Failure-to-Provide and Inadequate Environs not distinguished in this computation.

Bibliography

Abbott, Grace. 1938. *The Child and the State*. Chicago: The University of Chicago Press. Vol. 1, 1938*a;* vol. 2, 1938*b*.

Allen, H. D.; Kosciolek, E. J.; ten Bensel, R. W.; and Raile, R. B. 1969. "The Battered Child Syndrome, Part II: Social and Psychiatric Aspects." *Minnesota Medicine* 52 (January 1969): 155–56.

American Humane Association. 1978. *National Analysis of Official Child Neglect and Abuse Reporting: An Executive Summary*.

———, Children's Division. 1972. *A National Symposium on Child Abuse*. Denver, Colo.

American Social Science Association. 1876. *Proceedings of the Conference of Charities*. Albany: Joel Munsell.

Barrows, Isabel C., ed. 1889. *Proceedings of the National Conference of Charities and Correction*. Boston: Geo. H. Ellis.

Bell, Cynthia, and Mlyniec, Wallace J. 1974. "Preparing for a Neglect Proceeding: A Guide for the Social Worker." *Public Welfare* 32 (Fall 1974): 26–37.

Berkeley Planning Associates. 1977. *Executive Summary, Evaluation of the Joint OCD/SRS National Demonstration Program on Child Abuse and Neglect, 1974–1977*. December 1977. Mimeographed.

Billingsley, Andrew. 1964. "The Role of the Social Worker in a Child Protective Agency." *Child Welfare* 43 (1964): 472–92, 497.

———, and Giovannoni, Jeanne M. 1972. *Children of the Storm*. New York: Harcourt Brace Jovanovich.

Billingsley, A.; Giovannoni, J. M.; and Purvine, M. E. 1969. *Studies in Child Protective Services*. Mimeographed.

Blackstone, Sir William. 1793. *Commentaries on the Laws of England in Four Books*. 12th ed. With notes and additions by Edward Christian. Bk. 1, chap. 16: "Of Parent and Child." London.

BOARDMAN, HELEN. 1962. "A Project to Rescue Children from Inflicted Injuries." *Social Work* 7 (January 1962): 43–51.

BOEHM, BERNICE. 1962. "An Assessment of Family Adequacy in Protective Cases." *Child Welfare* 41 (1962): 10–16.

BOPP, WILLIAM J., and SCHULTZ, DONALD O. 1972. *A Short History of American Law Enforcement.* Springfield, Ill.: Charles C Thomas.

BRACE, CHARLES LORING. 1876. "The 'Placing Out' Plan for Homeless and Vagrant Children." *Proceedings of the Conference of Chartres, Saratoga, September, 1876.* Albany: Joel Munsell.

———. 1880. *Dangerous Classes of New York.* 3d ed. New York: Wynkoop and Hallenbeck.

BREMNER, ROBERT H., ed. 1970. *Children and Youth in America: A Documentary History.* Cambridge: Harvard University Press. Vol. 1, 1970a; vol. 2, 1970b; vol. 3, 1970c.

BRONFENBRENNER, URIE. 1958. "Socialization and Social Class Through Time and Space." In E. C. Maccoby, Newcomb, T. M, and Hartley, E. L., eds., *Readings in Social Psychology.* 3d ed. New York: Holt, Rinehart and Winston.

CAIN, V. 1978. "Concern for Children in Placement." Cited in 1977 Analysis of Child Abuse and Neglect, National Center on Child Abuse and Neglect.

CARSTENS, C. C. 1914. "The Laws for Child Protection." In S. M. Lindsay, ed., *Legislation for the Protection of Animals and Children.* New York: Columbia University.

Child Welfare League of America. 1973. *Standards for Child Protective Service.* Rev. ed. (1973 printing). New York: Child Welfare League of America.

COHEN, M. I.; MULFORD, R. M.; and PHILBRICK, E. 1967. *Neglecting Parents: A Study of Psychosocial Characteristics.* Denver: American Humane Association.

COHEN, STEPHEN, and SUSSMAN, ALAN. 1975. "The Incidence of Child Abuse in the U.S." *Child Welfare,* 1975, pp. 54–56, 432–443.

———. 1975. *Reporting Child Abuse and Neglect: Guidelines for Legislation.* Cambridge: Ballinger Publishing Co.

COLLINS, J. G. 1974. "The Role of the Law Enforcement Agency." In Helfer, Ray E., and Kempe, C. Henry, eds., *The Battered Child.* Chicago: University of Chicago Press.

CRONBACH, LEE J. 1951. "Coefficient Alpha and the Internal Structure of Tests." *Psychometrika* 16 (September 1951): 297–333.

DALY, BARBARA. 1969. "Willful Child Abuse and State Reporting Statutes." *University of Miami Law Review* 23 (1969): 283–346.

DAVENPORT-HILL, FLORENCE. 1889. *Children of the State.* London: Macmillan & Co.

DAVIS, A., and HAVINGSHURST, R. J. 1946. "Social Class and Color Differences in Childrearing." *American Sociological Review* 2 (1946): 698–710.

DeFrancis, Vincent. 1955. *The Fundamentals of Child Protection.* Denver: American Humane Association.

———. 1961. *Protective Services and Community Expectations.* Denver: Children's Division, American Humane Association. Presented Apr. 10, 1961.

———. 1963. *Child Abuse: Preview of a Nationwide Survey.* Denver: American Humane Association.

———. 1963. "Parents Who Abuse." *PTA Magazine,* November 1963.

———. 1965. *Protecting the Child Victim of Sex Crimes.* Children's Division, American Humane Association, Publication 28. Denver. Presented May 25, 1965.

DeFrancis, Vincent, and Lucht, Carroll L. 1974. *Child Abuse Legislation of the 1970s.* Denver: American Humane Association.

Elmer, Elizabeth. 1960. "Abused Young Children Seen in Hospitals." *Social Work* 5 (1960): 98–102.

Erlanger, Howard S. 1975. "Social Class Differences in Parents' Use of Physical Punishment." In S. K. Sternmetz and M. A. Strauss, eds., *Violence in the Family.* New York: Dodd, Mead and Co.

Evans, S. L.; Rinehart, J. B.; and Succop, R. A. ---- "Failure to Thrive: A Study of 45 Children and Their Families." *Journal of American Academy of Child Psychiatry* 2: (1963) 440–57.

Folks, Homer. 1902. *The Care of Destitute, Neglected and Delinquent Children.* New York: Macmillan.

Fox, Sanford J. 1971. *The Law of Juvenile Courts in a Nutshell.* St. Paul: West Publishing Co.

Garbino, James; Crouter, Ann; and Sherman, Deborah. 1977. "Using Report Data in Defining the Community Context of Child Abuse and Neglect." Paper for a workshop of the 2d National Conference on Child Abuse and Neglect, Houston, April 1977. Mimeographed.

Garrett, Karen Ann, and Rossi, Peter H. 1978. "Judging the Seriousness of Child Abuse." *Medical Anthropology* (Winter, part 3, 1978): 1–48.

Gelles, R. J. 1973. "Child Abuse Psychopathology: A Sociological Critique and Reformulation." *American Journal of Orthopsychiatry* 43 (July 1973): 611–21.

———. 1977. "Problems in Defining and Labeling Child Abuse." Paper presented to the Study Group on Problems in the Prediction of Child Abuse and Neglect. Wilmington, Del., June 27, 1977.

Gil, David. 1970. *Violence Against Children.* Cambridge: Harvard University Press.

———. 1976. *The Challenge of Social Equality.* Cambridge: Schenckman Press.

GIL, DAVID, and NOBLE, JOHN. 1967. *Public Knowledge, Attitudes and Opinions About Child Abuse in the United States*. Papers in Social Welfare, No. 14. Waltham, Mass., Florence Heller Graduate School for Advanced Studies in Social Welfare.

GIOVANNONI, J. M., and BILLINGSLEY, A. 1970. "Child Neglect Among the Poor: A Study of Parental Adequacy in Families of Three Ethnic Groups." *Child Welfare* 49 (April 1970): 196–204.

GIOVANNONI, J. M.; CONKLIN, J.; and IIYAMA, P. *Child Abuse and Neglect: Perspectives from Child Development Knowledge*. San Francisco: R&E Associates.

GOLDSTEIN, JOSEPH; FREUD, ANNA; and SOLNIT, ALBERT. 1973. *Beyond the Best Interests of the Child*. New York: Free Press. Revised 1979.

GROENEVELD, L. G., and GIOVANNONI, J. M. 1977a. "Variations in Child Abuse Reporting: The Influence of State and County Characteristics." Mimeographed.

———. 1977b. "The Deposition of Child Abuse and Neglect Cases." *Social Work Research and Abstracts* 13 (Summer 1977): 36–47.

HARMON, HARRY. 1967. *Modern Factor Analysis*. Chicago: University of Chicago Press.

HEAPS, WILLARD A. 1974. *Juvenile Justice*. New York: The Seabury Press.

HELFER, RAY E. 1974. "The Responsibility and Role of the Physician." In Ray E. Helfer and C. Henry Kempe, eds., *The Battered Child*. Chicago: University of Chicago Press.

———. 1975. *Child Abuse and Neglect: The Diagnostic Process and Treatment Programs*. Office of Child Development.

———, and KEMPE, C. HENRY. 1974. *The Battered Child*. Chicago: University of Chicago Press.

HOLMES, S. A.; BARNHARDT, C.; CANTONI, L.; and REYMER, E. 1975. "Working with the Parent in Child Abuse Cases." *Social Casework* 56 (1975): 3–12.

Institute of Judicial Administration, American Bar Association Juvenile Justice Standards Project. 1977. *Standards Relating to Abuse and Neglect*. Tentative draft. Cambridge: Ballinger Publishing Co.

ISAACS, JACOB L. 1972. "The Role of the Lawyer in Child Abuse Cases." In C. Henry Kempe and Ray E. Helfer, eds., *Helping the Battered Child and His Family*. Philadelphia: J. B. Lippincott.

KADUSHIN, ALFRED. 1974. *Child Welfare Services*. New York: Macmillan.

KAHN, ALFRED. 1951. *Police and Children: A Study of New York City's Juvenile Aid Bureau*. Citizen's Committee on the Children of New York City.

KATZ, SANFORD. 1971. *When Parents Fail: The Law's Response to Family Breakdown*. Boston: Beacon Press.

———. 1975. "Child Neglect Laws in America." *Family Law Quarterly* 9 (Spring 1975): 372.

KEMPE, C. HENRY, and HELFER, RAY E., eds. 1972. *Helping the Battered Child and His Family.* Philadelphia: J. B. Lippincott.

KEMPE, C. HENRY; SILVERMAN, FREDERIC N.; STEELE, BRANDT F.; DROEGEMUELLER, WILLIAM; and SILVER, HENRY K. 1962. "The Battered Child Syndrome." *Journal of the American Medical Association* 181 (1962): 4–11.

KNAPP, VRINDA S. 1975. "The Role of the Juvenile Police in the Protection of Neglected and Abused Children." Xerox University Microfilms, Ann Arbor. (Microfilm from University of Southern California, D.S.W., 1961)

KRAUSE, HARRY D. 1977. *Family Law in a Nutshell.* St. Paul: West Publishing Co.

LEVINE, MURRAY, and LEVINE, ADELINE. 1970. *A Social History of Helping Services.* New York: Appleton-Century-Crofts.

LINDSAY, SAMUEL M., ed. 1914. *Legislation for the Protection of Animals and Children.* Bulletin of Social Legislation No. 2. New York: Columbia University.

LENA, H. F., and WARKOV, S. 1978. "Occupation Perceptions of the Causes and Consequences of Child Abuse/Neglect." *Medical Anthropology* 2 (Winter, part 1, 1978):1–28.

MARTIN, BARCLAY. 1975. "Parent-Child Relations." In F. D. Horowitz and E. M. Hitherington, eds., *Review of Child Development Research.* Chicago: University of Chicago Press.

MARTIN, MARY PORTER. 1978. *1977 Analysis of Child Abuse and Neglect Research.* National Center on Child Abuse and Neglect, U.S. Children's Bureau, Administration for Children, Youth and Families, Office of Human Development Services, U.S. Department of Health, Education and Welfare.

McCREA, ROSWELL C. 1969. *The Humane Movement.* New York: Columbia University Press. (Reprinted by McGrath Publishing Co., College Park, Md.)

MEIER, ELIZABETH B. 1964. "Child Neglect." In Nathan Cohen, ed., *Social Work and Social Problems.* New York: National Association of Social Workers.

MILLER, DANIEL R., and SWANSON, GUY E. 1960. *Inner Conflict and Defense.* New York: Henry Holt.

MNOOKIN, ROBERT. 1972. "Health Care: In Whose Best Interests?" *Harvard Educational Review* 43 (November 1972): 5, 99, 638.

MORGAN, EDMUND S. 1966. *The Puritan Family.* New York: Harper & Row.

MULFORD, R. M. 1958. *Emotional Neglect of Children: A Challenge to Protective Services.* Denver: Children's Division, American Humane Association.

NAGI, SAAD Z. 1975. "The Structure and Performance of Programs on

Child Abuse and Neglect." Interim Report Submitted to the Office of Child Development, Department of Health, Education and Welfare, March 1975. (Grant No. OCD–CB–500–C–1.)

———. 1977. *Child Maltreatment in the United States.* New York: Columbia University Press.

NEWBERGER, E., ET AL. 1975. "Toward an Etiologic Classification of Pediatric Social Illness: A Descriptive Epidemiology of Child Abuse and Neglect, Failure to Thrive, Accidents and Poisonings in Children Under Four Years of Age." Paper presented at the Society for Research in Child Development Biennial Meeting, Denver, Apr. 11, 1975.

New York. 1914. *Report of the New York State Commission on Relief for Widowed Mothers.* Albany: J. B. Lyon.

NUNNALLY, JUM. 1967. *Psychometric Theory.* New York: McGraw–Hill.

OWINGS, CHLOE. 1925. *Women Police: A Study of the Development and Status of the Women Police Movement.* Publications of the Bureau of Social Hygiene. New York: Frederick H. Hitchcock.

PARKE, ROSS D., and COLLMER, CANDACE W. 1975. "Child Abuse: An Interdisciplinary Analysis." In Mavis Hetherington, ed., *Review of Child Development Research,* vol. 5. Chicago: University of Chicago Press.

PIGEON, HELEN D. 1949. *Principles and Methods of Dealing with Offenders.* Philadelphia: Pennsylvania Valley Publishers.

PITCHER, RUDOLPH A. 1972. "The Police." In C. Henry Kempe and Ray E. Helfer, eds., *Helping the Battered Child and His Family.* Philadelphia: J. B. Lippincott.

POLANSKY, NORMAN; BORGMAN, ROBERT D.; and DE SAIX, CHRISTINE. 1972. *Roots of Futility.* London: Jossey-Bass.

POLANSKY, NORMAN; CHALMERS, MARY ANN; BUTTENWEISER, ELIZABETH; and WILLIAMS, DAVID. 1977. "Assessing Adequacy of Child Care: An Urban Scale." University of Georgia, Athens. Mimeographed.

POLANSKY, NORMAN; HALLY, D.; and POLANSKY, N. F. 1975. *Profile of Neglect: A Survey of the State of Knowledge of Child Neglect.* Community Services Administration, Social and Rehabilitation Services, Department of Health, Education and Welfare.

POLANSKY, NORMAN, and WILLIAMS, DAVID P. 1978. "Class Orientations to Child Neglect." University of Georgia, Athens. Mimeographed.

RADBILL, SAMUEL X. 1974. "A History of Child Abuse and Infanticide." In Ray E. Helfer and C. Henry Kempe, eds., *The Battered Child.* Chicago: University of Chicago Press.

RICHMOND, MARY E., and HALL, FRED S. 1913. *A Study of Nine Hundred and Eighty-five Widows Known to Certain Charity Organization Societies in 1910.* New York: Russell Sage Foundation.

Rossi, Peter; Waite, Emily; Bass, Christine; and Berk, Richard E. 1974. "The Seriousness of Crime: Normative Structure and Individual Difference." *American Sociological Review* 39 (1974): 224–37.

Rummel, R. J. 1970. *Understanding Factor Analysis*. Evanston: Northwestern University Press.

Sanders, R. W. 1972. "Resistance to Dealing with Parents of Battered Children." *Pediatrics* 50 (December 1972): 853–57.

Scheff, T. J. 1965. "Decision Rules: Types of Error and Their Consequences in Medical Diagnosis." In F. Mesarik and P. Ratoosh, eds., *Mathematical Explorations in Behavioral Science*. Homewood, Ill.: Dorsey Press.

Schlossman, Steven L. 1977. *Love and the American Delinquent: The Theory and Practice of "Progressive" Juvenile Justice*. Chicago: University of Chicago Press.

Sellin, Thorsten, and Wolfgang, Marvin E. 1964. *The Measurement of Delinquency*. New York: John Wiley & Sons.

Siegel, Sidney. 1956. *Nonparametric Statistics*. New York: McGraw-Hill.

Silver, L. B. 1968. "Child Abuse Syndrome: A Review." *Medical Times* 96 (August 1968): 803–20.

Silver, L. B.; Barton, W.; and Dublin, C. C. 1967. "Child Abuse Laws: Are They Enough?" *Journal of the American Medical Association* 194 (Jan. 9, 1967): 65–68.

Simons, B.; Downs, E. F.; Hurster, M. M.; and Archer, M. 1966. "Child Abuse: Epidemiologic Study of Medically Reported Cases." *New York State Journal of Medicine* 66 (Oct. 1, 1966): 2783–88.

Streshinsky, Naomi; Billingsley, Andrew; and Gurgin, Vonnie. 1966. "A Study of Social Work Protective Services: It's Not What You Know, It's Where You Work." *Child Welfare* 45 (October 1966): 444–50, 471.

Tatsuoka, Maurice M. 1971 *Multivariate Analysis*. New York: Wiley.

ten Broeck, Jacobus. 1964 and 1965. *California's Dual System of Family Law: Its Origin, Development and Present Status*. Berkeley: University of California, Department of Political Science. Reprinted from *Stanford Law Review* 16 (March 1964), 16 (July 1964), and 17 (April 1965).

U.S., Children's Bureau. 1919. "Standards of Child Welfare: A Report of the Children's Bureau Conferences, May to June 1919." Conference Series 1, Bureau Publication No. 60.

U.S., Congress, Senate. 1909. *Proceedings of the Conference on the Care of Dependent Children Held at Washington, D.C., January 1909*. 60th Congress, 2d session. Senate Document No. 721.

University of Chicago Faculty of the School of Social Service Administration, eds. 1938. *The Child and the State*. Vol. 1: *Legal Status in the Family Apprenticeship and Child Labor*. Chicago: University of Chicago Press.

WALD, MICHAEL. 1975. "State Intervention on Behalf of 'Neglected' Children: A Search for Realistic Standards." *Stanford Law Review* 27 (April 1975): 985–1040.

WHITING, LEILA. 1976. "Defining Emotional Neglect." *Children Today* January–February 1976, pp. 2–5.

WILSON, THELMA GARRETT. 1960. *Ventura Ventures into Child Protective Service*. Denver: American Humane Association.

WINER, B. J. 1971. *Statistical Procedures in Experimental Design*, 2nd ed. New York: McGraw-Hill.

WOLFGANG, MARVIN E., and FERRACUTI, FRANCO. 1967. *The Subculture of Violence: Towards an Integrated Theory in Criminology*. London: Tavistock Publications.

WRIGHT, L. 1970. "Psychologic Aspects of the Battered Child Syndrome." *Southern Medical Bulletin* 58 (June 1970): pp. 14–18.

YOUNG, LEONTINE R. 1964. *Wednesday's Children: A Study of Child Neglect and Abuse*. New York: McGraw-Hill.

LAWS AND COURT DECISIONS CITED IN THE TEXT

Education Code, pt. 2, div. 6, section 6902, Deering's California Codes, Annotated Education.

California Welfare and Institutions Code, chap. 1068, art. 6, secs. 300b and d, and chap. 2, art. 4, sec. 5250, Deering's California Codes, W&I Code, Annotated. San Francisco: Bancroft-Whitney Co., 1969.

The Social Security Act, Title XX, sec. 2002.

Ingraham v. *Wright*, 97, S. CT. 1401, 1977.

Illinois Review Statutes, chap. 37, 705–9.

California Penal Code, sec. 11161.5, sec. 273A.

Child Abuse and Neglect Legislation, 93d Congress, S. 1191, P.L. 93–247.

Child Abuse Prevention Act, 1973. Hearings before the Subcommittee on Children and Youth of the Committee on Labor and Public Welfare, U.S. Senate, 93d Congress, 1st sess., S. 1191.

Lindsay v. *Lindsay*, L57 Illinois 328 (1913).

In re Gault, 387, U.S. 1, 1967, 87 S. Ct., 1428, 18.

The People v. *Turner*, 55 Illinois 280 (1870).

Ex Parte Crouse, 4 Wharton (Pa.), 9 (1838).

Connecticut Laws, 1919, chap. 323, sec. 9.

Laws of Illinois. "An Act to Regulate the Treatment and Control of Dependent Neglected and Delinquent Children," sec. 1–21, 1899.

"In the Matter of Gault: Excerpts from the United States Supreme Court Decision and from the Dissent." *Current History* 53 (August 1967): 112–13.

Federal Register, part 2, Jan. 23, 1978, p. 3244.

L. Ed. zd. 527 (1967), 234.

Index